VEGETABLE COOKERY

Lou Seibert Pappas

HPBooks

ANOTHER BEST-SELLING VOLUME FROM HPBOOKS®

Executive Editor: Rick Bailey; Editorial Director: Veronica Durie; Editor: Retha M. Davis; Art Director: Don Burton; Book Design: Kathleen Koopman; Typography: Cindy Coatsworth, Michelle Claridge; Food Stylist: Mable Hoffman; Photography: George de Gennaro Studios

Published by HPBooks®, P.O. Box 5367, Tucson, AZ 85703 602/888-2150
ISBN 0-89586-193-3
Library of Congress Catalog Card Number 82-82688
©1982 Fisher Publishing, Inc. Printed in the U.S.A.

COVER PHOTO: Butter-Glazed Vegetables, page 156.

CONTENTS

Vegetable Basics 5
Know Your Vegetables 9
Vegetable Appetizers 31
Hot & Cold Soups 44
Salads 63
Eggs & Soufflés 82
Pastries & Pasta 94
Main Dishes 112
Side Dishes 132
Sauces & Relishes 164
Breads & Desserts 173
Index 187

Lou Seibert Pappas

An interest in foods developed in early childhood for Lou Seibert Pappas. Her mother was a fine bread and pastry maker and her father worked in food marketing. Lou grew up knowing and handling a wide variety of produce and other fresh foods.

Lou's growing interest in the world of food took her to Oregon State University to graduate with a degree in Home Economics and Journalism. Her professional food career began as a home economist and food stylist for Sunset Magazine. During her 30 years in the food industry, she served as a food consultant for many Western food firms.

Currently, Lou is food editor for the Peninsula Times Tribune in Palo Alto, California. Her readers enjoy her food news, creative recipes and insights into the national and international aspects of food through weekly features. Her writing also appears in Gourmet and Cuisine magazines.

Lou has authored numerous cookbooks including "Greek Cooking," "Egg Cookery," "Bread Baking" and "Gourmet Cooking the Slim Way."

Lou and husband Nicholas enjoy traveling, with Europe a favorite destination. More than 10 month-long trips have provided Lou opportunity to look into kitchens and visit with famous chefs throughout the Western world.

Lou enjoys creating new recipes with three sons and a daughter always willing to help out or taste. Food is a family affair in the Pappas house and everyone gets involved.

Lou also shares her talents and knowledge through cooking classes and workshops.

VEGETABLE BASICS

Cooks today are discovering that roots, shoots, stalks, leaves, seeds and pods lend delicious flavors, exciting variety and valuable nutrients to any meal. Vegetables of every kind are finding a new prominence at the table, both at home and in restaurants. We are discovering what Middle Eastern and Asian cooks have known for a long time: Vegetables should be prized and used to create superb dishes and not treated merely as tag-along accompaniments.

Fields and gardens across the world contribute a varied and abundant source of vegetables. With consumers demanding top-quality, fresh food for healthy living, vegetables receive critical appraisal. Producers and marketers are working continually to meet higher standards. Through improved handling and transportation, a wide variety of quality produce is available in all markets. New interest in vegetables has spurred producers to experiment with new or previously little known vegetables such as jícama, fava beans and Belgian endive.

New hybrids such as Sugar Snap peas and classics like Jerusalem artichokes, chayote and okra are enjoying a culinary revival. Oriental treats like the shiitake and enoki mushrooms are being cultivated domestically. Spaghetti squash, introduced to the market in 1930, only now is becoming popular. Crunchy jícama is being used increasingly in salads and as a vegetable dipper.

Helping to spark this interest in vegetable cookery are restaurateurs and consumers whose travels have inspired interest in ethnic cooking. As international cuisines enter the kitchen, exciting dishes of good cooks from across the world can easily be duplicated. Provencal ratatouille, Greek spinach pie, Indian curries, Oriental stir-fry dishes and Italian pesto delight palates anywhere.

Grocery staples of yesterday—potatoes, carrots, cabbage and onions—are no longer enough. Vegetables such as slender French green-beans, Italian licorice-flavored fennel, Chinese daikon, Belgian endive and celeriac greet the shopper. Variety is suddenly a key to produce shopping.

Interest in home gardening is increasing, providing an abundance of just-picked vegetables for the creative cook. Garden seeds are available for exotic as well as more common vegetables. Gardens are producing golden tomatoes, purple string beans, Chinese cabbage, sorrel, spaghetti squash and Sugar Snap peas. Cooks savor the bountiful harvest and enjoy creating a potpourri of dishes. For further information on home vegetable gardening, refer to *Vegetables, How to Select, Grow and Enjoy*, published by HPBooks.

In addition to the enjoyment received, the benefits from cooking with vegetables are many: you will have the opportunity to try many creative recipe ideas and produce bright colorful dishes to serve friends and family. Delicious vegetable dishes are good for you and your budget.

Techniques used in vegetable cookery are many. All can be easily mastered. A key point to remember is to select fresh vegetables in season when possible. If not available fresh, choose a quality alternative from frozen, canned or dried vegetables. Then select the proper cooking method. Cook to the peak of perfection. Then serve and enjoy!

This collection of recipes reaches into all corners of the world. It's an array of dishes: appetizers, soups, salads, main and side dishes and desserts. Enjoy the opportunity to create new dishes with favorite vegetables. Experiment and discover the delicious flavors and textures of new vegetables.

NUTRITION

Vegetables are a storehouse of good nutrition. They supply many essential nutrients in a balanced diet including carbohydrates, vitamins and minerals. In addition, some vegetables are important sources of added protein and fat. Quantities of each nutrient will vary in different vegetables, therefore it's wise to serve a variety of vegetables to be sure all nutrients are included in the diet.

Green leafy vegetables are rich in vitamins A and C. Other green vegetables, such as peas, beans and kale, contain B vitamins. Minerals are also found in leafy vegetables. They are particularly high in iron and calcium. In general, leaf and stem vegetables rank above other vegetables as sources of these two elements. Stem vegetables are similar to leafy vegetables in nutritive value. Deep-green color generally indicates high nutritive value. For example, green asparagus and green celery are higher in vitamin A and iron than the bleached varieties.

Roots and tubers are high in vitamins. A single medium potato contains 1/3 of the daily adult requirement of vitamin C and some vitamin B. Peas and dried beans contain essential protein. Carrots and sweet potatoes are prime sources of vitamin A. Cauliflower is a good source of vitamin C and broccoli has vitamins A and C plus iron.

Considered as a group, vegetables are low-calorie. The range of caloric value is quite varied. Examples of vegetables considered low in calories are cooked asparagus at 35 calories per cup or cooked cabbage at 30 calories per cup. Peas are considered average at 110 calories per cup. A vegetable considered high in calories would be lima beans at 170 calories per cup of cooked beans.

Today's methods of food preservation, both commercial and home-style, help retain valuable vegetable nutrients. However, processed vegetables will never replace the quality of fresh. Whether frozen, canned or dried, preserved vegetables help in adding variety to the year-round menu.

Vegetables are an important part of our daily diet. They make major contributions to the health and well-being of our bodies.

TIPS FOR BUYING VEGETABLES

Freshness is the key to succulent, tender and full-flavored vegetables. Whenever possible, buy during the peak season to obtain the finest quality available. With modern transportation and improved production techniques, many vegetables are now available year round.

When purchasing fresh vegetables, check for signs of freshness including bright natural colors, crispness and firmness. Avoid vegetables with wilted, weathered or leathered looks or any signs of decay or spoilage. To avoid spoilage or waste, keep in mind how soon you plan to use the vegetables.

TIPS FOR STORING VEGETABLES

Proper storage is important to maintain fresh quality. Wash vegetables just before preparation. Washing prior to storage increases opportunity for bacterial growth and vegetable deterioration.

Certain fruits and vegetables should not be stored together. As they ripen, apples give off ethylene gas which makes carrots bitter. Onions hasten the spoilage of potatoes.

Some vegetables, such as potatoes, winter squash, sweet potatoes and rutabagas should be stored outside the refrigerator. Dampness will cause these vegetables to rot.

Other vegetables are best stored at 50F (10C). These include eggplant, tomatoes, peppers, cucumbers and okra. If kept too warm, they will rapidly decay. Often the only solution is to refrigerate them.

Perishable and semi-perishable vegetables should be refrigerated as soon as possible. Prepare and serve them as soon as possible. Store these vegetables in perforated plastic bags in the coldest part of your refrigerator.

Refrigerator storage time for vegetables varies greatly, depending on freshness at time of picking or purchase. Refer to Know Your Vegetables, page 9, for specific storage tips on each vegetable.

BASIC VEGETABLE PREPARATION

Vegetables should be prepared just prior to use. Many vegetables need only to be washed or scrubbed. Others require removal of outer skin or core. If skin must be removed, pare as thinly as possible to retain as much of the nutrient value as possible. To preserve nutrients, avoid soaking vegetables in water for long periods of time.

If vegetables are likely to discolor, sprinkle

with lemon juice or place briefly in acidulated water. An easy combination for acidulated water is 1 quart of water to 1 teaspoon lemon juice.

For even cooking, cut vegetables in uniform-size pieces. To add interest to vegetable dishes, be creative in the ways you cut vegetables. Try shapes such as wedges, slices, half-moons, circles, spears, cubes, diagonal slices and matchsticks or julienne pieces.

If any vegetables have a wax coating, such as rutabagas, cucumbers or turnips, the skin must be removed.

COOKING TECHNIQUES
Vegetables can be cooked in a variety of ways. Some methods are more suitable than others for individual vegetables. Careful attention should be given to maintain flavor, color and nutrients during cooking.

Many vegetables contain natural acids. As the vegetable is cooked, the acid is released from the cells. Unless allowed to escape, such as in an uncovered saucepan, acid comes in contact with other parts of the vegetable with varying results. In green vegetables, it destroys the bright green of chlorophyll. In red vegetables such as beets or red cabbage, this acid or the addition of vinegar or lemon juice brightens the natural red color. Acid does not affect yellow or orange vegetables and preserves the white color in off-white vegetables such as cauliflower. Cooking of these vegetables can be done in a covered saucepan.

A flavor-enhancing technique is to salt vegetables such as eggplant and zucchini before cooking. Sprinkle sliced or grated vegetable lightly with salt. Let stand 15 to 30 minutes. Rinse well and pat dry with paper towel. This helps leach out excess moisture and bitter juices. Eggplant slices that have been pre-salted absorb less fat during cooking. Zucchini has a sweeter flavor.

Another way to enhance vegetable flavors is through the use of butter or margarine. Throughout this book, recipes call for butter in cooking and seasoning vegetables. Margarine may be substituted, if desired.

Cooking times cannot be given with accuracy. Many variables exist which affect timing. Some factors include variety and maturity of the vegetable, time and temperature at which it was harvested and stored, and the size of pieces being cooked. The cooking temperature is also a variable.

Overcooking is responsible for more undesirable flavors and faded unattractive colors in vegetables than anything else. Many vegetables are best when cooked to a crisp-tender or al dente stage. That means that it is tender, but still firm to the bite. Consider peeling, trimming or cutting vegetables diagonally or shredding them to speed up cooking. Peel stalks of asparagus and broccoli to eliminate extra cellulose and thus speed up cooking time.

Here is a brief description of the basic and most commonly used vegetable cookery methods.

BOILING
Boiling is the most frequently used vegetable-cooking technique, but there is much discussion between cooks over the two methods used. Some prefer a large amount of water in an uncovered pan; others like a small amount of water in a covered pan. Each method has its merits. Cooking green and strong-flavored vegetables in a large amount of boiling water in an uncovered pan preserves natural color, flavor and texture. Alternatively, using a small amount of water in a covered pan preserves more nutrients. Green vegetables turn a dull olive color when overcooked in a covered pan.

To boil vegetables, first select the desired method. Use either the open-pan, deep-water method allowing about 2 quarts of water per pound of vegetables, or a covered pan and shallow water, using about 1 cup of water per pound of vegetables. In either case, bring water to a boil. Add vegetables to boiling water. Begin timing when water returns to a gentle boil. Boil until vegetables are crisp-tender.

Some vegetables, including artichokes, asparagus, red cabbage and celeriac, discolor if prepared in cast-iron or aluminum pans. Select stainless-steel, enameled or glass saucepans for cooking these vegetables.

PARBOILING
Parboil means to cook partially. Generally it is done using the boiling method and reducing the cooking time by 2/3. Cooking is generally completed using another method.

BLANCHING

Blanching means to precook by plunging into boiling water, generally for a very short time, 30 seconds to 2 minutes. This method is used for inactivating enzymes in vegetables for canning, freezing and drying. It is also used to aid in removing skins from tomatoes, onions and other vegetables and fruit. After blanching, vegetables are generally plunged into an ice-water bath, also known as *refreshing*.

STEAMING

Steaming is cooking over boiling liquid, generally water. Vegetables that can be boiled can also be steamed; however, steaming takes longer. To shorten steaming time, cut thick vegetables into thin pieces. To steam, place vegetables in a steamer rack, colander or in a specially designed steaming pan. Place in a pan with a small amount of water or other liquid and cover. Bring to a boil, reduce heat and simmer until crisp-tender. Steaming can also be done in a wok using a specially designed rack for vegetables.

MICROWAVE METHOD

Vegetables cooked in a microwave oven retain their bright colors, flavors and texture. By using a small amount or no liquid in cooking, nutrient loss is minimized. Most vegetables should be covered for microwave cooking. Vegetables with natural coverings such as potatoes or squash should be pierced to allow steam to escape. Cooking times will vary based on size, quantity and temperature of vegetable being cooked and desired level of doneness. Stir or rearrange vegetables during cooking to ensure even doneness throughout. Salt vegetables after cooking to avoid moisture loss and toughening. Blanch vegetables in the microwave for freezing. For additional information, refer to your microwave oven Use & Care Guide or *Microwave Cookbook* published by HPBooks.

SAUTÉING & STIR-FRYING

Certain vegetables can be quickly sautéed or stir-fried in a skillet or wok using high heat and a small amount of hot oil or fat. The result is vegetables with bright colors and pleasing crisp-tender textures. For successful stir-frying, care must be taken in preparing vegetables. Here's how to achieve even cooking with a blend of vegetables: Vegetables which take longer to cook, such as carrots, should be cut in smaller pieces. Cut fast-cooking vegetables in larger pieces. Start by cooking the slowest-cooking vegetables first. Then add each vegetable in order of longest cooking time. Some such as carrots or cauliflower may need to be parboiled.

DEEP-FRYING

Deep-frying is achieved by cooking cut vegetables or batter-dipped vegetables in oil heated to 375F (190C). At this temperature, a 1-inch cube of bread will turn golden brown in 50 seconds. The Japanese and Italians favor batter-coating their vegetables before frying them for tempura-style vegetables or fritters. Deep-frying vegetables results in a crunchy, crisp outer layer with a moist succulent center.

BRAISING/STEWING

Braising is a method of cooking slowly in a covered utensil in a small amount of fat and liquid. A variety of vegetables can be cooked in this way and a delicious blend of flavors results. Often these dishes are equally good served hot or cold.

BAKING

One of the simplest forms of vegetable cookery is baking. Baking is cooking in an oven or oven-type appliance with dry heat. Vegetables can be baked covered or uncovered. This method need not be reserved for classics, such as potatoes and winter squash which are delicious baked whole in their skins. Try something new with whole onions or heads of garlic. These vegetables become sweet and succulent during oven baking. Natural vegetable skins, a coating of oil or wrapping with foil helps retain moistness during baking.

BROILING/GRILLING

Another easy cooking method is broiling or grilling. Cooking is done by direct dry heat. Vegetable surfaces generally need some protection with this cooking method. Potatoes should be wrapped in foil. Ears of corn with husks still attached should be soaked in cold water, then drained before grilling. Cut vegetables should have their cut surfaces brushed with oil to protect from charring.

PRESSURE COOKING

Vegetables can be cooked quickly in a pressure cooker with minimal nutrient loss. This method cooks vegetables in an air-tight container at a high temperature under steam pressure, usually 15 pounds. Follow manufacturer's directions exactly when using your pressure cooker.

ARTICHOKE, GLOBE

Available: year round; peak: spring through early summer

Selection: Choose plump, bright-green globular artichokes with compact tightly closed leaves. Surface brown spots may be due to frost and do not affect quality or flavor. Size is not a quality factor when selecting artichokes. Artichokes 1 to 1-1/2 inches or less in size are generally called *artichoke hearts* or *baby artichokes*.

Storage: Store unwashed in perforated plastic bag in refrigerator 1 to 2 weeks.

Preparation: Trim with stainless-steel knives or scissors to prevent discoloration of cut surface. Rub cut surfaces with half a lemon or drop into acidulated water. Cook in a stainless-steel, enamel, tin-lined copper or glass saucepan to prevent discoloration. To prepare whole for boiling or steaming, trim stem flush with base of choke. Artichokes should stand upright. Snap off small leaves at the stem end. Trim off top 3/4 to 1 inch from artichoke. Using scissors, cut 1/2 inch off tip of each remaining leaf. After cooking, the fuzzy choke center may be removed with a spoon, melon-baller or tip of peeler. For stuffing, prepare as given above up to cooking. Open artichoke gently with your hands. Remove fuzzy choke center with spoon, melon-baller or tip of peeler. Wash under cold running water. Rub again with lemon. Insert stuffing between leaves and proceed with recipe.

Boil	Steam	Stir-Fry Sauté	Braise Stew	Bake	Deep-Fry	Grill Broil	Pressure Cook	Microwave	Raw
✔	✔	✔	✔	✔	✔		✔	✔	✔

ARTICHOKE, JERUSALEM (Sunchokes)

Available: year round; peak: fall through spring

Selection: Choose firm tubers, about 2 inches long, free from soft spots or blemishes. Sunchoke is a marketing name for Jerusalem artichoke. These small, lumpy, branched tubers are neither native to Jerusalem nor are they artichokes. They do have a similar taste to artichokes. Botanically, they are edible tubers of a variety of sunflower. In appearance, they resemble gingerroot.

Storage: Store unwashed in perforated plastic bag in refrigerator 3 to 4 days.

Preparation: Scrub well with stiff brush. Peel and use raw in salads or cook in skin and then peel. Skin may also be left on. To keep peeled artichoke from discoloring, place in acidulated water.

Boil	Steam	Stir-Fry Sauté	Braise Stew	Bake	Deep-Fry	Grill Broil	Pressure Cook	Microwave	Raw
✔	✔	✔	✔	✔	✔		✔	✔	✔

ASPARAGUS

Available: spring through early summer

Selection: Choose straight, firm stalks with compact, closed bud clusters. Stalks should be green from tips to as close to root end as possible and free from blemishes. Stalk size varies from very thin to 1-inch thick. Generally best stalks are 1/2- to 3/4-inch thick. White or blanched asparagus is a forced variety cultivated in darkness to develop the white color.

Storage: Wrap ends of stalks in moist towel or paper towel or stand in a small amount of cold water. Store unwashed in perforated plastic bag in refrigerator 2 to 3 days.

Preparation: Snap off or trim woody ends. Use a vegetable peeler to remove tough outer stem as far as tips. Or slice asparagus thinly on diagonal for stir-fry dishes. Cook as whole spears or cut-up.

Boil	Steam	Stir-Fry Sauté	Braise Stew	Bake	Deep-Fry	Grill Broil	Pressure Cook	Microwave	Raw
✔	✔	✔		✔	✔		✔	✔	✔

BEANS, DRIED

Available: year round

Selection: Choose dried beans which are uniform in size and free from foreign material. Discard beans that are wrinkled or discolored.

Storage: Store dried beans in a tightly covered container in a cool, dry place.

Preparation: Soak beans overnight in water or place beans in a saucepan with water to cover. Bring to a boil and boil 2 minutes. Remove from heat and let stand 1 hour.

Boil	Steam	Stir-Fry Sauté	Braise Stew	Bake	Deep-Fry	Grill Broil	Pressure Cook	Microwave	Raw
✔			✔	✔			✔	✔	

BEANS, GREEN, LIMA, WAX

Available: year round; peak: early summer through fall

Selection: Choose young, tender beans with clean, crisp, firm pods. Colors will vary depending on variety.

Storage: Store unwashed in perforated plastic bag in refrigerator 1 to 2 days.

Preparation: Wash beans in cold water. Remove ends and strings from green or wax beans. Leave whole, cut in 1-inch pieces or cut lengthwise. Lima beans in pods should be podded. Wash and cook using desired method.

Boil	Steam	Stir-Fry Sauté	Braise Stew	Bake	Deep-Fry	Grill Broil	Pressure Cook	Microwave	Raw
✔	✔	✔	✔	✔			✔	✔	

Left to Right: Edible Pea Pods, Bean Sprouts (Mung), Garbanzo Beans (Cici), Green Beans, Fava or Broad Beans, Black-Eyed Peas

BEAN SPROUTS

Available: year round

Selection: Choose crisp, clean, plump, fresh-looking sprouts with bean buds attached.

Storage: Store unwashed in perforated plastic bag in refrigerator 3 to 4 days.

Preparation: Rinse sprouts in cold water prior to using. Drain well. Use in salads, stir-fry or other dishes.

Boil	Steam	Stir-Fry Sauté	Braise Stew	Bake	Deep-Fry	Grill Broil	Pressure Cook	Microwave	Raw
✔	✔	✔							✔

BEET GREENS - see Greens

BEETS

Available: year round; peak: late spring through fall

Selection: Choose smooth, firm, round, small to medium-size beets with slender tap root. Flesh should be deep red and free from cracks. Attached greens should be crisp and fresh-looking.

Storage: Store unwashed in perforated plastic bag in refrigerator up to 1 week. Beets without attached greens can be stored slightly longer.

Preparation: Scrub gently to avoid breaking surface skin. Do not remove tap root until after cooking. Cook in the skin. Cool. Skins will easily slide off. Slice, dice, julienne or use whole.

Boil	Steam	Stir-Fry Sauté	Braise Stew	Bake	Deep-Fry	Grill Broil	Pressure Cook	Microwave	Raw
✔		✔	✔	✔			✔	✔	

BOK CHOY - see Chinese Cabbage

BROCCOLI

Available: year round; peak: fall through spring

Selection: Choose firm, compact clusters of small deep-green or purple-green flower buds. Avoid yellowing flower buds. Stalks should be thick and firm, but not woody.

Storage: Store unwashed in perforated plastic bag in refrigerator up to 1 week.

Preparation: Break or cut into flowerets. Remove tough outer skin of each stalk by peeling from bottom up to flowerets. If stalks are thick, slit several times for more even cooking.

Boil	Steam	Stir-Fry Sauté	Braise Stew	Bake	Deep-Fry	Grill Broil	Pressure Cook	Microwave	Raw
✔	✔	✔			✔		✔	✔	✔

BRUSSELS SPROUTS

Available: fall through spring

Selection: Choose firm, compact, small to medium-size heads with tight-fitting outer leaves. Color should be bright green. Avoid wilted or yellowing heads or those with ragged leaves.

Storage: Store unwashed in perforated plastic bag in refrigerator 3 to 4 days.

Preparation: Remove loose, wilted or yellowed outer leaves. Using a paring knife, make 2 diagonal cuts in base of each sprout. This promotes even cooking.

Boil	Steam	Stir-Fry Sauté	Braise Stew	Bake	Deep-Fry	Grill Broil	Pressure Cook	Microwave	Raw
✔	✔	✔	✔		✔		✔	✔	

CABBAGE

Available: year round; peak: late fall through early summer

Selection: Choose firm, hard heads, heavy for their size. Color should be bright red or green. Savoy cabbage or crinkle-edge cabbage will have loosely formed heads. Avoid wilted, yellow leaves or serious blemishes.

Storage: Store unwashed in perforated plastic bag in refrigerator 1 to 2 weeks.

Preparation: Wash and trim cabbage before using. If trimming red cabbage, select a stainless-steel knife to prevent any discoloration. When stuffing parboiled cabbage leaves, trim veins of each precooked leaf if they are large and stick out from the surface of the leaf. Use a small paring knife to whittle vein flush with leaf surface.

Boil	Steam	Stir-Fry Sauté	Braise Stew	Bake	Deep-Fry	Grill Broil	Pressure Cook	Microwave	Raw
✔	✔	✔	✔				✔	✔	✔

CABBAGE, CHINESE (Napa Cabbage and Bok Choy)

Available: year round; peak: fall through late winter

Selection: Bok choy is the loose-leaf variety of Chinese cabbage. Choose large dark-green leaves with thick, succulent, celery-like white stems. Leaves should be shiny. Napa cabbage has an elongated head. Choose large, oval-shaped, light-green heads with crinkled, close-fitting leaves.

Storage: Store unwashed in perforated plastic bag in refrigerator 3 to 4 days.

Preparation: Wash leaves well. Slice for use in salads or stir-fry.

Boil	Steam	Stir-Fry Sauté	Braise Stew	Bake	Deep-Fry	Grill Broil	Pressure Cook	Microwave	Raw
✔	✔	✔	✔					✔	✔

Left to Right: Savoy Cabbage, Red Cabbage, Green Cabbage, Napa or Chinese Cabbage

CARROTS

Available: year round; winter best

Selection: Choose well-shaped, clean, firm, smooth, bright-orange carrots. Avoid blemishes, splits or other skin damage. Attached greens should be fresh-looking.

Storage: Store unwashed in perforated plastic bag in refrigerator 1 to 2 weeks.

Preparation: Wash and trim well. Scrub well with a brush or peel as desired. Cook whole or in desired shape and size.

Boil	Steam	Stir-Fry Sauté	Braise Stew	Bake	Deep-Fry	Grill Broil	Pressure Cook	Microwave	Raw
✔	✔	✔	✔	✔	✔	✔	✔	✔	✔

CAULIFLOWER

Available: year round; peak: fall through winter

Selection: Choose clean, white to creamy-white, heavy, compact heads. Avoid discolored spots or any speckled appearance.

Storage: Store unwashed in perforated plastic bag in refrigerator up to 1 week.

Preparation: Peel off outer green leaves. Remove stem end and cut out woody core. Cauliflower may be cooked whole or broken into flowerets.

Boil	Steam	Stir-Fry Sauté	Braise Stew	Bake	Deep-Fry	Grill Broil	Pressure Cook	Microwave	Raw
✔	✔	✔	✔		✔		✔	✔	✔

CELERIAC (Celery Root)

Available: fall through early spring

Selection: Choose small celeriacs because larger ones tend to be woody. Look for smooth, firm bulbs, heavy for their size with few rootlets.

Storage: Store unwashed in perforated plastic bag in refrigerator up to 1 week.

Preparation: Peel skin and 1/8 inch of root or slice and remove outer skin. To keep peeled celeriac from discoloring, place in acidulated water.

Boil	Steam	Stir-Fry Sauté	Braise Stew	Bake	Deep-Fry	Grill Broil	Pressure Cook	Microwave	Raw
✔	✔	✔	✔		✔				✔

CELERY

Available: year round

Selection: Choose a firm bunch with crisp medium-size stalks. Leaves should be light green and fresh-looking. Avoid rubbery stalks or wilted leaves.

Storage: Store unwashed in perforated plastic bag in refrigerator up to 1 week.

Preparation: Separate into stalks. Trim or remove leaves. Wash well in cold water.

Boil	Steam	Stir-Fry Sauté	Braise Stew	Bake	Deep-Fry	Grill Broil	Pressure Cook	Microwave	Raw
✔	✔	✔	✔			✔	✔	✔	✔

CHARD, SWISS

Available: spring through winter; peak: summer through early fall

Selection: Choose chard with white stalks and dark-green leaves. Leaves should be crisp and unblemished. Yellow leaves indicate overmaturity.

Storage: Store unwashed in perforated plastic bag in refrigerator up to 2 days.

Preparation: Wash well under cold running water. Remove leaves from chard stems. Cook separately because leaves cook much more quickly than stems.

Boil	Steam	Stir-Fry Sauté	Braise Stew	Bake	Deep-Fry	Grill Broil	Pressure Cook	Microwave	Raw
✔	✔	✔	✔		✔		✔	✔	

Left to Right: Bok Choy, Celery Hearts, Asparagus, Red Swiss Chard, Green Swiss Chard

CHAYOTE

Available: year round; peak: fall through midspring

Selection: Choose smooth, light-green chayote about the size of a large pear. Avoid skin blemishes.

Storage: Store unwashed in perforated plastic bag in refrigerator 3 to 4 days.

Preparation: Wash well, trim ends. Skin is tender and does not need to be removed. Inner seed can be cooked and eaten or discarded.

Boil	Steam	Stir-Fry Sauté	Braise Stew	Bake	Deep-Fry	Grill Broil	Pressure Cook	Microwave	Raw
✔	✔	✔	✔					✔	✔

CHICORY

Available: year round; peak: midspring through early fall

Selection: Choose dark-green leaves, similar in shape to spinach.

Storage: Store unwashed in perforated plastic bag in refrigerator up to 2 days.

Preparation: Wash leaves well. Trim bruised leaves or tough stem ends.

Boil	Steam	Stir-Fry Sauté	Braise Stew	Bake	Deep-Fry	Grill Broil	Pressure Cook	Microwave	Raw
									✔

COLLARDS - see Greens

CORN, SWEET

Available: summer and early fall

Selection: Choose corn with bright-green husks, free from decay or injury. Ears should have even rows with plump white or yellow kernels. Dry or yellow husks indicate stale corn.

Storage: For best flavor, cook corn as soon as possible. If necessary to store, keep in husks in coldest part of refrigerator.

Preparation: Remove husks and silks. Rinse cob well. Cook on cob or remove kernels using a sharp knife.

Boil	Steam	Stir-Fry Sauté	Braise Stew	Bake	Deep-Fry	Grill Broil	Pressure Cook	Microwave	Raw
✔	✔	✔	✔	✔		✔	✔	✔	

CUCUMBER

Available: year round; peak: late spring through summer

Selection: Choose firm, deep-green, well-shaped cucumbers, not too large in diameter. Small areas of white are not a negative sign. Avoid very large cucumbers as they may be seedy. Note: A very long European-type cucumber is sold in some market areas.

Storage: Ideal storage is at 50F (10C), however can be refrigerated. Will keep up to 1 week.

Preparation: Remove thin layer of outer skin. If large, cut in half and remove inner seeds. If desired, salt lightly. Let stand 15 to 30 minutes in colander. Rinse well and pat dry with paper towel. This removes excess moisture and any bitter taste.

Boil	Steam	Stir-Fry Sauté	Braise Stew	Bake	Deep-Fry	Grill Broil	Pressure Cook	Microwave	Raw
✔	✔	✔	✔	✔	✔				✔

DANDELION - see Greens

EGGPLANT

Available: year round; peak: late summer through early fall

Selection: Choose firm, smooth, shiny eggplant with a rich deep-purple color. Should be heavy for its size. Soft or flabby eggplant indicates over-ripeness. Avoid brown spots which indicate decay.

Storage: Ideal storage is at 50F (10C), however can be refrigerated. Will keep up to 2 days.

Preparation: Wash well. Trim ends and cut into desired size pieces or leave whole for stuffing. If tender, it is not necessary to remove outer skin. If desired, salt lightly. Let stand 15 to 30 minutes in colander. Rinse well and pat dry with paper towel. This removes excess moisture and any bitter taste.

Boil	Steam	Stir-Fry Sauté	Braise Stew	Bake	Deep-Fry	Grill Broil	Pressure Cook	Microwave	Raw
✔	✔	✔	✔	✔	✔	✔		✔	

ENDIVE (Batavian Endive)

Available: year round; peak: midspring through early fall

Selection: Choose loose heads with dark-green outer leaves. Leaves get progressively lighter toward center. Endive has curly narrow leaves and gives a bittersweet flavor to salads. It is often erroneously called *chicory*.

Storage: Store unwashed in perforated plastic bag in refrigerator up to 2 days.

Preparation: Wash leaves well. Trim bruised leaves or tough stem ends.

Boil	Steam	Stir-Fry Sauté	Braise Stew	Bake	Deep-Fry	Grill Broil	Pressure Cook	Microwave	Raw
									✔

ENDIVE, BELGIAN (Witloof Chicory, French Endive or Chicons)

Available: fall through midspring

Selection: Choose 5- to 6-inch-long, firm, compact heads. Color should be white, shading to yellow at tips. Avoid discolored leaves. Belgian endive is a forced variety of chicory cultivated in darkness to develop a compact cluster of blanched leaves.

Storage: Store unwashed in perforated plastic bag in refrigerator 1 to 2 days.

Preparation: Insert a small sharp knife in base of the endive. Cut in a circular motion to remove bitter core.

Boil	Steam	Stir-Fry Sauté	Braise Stew	Bake	Deep-Fry	Grill Broil	Pressure Cook	Microwave	Raw
✔	✔	✔	✔					✔	✔

ESCAROLE

Available: year round; peak: midspring through early fall

Selection: Choose loose heads with dark-green outer leaves. Leaves get progressively lighter toward center. Escarole is actually endive with broad smooth leaves.

Storage: Store unwashed in perforated plastic bag in refrigerator up to 2 days.

Preparation: Wash leaves well. Trim bruised leaves or tough stem ends.

Boil	Steam	Stir-Fry Sauté	Braise Stew	Bake	Deep-Fry	Grill Broil	Pressure Cook	Microwave	Raw
									✔

FENNEL (Finocchio, Anise)

Available: midfall through midspring

Selection: Choose firm, compact bulbs with a greenish-white base. Stalks should be crisp, rigid and green.

Storage: Store unwashed in perforated plastic bag in refrigerator up to 1 week.

Preparation: Remove leaves and any stalks near base of bulb. Remove strings from bulb.

Boil	Steam	Stir-Fry Sauté	Braise Stew	Bake	Deep-Fry	Grill Broil	Pressure Cook	Microwave	Raw
✔	✔	✔	✔	✔		✔		✔	✔

GARLIC

Available: year round

Selection: Choose loose rather than packaged bulbs which are plump, firm and dry. Avoid browning or soft spots.

Storage: Hang bulbs in basket or net bag in cool (50F, 10C), dark, dry location. For best flavor, keep no longer than 2 to 3 weeks.

Preparation: To peel, separate bulb into cloves. Place a clove flat on a board. Lay a chef's knife or cleaver on top, parallel to board, and with the fist of the other hand, thump blade to split garlic skin. Remove skin.

Boil	Steam	Stir-Fry Sauté	Braise Stew	Bake	Deep-Fry	Grill Broil	Pressure Cook	Microwave	Raw
✔	✔	✔	✔	✔					✔

GINGERROOT

Available: year round

Selection: Choose firm, fresh-looking roots. Avoid any sign of decay.

Storage: Store unwashed in perforated plastic bag in refrigerator 2 to 3 weeks or store in tightly sealed container in freezer.

Preparation: Scrub well with brush and peel. Dice, grate, slice, chop or shred amount needed.

Boil	Steam	Stir-Fry Sauté	Braise Stew	Bake	Deep-Fry	Grill Broil	Pressure Cook	Microwave	Raw
									✔

Left to Right: Beet Greens, Collard Greens, Kale, Mustard Greens, Turnip Greens

GREENS, BEET, COLLARD, DANDELION, MUSTARD, SORREL, TURNIP

Available: year round; peak: midwinter through midspring

Selection: Choose fresh, young, tender but crisp leaves free from blemishes with good, healthy color. Avoid leaves with coarse stems.

Storage: For best results, use greens immediately. If necessary to store, place unwashed in perforated plastic bag in refrigerator 1 day.

Preparation: Wash thoroughly in ice-cold water. Drain well in a colander. For salad, dry greens in a salad spinner or basket or pat dry with paper towel. Trim bruised leaves or tough stem ends.

Boil	Steam	Stir-Fry Sauté	Braise Stew	Bake	Deep-Fry	Grill Broil	Pressure Cook	Microwave	Raw
✔	✔	✔	✔					✔	✔

JÍCAMA

Available: year round; peak: late fall through spring

Selection: Choose clean, firm, well-shaped roots. Avoid blemishes or cuts.

Storage: Store unwashed in perforated plastic bag in refrigerator up to 2 weeks. Cover any cut edges with plastic film to prevent drying.

Preparation: Remove outer skin. Wash well. Use raw in salads and as a substitute for water chestnuts.

Boil	Steam	Stir-Fry Sauté	Braise Stew	Bake	Deep-Fry	Grill Broil	Pressure Cook	Microwave	Raw
		✔	✔					✔	✔

KALE

Available: year round; peak: winter through early spring

Selection: Choose crisp, firm leaves ranging in color from light green to blue green. Younger shoots and leaves have a sweet flavor. Older leaves are more bitter.

Storage: Store unwashed in perforated plastic bag in refrigerator up to 2 days.

Preparation: Wash leaves well. Trim bruised leaves or tough stem ends.

Boil	Steam	Stir-Fry Sauté	Braise Stew	Bake	Deep-Fry	Grill Broil	Pressure Cook	Microwave	Raw
✔	✔	✔	✔					✔	✔

KOHLRABI

Available: year round; peak: summer through early fall

Selection: Choose firm, fresh, smooth-skinned bulbs, about 3 inches in size or less. Larger bulbs are stronger in flavor.

Storage: Store unwashed in perforated plastic bag in refrigerator up to 1 week.

Preparation: Wash well. Remove tough outer skin. Cut in desired shape or size.

Boil	Steam	Stir-Fry Sauté	Braise Stew	Bake	Deep-Fry	Grill Broil	Pressure Cook	Microwave	Raw
✔	✔	✔						✔	✔

LEEKS

Available: year round; peak: spring through midfall

Selection: Choose young, small leeks with vivid-green tops. Yellow leaves suggest age.

Storage: Remove any brown or limp tops. Store unwashed in perforated plastic bag in refrigerator 3 to 5 days.

Preparation: To clean thoroughly, cut off root end, quarter lengthwise and hold under cold running water to remove sand and grit.

Boil	Steam	Stir-Fry Sauté	Braise Stew	Bake	Deep-Fry	Grill Broil	Pressure Cook	Microwave	Raw
✔	✔	✔	✔	✔	✔			✔	✔

LETTUCE

Available: year round

Selection: Choose well-shaped heads with bright, fresh-looking leaves. There are many varieties of lettuce. Here are some of the more common ones which should be available at your local market: Crisp head or iceberg lettuce should have solid heads of tightly wrapped pale-green leaves. Select it for shredding and including in Mexican dishes such as tacos. It retains crispness well. Romaine or cos lettuce should be tall, stiff and cylindrical with crisp, medium- to dark-green leaves in loosely folded heads. Choice leaves are found in the center and are a pale yellow-green. This lettuce is a basic ingredient for Caesar salads. Butterhead, Buttercrunch, Boston or Bibb should be soft with loosely clustered light-green leaves. They are prized for their subtle fresh flavors. Loose-leaf or bunching lettuce does not form into heads. It should have tender leaves shaped in loose clusters shading from light to dark green. Some varieties have red-tipped leaves. Leaves may be smooth, crinkled or curled. Avoid lettuce showing signs of decay or damage.

Storage: Store unwashed in perforated plastic bag in refrigerator. Iceberg and romaine will keep up to 1 week. Store other lettuce no longer than 2 days.

Preparation: Wash thoroughly in ice-cold water. Drain well. For salad, dry greens in a salad spinner or basket or pat dry with paper towel. Trim bruised leaves and tough stem ends.

Boil	Steam	Stir-Fry Sauté	Braise Stew	Bake	Deep-Fry	Grill Broil	Pressure Cook	Microwave	Raw
✔	✔	✔	✔						✔

Left to Right: Romaine, Curly Endive, Boston Lettuce, Belgian Endive, Escarole, Cilantro

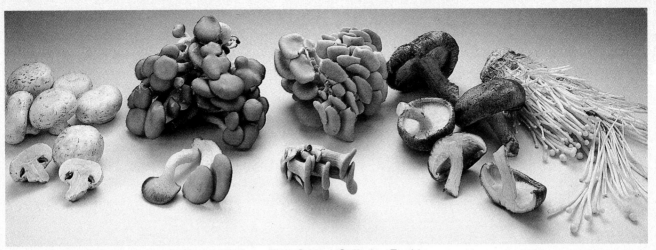

Left to Right: Champignon de Paris, Abalone, Tree Oyster, Shiitake, Enoki

MUSHROOMS

Available: year round

Selection: Choose caps that are completely closed over the stem showing no gills. Open caps indicate older mushrooms. Mushrooms should be firm, even-shaped and unbruised. Avoid wilted, slick or wrinkled mushrooms. One variety, Champignon de Paris, makes up most of the commercially grown mushroom crop. Colors range from white or off-white to tan and sizes range from 3/4 inch to 3 inches. Of all mushrooms, they have the mildest flavor and aroma. New mushroom varieties are appearing in some markets. Enoki mushrooms have long thin stems topped by pinhead button caps. They have a mild sweet flavor and crisp texture. Shiitake, meaty-flavored dark-brown mushrooms, are favored for Oriental dishes. They range in size from 2 to 4 inches across. Abalone mushrooms grow in clusters. The are a gray to deep-brown color and have a sweet flavor. A close relative is the Tree Oyster mushroom, also grown in clusters. Tree Oyster mushrooms are pearl-white to gray in color and have a slightly bitter flavor when eaten raw. They have a crunchy texture when slightly cooked.

Storage: Store in a paper bag in refrigerator to allow mushrooms to breathe and avoid absorbing moisture. Moisture causes mushrooms to deteriorate quickly.

Preparation: Trim stems. Wipe off dirt with damp cloth. Do not soak in water. If extremely dirty, rinse gently in cold water. Pat dry with paper towel.

Boil	Steam	Stir-Fry Sauté	Braise Stew	Bake	Deep-Fry	Grill Broil	Pressure Cook	Microwave	Raw
	✔	✔	✔	✔	✔	✔		✔	✔

MUSTARD GREENS - See Greens

OKRA

Available: year round; peak: late spring through early fall

Selection: Choose fresh, tender, bright-green pods with a moderately firm texture. Size ranges from 3 to 7 inches, depending on variety. Avoid dry, dull or shriveled pods.

Storage: Ideal storage is at 50F (10C), however can be refrigerated in perforated plastic bag up to 2 days.

Preparation: Wash well in cold water. Remove stem ends with a knife, being careful not to pierce the inner tissue which contains a natural thickening agent. If using okra in soups, it is desirable to pierce the inner tissue to release this sap before cooking so it will thicken soup during cooking. Avoid cooking okra in iron, copper, brass or tin because okra will discolor.

Boil	Steam	Stir-Fry Sauté	Braise Stew	Bake	Deep-Fry	Grill Broil	Pressure Cook	Microwave	Raw
✔	✔	✔	✔		✔		✔	✔	

ONIONS

Available: year round

Selection: Choose dry onions that are firm, clean, well-shaped and heavy for their size. The protective papery skins should be dry and glistening. Onions should be free of green sprouts. Green onions should have firm white bulbs with crisp, bright-green tops.

Storage: Hang bulbs in basket or net bag in cool (50F, 10C), dark, dry location. Will keep several months.

Preparation: Remove top and base of onions. Plunge into boiling water 30 seconds to aid in removing skins. Pull off skins. Remove thin membrane. When cooking small boiling onions, cut 1/8-inch-deep crosses in the root-ends to prevent bursting during cooking.

Boil	Steam	Stir-Fry Sauté	Braise Stew	Bake	Deep-Fry	Grill Broil	Pressure Cook	Microwave	Raw
✔	✔	✔	✔	✔	✔	✔	✔	✔	✔

Left to Right: Spanish Onion, Garlic, Green Onions, Shallots, Leeks, Red Onions

PARSLEY

Available: year round

Selection: Choose crisp, fresh parsley, free from blemishes. Avoid browning around edges.

Storage: Store unwashed in perforated plastic bag in refrigerator up to 1 week.

Preparation: Wash well in cold water. Shake dry. Use as a garnish or in salads.

Boil	Steam	Stir-Fry Sauté	Braise Stew	Bake	Deep-Fry	Grill Broil	Pressure Cook	Microwave	Raw
					✔				✔

PARSNIPS

Available: year round; peak: fall through early winter

Selection: Choose smooth, clean, small to medium roots that are firm, well-shaped and without visible blemishes. Avoid large roots as they tend to be woody.

Storage: Store unwashed in perforated plastic bag in refrigerator up to 1 week.

Preparation: Remove outer skin. Leave whole or cut in pieces. Split larger ones in half, then remove tough core.

Boil	Steam	Stir-Fry Sauté	Braise Stew	Bake	Deep-Fry	Grill Broil	Pressure Cook	Microwave	Raw
✔	✔	✔	✔		✔		✔	✔	

PEA PODS, EDIBLE (Chinese Pea Pods, Snow Peas, Sugar Peas, or Snap Peas)

Available: year round; peak: spring through early fall

Selection: Choose bright-green, crisp and tender pods. An outline of immature peas may show. Sugar Snap peas have a thicker pod than other edible pods and peas are more fully developed.

Storage: Store unwashed in perforated plastic bag in refrigerator 1 to 2 days.

Preparation: Cut off stem-end leaving string attached. Continue to pull string down outside edge to remove it.

Boil	Steam	Stir-Fry Sauté	Braise Stew	Bake	Deep-Fry	Grill Broil	Pressure Cook	Microwave	Raw
✔	✔	✔	✔					✔	✔

PEAS

Available: year round; peak: early spring through midsummer

Selection: Choose bright-green, well-filled pods. Rub 2 pods against each other; if young they will squeak. Avoid pods with a rubber-like or leathery feel.

Storage: Store in pods in perforated plastic bag in refrigerator 1 to 2 days.

Preparation: Shell peas by popping open each pod with thumb or finger. Run thumb through pod to remove peas. Discard pods.

Boil	Steam	Stir-Fry Sauté	Braise Stew	Bake	Deep-Fry	Grill Broil	Pressure Cook	Microwave	Raw
✔	✔	✔	✔				✔	✔	

PEPPERS, SWEET BELL OR HOT

Available: year round; peak: summer through early fall

Selection: Choose glossy peppers, avoiding cracks or bruises. They should be firm, heavy for their size and well-shaped. Red bell peppers are fully matured green bell peppers.

Storage: Ideal storage is at 50F (10C), however can be refrigerated. Will keep up to 1 week.

Preparation: Split, remove seeds and pith.

Boil	Steam	Stir-Fry Sauté	Braise Stew	Bake	Deep-Fry	Grill Broil	Pressure Cook	Microwave	Raw
✔	✔	✔	✔	✔	✔	✔		✔	✔

POTATOES, SWEET

Available: year round; peak: fall through early winter

Selection: Choose uniformly shaped, plump, firm potatoes. Avoid decay, soft spots, or shriveled areas. Colors range from pale to deep yellow to dark brownish-red. As a rule, darker skin means a sweeter, moister flesh. It is the dark-skinned sweet potatoes that are referred to erroneously as *yams*.

Storage: At room temperature, keep 1 week; between 50 to 60F (10 to 15C), keep up to 2 months.

Preparation: Scrub well. Trim ends and woody areas. Peel before or after cooking, depending on use.

Boil	Steam	Stir-Fry Sauté	Braise Stew	Bake	Deep-Fry	Grill Broil	Pressure Cook	Microwave	Raw
✔		✔	✔	✔	✔	✔	✔	✔	

POTATOES, WHITE

Available: year round
New Potatoes—midwinter through early spring

Selection: Choose firm, uniform, smooth, well-shaped potatoes. Avoid blemishes, sprouting, decay or cuts from harvesting. Green color indicates sunburn or exposure to light and should be avoided. Potatoes should have shallow eyes. There are 2 basic types of potatoes: waxy and nonwaxy or mealy. Nonwaxy potatoes or Russet variety, also known as *Idaho bakers,* are especially good for baking, mashing and frying. Nonwaxy potatoes lose their shape when boiled, therefore are poor choices for salads, scalloped potatoes, or other dishes requiring distinct pieces. Waxy potatoes such as round-white, round-red or long-white are higher in sugar content and lower in starch. They hold their shape well if not overcooked. New potatoes are freshly harvested, generally available in midwinter and early spring. Their skin often appears to be peeling, but this does not affect quality. Select new potatoes using guidelines listed above.

Storage: At room temperature, keep 1 week; between 50 to 60F (10 to 15C), keep up to 2 months. Store in a dark location, avoiding direct light which causes potatoes to turn green and bitter.

Preparation: If using potatoes with skin on, scrub with brush to remove surface dirt. Or, peel to remove outer skin. Cut into desired shape or size. To keep pecled potatoes white, place in a bowl of cold water.

Boil	Steam	Stir-Fry Sauté	Braise Stew	Bake	Deep-Fry	Grill Broil	Pressure Cook	Microwave	Raw
✔	✔	✔	✔	✔	✔	✔	✔	✔	

PUMPKIN

Available: fall through early winter

Selection: Choose those with a hard, deep-orange-colored rind.

Storage: Store in a cool, dry location up to 3 months.

Preparation: Split in half. Remove seeds and seed fibers and bake. Or, cut into smaller pieces, peel, then bake or boil. Can also be cooked whole, however seeds should be removed through an opening in the top. Whole pumpkin can then be used as a tureen or serving bowl.

Boil	Steam	Stir-Fry Sauté	Braise Stew	Bake	Deep-Fry	Grill Broil	Pressure Cook	Microwave	Raw
	✔			✔			✔	✔	

RADISHES

Available: year round

Selection: Choose firm, well-shaped radishes, free from cuts or splits. Attached greens should be fresh-looking. Size will range from small, round 1-inch to jumbo-size daikon or Oriental radish.

Storage: Store unwashed in perforated plastic bag in refrigerator 1 to 2 weeks.

Preparation: Wash well. Remove any attached greens, stem and root ends. Slice or serve whole.

Boil	Steam	Stir-Fry Sauté	Braise Stew	Bake	Deep-Fry	Grill Broil	Pressure Cook	Microwave	Raw
✔	✔							✔	✔

Left to Right: Jerusalem Artichokes, Turnips, Jicama, Parsnips, Rutabagas

RUTABAGA

Available: year round; peak: fall through early spring

Selection: Choose small to medium-size rutabagas that are smooth, firm and clean. Avoid bruises. They should be heavy for their size.

Storage: At room temperature, keep 1 week; between 50 to 60F (10 to 15C), keep up to 2 months. Can also be stored in a perforated plastic bag in refrigerator.

Preparation: Remove thick outer skin. Often there is a thin wax coating to preserve moisture and prevent shriveling. This must be removed before cooking.

Boil	Steam	Stir-Fry Sauté	Braise Stew	Bake	Deep-Fry	Grill Broil	Pressure Cook	Microwave	Raw
✔	✔	✔	✔	✔			✔	✔	✔

SALSIFY

Available: year round; peak: midsummer through fall

Selection: Choose firm, clean roots. Avoid cuts from harvesting.

Storage: Store unwashed in perforated plastic bag in refrigerator up to 4 days. Use as soon as possible as flavor deteriorates quickly.

Preparation: Remove outer skin. To keep peeled salsify from discoloring, place in acidulated water.

Boil	Steam	Stir-Fry Sauté	Braise Stew	Bake	Deep-Fry	Grill Broil	Pressure Cook	Microwave	Raw
✔	✔	✔	✔		✔				

SHALLOTS

Available: year round

Selection: Choose firm, clean, well-shaped bulbs which are heavy for their size. Protective papery skins should be dry and glistening.

Storage: Hang bulbs in basket or net bag in cool (50F, 10C), dark, dry location. Will keep several months.

Preparation: Remove top and base. Peel with fingers to remove dry skins and 1 layer of flesh.

Boil	Steam	Stir-Fry Sauté	Braise Stew	Bake	Deep-Fry	Grill Broil	Pressure Cook	Microwave	Raw
✔	✔	✔	✔	✔					✔

SORREL - see Greens

SPINACH

Available: year round; peak: spring through early summer

Selection: Choose large, fresh-looking bunches with dark-green color. Avoid wilted, yellow or limp leaves.

Storage: Store unwashed in perforated plastic bag in refrigerator 1 to 2 days.

Preparation: Wash well in several changes of cold water to remove grit and sand. Drain well. Trim bruised leaves or tough stem ends.

Boil	Steam	Stir-Fry Sauté	Braise Stew	Bake	Deep-Fry	Grill Broil	Pressure Cook	Microwave	Raw
✔	✔	✔	✔		✔		✔	✔	✔

Left to Right: Chayote, Yellow Crookneck, Yellow Straightneck, Zucchini, Pattypan

SQUASH, SUMMER

Available: year round; peak: late spring through early fall

Selection: Choose summer varieties that are tender, well-formed, firm and fresh in appearance. Avoid any with a hard dull rind. Summer squash are picked while young. Common varieties of summer squash include the cylindrical green zucchini, ideally 4 to 6 inches long and 1 to 1-1/2 inches in diameter. A similar squash is Cocozelle, identified by white striping on green skin. Italian Marrow is a slender, bright-green squash. Yellow Crookneck has a crane-shaped neck and is best under 6 inches long. Yellow Straightneck is just that, without a curve. Pattypan, also called scalloped squash, has a bowl-shape and definite scalloped design around its circumference. Its color may be yellow, white or pale green.

Storage: Store unwashed in perforated plastic bag in refrigerator 3 to 4 days.

Preparation: Rinse and trim ends. Young, tender squash do not need to be peeled. If desired, salt lightly after cutting into desired-size pieces. Let stand 15 to 30 minutes in colander. Rinse well and pat dry with paper towel. This removes excess moisture and any bitter taste.

Boil	Steam	Stir-Fry Sauté	Braise Stew	Bake	Deep-Fry	Grill Broil	Pressure Cook	Microwave	Raw
✔	✔	✔	✔	✔	✔	✔	✔	✔	✔

SQUASH, WINTER

Available: late summer through early spring

Selection: Choose winter varieties with a hard, deep-colored rind. Squash heavy for their size indicate good maturity. Winter squash are mature with a hard rind that protects the firm, fibrous inside flesh. There are several common varieties of winter squash. Banana squash, averaging 10 to 15 pounds, is cylindrically shaped with olive-gray skin and bright-orange flesh. Hubbard squash is big, averaging around 12 pounds each, with a thick bumpy skin from dark-green to deep-orange and yellow-orange flesh. Acorn, also known as Table Queen, Danish or Des Moines, is a convenient size, weighing 1 to 2 pounds. It has distinct ribs running the length of its hard blackish-green or golden-yellow skin. Butternut is readily identified by its bulbous end and pale creamy skin. Inside is a choice fine-textured deep-orange flesh. Buttercup is a turban squash with a bulb-like cap swelling from its blossom end. The gray-flecked green rind encloses yellowish-orange flesh. Spaghetti squash ranges in size from 2-1/2 to 5 or more pounds. It has a golden-yellow oval exterior. When cooked, the inner flesh separates into spaghetti-like strands.

Storage: Store in a cool, dry location up to 3 months.

Preparation: To split, snap off stem. Lay squash on a cutting board. Push the blade of a chef's knife into shell. With a mallet, strike the knife spine near the handle to force blade into the squash. Continue to tap gently until squash splits in half. Scoop out seeds with a sturdy spoon. Bake in the rind or cut in small pieces and remove rind. To prepare whole spaghetti squash, wash outer surface. Pierce with fork several times to allow steam to escape. Bake according to recipe instructions. Cut squash in half and remove seeds.

Boil	Steam	Stir-Fry Sauté	Braise Stew	Bake	Deep-Fry	Grill Broil	Pressure Cook	Microwave	Raw
✔	✔	✔	✔	✔			✔	✔	✔

Left to Right: Acorn (Des Moines or Table Queen), Banana, Butternut, Spaghetti, Dumpling

SWEET CORN - see Corn

SWEET POTATOES - see Potatoes

SWISS CHARD - see Chard

TOMATOES

Available: year round; peak: late spring through summer

Selection: Choose those that are well-formed, smooth, slightly soft with an overall rich red color. When available, vine-ripened tomatoes offer the best flavor by far.

Storage: Ideal storage is at 50F (10C), however can be refrigerated up to 5 days. Chilling reduces flavor. To ripen green or under-ripe tomatoes, place them in a paper bag or wrap in newspaper. Keep at room temperature or about 65F (20C).

Preparation: To peel tomatoes with ease, remove core. At the opposite side slash skin in a cross. Lower tomatoes into boiling water 30 to 60 seconds to blanch. Cool under cold water. Drain well and peel starting with a slashed section. To seed tomatoes, cut in half. Gently squeeze to remove seeds.

Boil	Steam	Stir-Fry Sauté	Braise Stew	Bake	Deep-Fry	Grill Broil	Pressure Cook	Microwave	Raw
		✔	✔	✔	✔	✔	✔	✔	✔

TURNIP GREENS - see Greens

TURNIPS

Available: year round; peak: fall through early spring

Selection: Choose small to medium size, smooth, clean, firm and slightly rounded turnips.

Storage: Store unwashed in perforated plastic bag in refrigerator up to 1 week.

Preparation: Wash well. Remove outer skin. Cut into desired shape or size.

Boil	Steam	Stir-Fry Sauté	Braise Stew	Bake	Deep-Fry	Grill Broil	Pressure Cook	Microwave	Raw
✔	✔	✔	✔	✔	✔	✔	✔	✔	✔

WATERCRESS

Available: year round

Selection: Choose fresh, crisp, dark-green glossy leaves. Avoid yellow or wilted leaves.

Storage: Store unwashed in perforated plastic bag in refrigerator 4 to 5 days or place in a container with stems in water. Cover with a plastic bag and refrigerate.

Preparation: Wash well in cold water. Drain well. Trim bruised leaves or tough stem ends.

Boil	Steam	Stir-Fry Sauté	Braise Stew	Bake	Deep-Fry	Grill Broil	Pressure Cook	Microwave	Raw
									✔

VEGETABLE APPETIZERS

Appetizers make an impact. They set the stage for the menu that follows. With a true purpose to whet the appetite, a thoughtfully chosen, savory morsel is often more welcome than a quantity of tidbits. In fact, an endless array of appetizers as a dinner prelude is disappearing in favor of a first-course appetizer served at the table.

Place appetizers strategically so they work for you. People will introduce themselves over a plate of Stuffed Mushrooms or as they dip into a fondue pot of Hot Garlic & Anchovy Sauce. Before you know it, your guests are feeling totally at ease.

New vegetable choices spark interest and enhance any occasion. Introduce one or more to set a mood. Offer meaty Oriental shiitake mushrooms sealed under a layer of goat cheese in Grilled Shiitake Mushrooms with Cheese. Or serve Sugar Snap peas spread with a herb-flavored cheese in the Stuffed-Vegetable Platter.

This appetizer selection is world-wide, with ethnic specialties from many lands. Nosegays of vegetables tucked in a wicker basket provide vitamin-packed crunchy dipping for the Provençal Mayonnaise. Japanese Tempura is delightful as a starter with its crisp, delicate coating encasing an array of vegetables or seafood. From the Greek cuisine come Dolmas, grape leaves rolled around a tasty stuffing of rice and pine nuts.

Mushrooms enhance many specialties. Try nut-flavored Mushroom & Almond Pâté, or Tiny Mushroom Pastries with flaky cream-cheese pastry.

Appetizer choices vary with the seasons, availability of vegetables and personal preferences. With vegetables starring in the introductory role, any meal or social event begins with flair and lightness.

Mediterranean-Style Theatre Party

Garbanzo-Sesame Spread, page 33
Lavosh and Pita Bread
Provençal Mayonnaise with
Vegetable Dippers, page 35
Dolmas, page 36
Hot Mushroom & Sausage Triangles, page 42
Florentine Meatballs, page 41

Blue-Cheese Dip with Vegetables

For a festive first course, spoon dip into small stoneware dishes making individual servings.

**3 oz. natural cream cheese or
 packaged cream cheese, room temperature**
1 cup dairy sour cream
3/4 teaspoon Worcestershire sauce
**1 tablespoon finely chopped chives or
 green onions**
2 tablespoons chopped fresh parsley

1 garlic clove, minced
1/8 teaspoon salt
1/8 teaspoon freshly ground pepper
Dash hot-pepper sauce
1/4 lb. blue cheese, room temperature
Assorted raw vegetables

In a small bowl, beat together cream cheese, sour cream and Worcestershire sauce. Mix in chives or green onions, parsley, garlic, salt, pepper and hot-pepper sauce. Crumble in blue cheese. Mix well. Spoon into a medium bowl. Cover and refrigerate. Serve with assorted raw vegetables. Makes 1-1/2 cups.

Green Goddess Dip

Serve as an appetizer dip, salad dressing or sauce for vegetables.

1 egg
1 tablespoon lemon juice
2 tablespoons white-wine vinegar
2 teaspoons Dijon-style mustard
3/4 teaspoon salt
1/4 teaspoon white pepper
7/8 cup safflower oil

1/2 cup minced fresh parsley
2 tablespoons minced chives
2 green onions, chopped
3 anchovy fillets, chopped
1/3 cup dairy sour cream
Assorted vegetables, raw or cooked

In a blender or food processor fitted with a steel blade, place egg, lemon juice, vinegar, mustard, salt and white pepper. Process until blended. With motor running, slowly pour in oil. Add parsley, chives, green onions and anchovies. Process until minced. Add sour cream. Process 10 seconds just to mix in. Place mixture in a small bowl. Cover and refrigerate. Serve with assorted vegetables. Makes 1-1/2 cups.

Hot Garlic & Anchovy Sauce

In the Piedmont region of Italy, this vegetable dip is known as Bagna Caôda.

2 cups whipping cream
3 tablespoons unsalted butter
4 to 5 garlic cloves, minced

6 anchovy fillets, finely chopped
Assorted raw vegetables

In a medium, heavy saucepan, bring cream to a boil over medium heat. Reduce heat. Cook cream over low heat until reduced to 1 cup, 5 to 10 minutes. Stir frequently to prevent boil-over. As a precaution, place a special disc that prevents boil-over in the bottom of the saucepan. In a small saucepan, melt butter over medium heat. Add garlic and anchovies. Cook 1 minute. Stir in reduced cream. Heat through. Place in a fondue pot or warming dish. Serve with assorted raw vegetables. Makes 1-1/4 cups.

Eggplant Caviar

Create a smoky flavored mock caviar using cooked eggplant and seasonings.

1 large eggplant
2 tablespoons olive oil
1/4 lb. mushrooms, chopped
2 green onions, chopped, white part only
2 tablespoons lemon juice
2 garlic cloves, chopped
1/2 cup plain yogurt
1/4 teaspoon salt

1/4 teaspoon freshly ground pepper
2 tablespoons minced fresh parsley
Grape leaves or romaine lettuce leaves
1/4 cup shelled pistachios or
  toasted chopped walnuts
Cherry tomatoes or ripe olives
Lavosh or sesame-seed crackers

Preheat oven to 400F (205C). Place whole eggplant in an 8-inch square or round 9-inch baking dish. Bake 40 to 45 minutes or until soft. Spear softened eggplant with a fork. Hold eggplant over gas flame to char the outer skin lightly and lend a smoky flavor. Or, place under a broiler to char skin. Immediately dip eggplant in a bowl of cold water. Prick skin with a fork and squeeze out juices. Peel off and discard skin. Cool peeled eggplant; set aside. Heat oil in a large skillet over medium-high heat. Add mushrooms and green onions. Sauté until soft, 2 to 3 minutes. Cool. Dice eggplant pulp. In a blender or food processor fitted with a steel blade, place eggplant pulp, mushrooms and green onions, lemon juice, garlic, yogurt, salt, pepper and parsley. Process until smooth. Line a medium bowl with grape leaves or romaine leaves. Spoon eggplant spread into bowl. Cover and refrigerate. Before serving, sprinkle with pistachios or walnuts. Garnish with tomatoes or olives. Serve with lavosh or sesame-seed crackers. Makes 2 to 2-1/2 cups.

Garbanzo-Sesame Spread

Sesame-seed paste adds flavor to this spread. Serve with lavosh, a bubbly Armenian bread.

1 (1-lb.) can garbanzo beans
1/3 cup lemon juice
1/3 cup tahini (sesame-seed paste)
2 garlic cloves
3/4 teaspoon ground cumin
3 tablespoons chopped green onion
1/4 teaspoon salt

1/4 teaspoon freshly ground pepper
2 tablespoons chopped fresh cilantro or
  Italian flat-leaf parsley
3 tablespoons pomegranate seeds or
  1/2 cup dry black Greek olives
Lavosh or pita bread

Drain garbanzo beans, reserving juice. In a blender or food processor fitted with a steel blade, combine beans, lemon juice, tahini, garlic, cumin, green onion, salt and pepper. Process until smooth. If mixture is too stiff, add 1 to 2 tablespoons reserved bean juice. Place bean spread in a medium bowl. Cover and refrigerate. Place on serving plate. Using a spatula, form chilled spread into a pyramid shape. Sprinkle with cilantro or parsley. Garnish with pomegranate seeds or olives. Serve with lavosh or pita bread. Makes 2 cups.

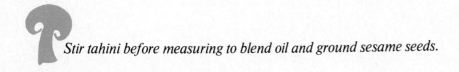

Stir tahini before measuring to blend oil and ground sesame seeds.

Hot Artichoke Dip & Rye Wafers

Make your own rye crackers to serve with any dip or cheese spread.

Rye Wafers, see below
1 (10-oz.) jar artichoke hearts in brine,
   drained
1/2 cup mayonnaise

1/2 cup freshly grated Romano cheese
   (1-1/2 oz.)
1/2 cup shredded Jarlsberg or
   Swiss cheese (2 oz.)

Rye Wafers:
1 cup rye flour
1 cup plus 2 tablespoons water

Coarse salt or sesame seeds

Prepare Rye Wafers. Preheat oven to 375F (190C). In a medium bowl, coarsely mash artichoke hearts. Stir in mayonnaise and cheeses. Spoon into a 1-quart ovenproof serving dish. Bake 20 to 25 minutes or until heated through. Serve warm with Rye Wafers. Makes 2-1/2 cups.

Rye Wafers:
Preheat oven to 350F (175C). Lightly butter 2 non-stick-surface baking sheets or line baking sheets with parchment paper. In a blender or food processor fitted with a steel blade, combine rye flour and water. Process until smooth. Batter should be consistency of thin pancake batter. Pour batter onto baking sheets in 1-1/2-inch circles. Sprinkle circles of batter lightly with coarse salt or sesame seeds. Bake 18 to 20 minutes or until golden brown. Remove wafers to a rack. Cool completely. Makes about 50 wafers.

Mushroom & Almond Pâté

Toasted almonds give this creamy vegetable spread a delicious nutty flavor.

1/2 cup blanched almonds
2 tablespoons butter
2 green onions finely chopped,
   white part only
1/2 lb. mushrooms, chopped
1 garlic clove, minced
1-1/2 teaspoons lemon juice

1/2 teaspoon chopped fresh tarragon or
   1/8 teaspoon dried leaf tarragon
1/4 teaspoon salt
1/4 teaspoon freshly ground pepper
1/4 cup dairy sour cream
4 to 5 sprigs parsley
Crisp crackers, flatbread or rye wafers

Preheat oven to 300F (150C). Spread almonds in a 9-inch pie dish. Bake 10 to 15 minutes or until golden brown; set aside. Melt 1 tablespoon butter in a large skillet over medium heat. Add green onions. Sauté until lightly browned, 4 to 5 minutes. Add remaining butter, mushrooms, garlic, lemon juice, tarragon, salt and pepper. Cook over high heat 2 minutes. With a slotted spoon, remove vegetables to a bowl. Cook pan juices over high heat until reduced to 1 tablespoon. Place toasted almonds in a blender or food processor fitted with a steel blade. Process until finely ground. Add mushroom mixture, pan juices and sour cream. Process until nearly smooth. Spoon into a serving dish. Cover and refrigerate until chilled, about 3 hours. Garnish with parsley. Serve with crackers, flatbread or rye wafers. Makes 1-1/3 cups.

Variation

Add 2 tablespoons sherry to almonds in blender or food processor. Then add mushroom mixture.

Herb Cream Cheese   Photo on pages 74 and 75.

When seasoned with herbs, natural cream cheese resembles imported Boursin.

3/4 lb. natural cream cheese or packaged
   cream cheese, room temperature
3 tablespoons dairy sour cream
1/3 cup whipping cream
3 tablespoons minced fresh parsley
2 teaspoons chopped fresh tarragon or
   1/2 teaspoon dried leaf tarragon
Toppings: 1 tablespoon coarsely ground pepper,
   1 tablespoon toasted finely chopped walnuts or filberts,
   1 tablespoon Herbs of Provence, page 111, or
   1 tablespoon minced fresh tarragon,
   fresh parsley or chives

2 green onions, minced
2 garlic cloves, minced
1/8 teaspoon salt
Few drops hot-pepper sauce
Assorted raw vegetables

In a medium bowl, blend cream cheese and sour cream. Add whipping cream. Beat until smooth. Mix in parsley, tarragon, green onions, garlic, salt and hot-pepper sauce. Shape into 3 rounds on a plate, spoon into individual crocks or place in a serving dish. Cover and refrigerate. When ready to serve, sprinkle with desired topping. Serve with assorted raw vegetables. Makes about 2 cups.

Provençal Mayonnaise

Make an attractive arrangement of raw vegetables to serve with this tasty dip.

2 egg yolks
1-1/2 tablespoons white-wine vinegar
1-1/2 tablespoons lemon juice
1 teaspoon dry mustard
1 teaspoon salt
1/4 teaspoon white pepper
2/3 cup safflower oil

1/3 cup olive oil
3 tablespoons capers, chopped
1 garlic clove, minced
4 anchovy fillets, finely chopped
3 tablespoons chopped fresh parsley
1/2 teaspoon grated lemon peel
Assorted raw vegetables

In a blender container or food processor fitted with a steel blade, place egg yolks, vinegar, lemon juice, mustard, salt and white pepper. Process until smooth. With motor running, slowly pour in safflower oil and olive oil. Process until smooth. Add capers, garlic, anchovies, parsley and lemon peel. Process until finely minced. Pour into a small bowl. Cover and refrigerate. Serve with assorted raw vegetables. Makes 1-1/3 cups.

 It is important to pour oil in a slow steady stream to ensure smooth creamy mayonnaise.

How To Make Dolmas

1/Drop grape leaves into boiling water. Lift blanched leaves from water with a slotted spoon. Drain well.

2/Place 1 teaspoon rice mixture in center of each leaf, shiny surface down. Fold like an envelope. Roll up loosely.

Dolmas

Pilaf-stuffed grape leaves make a delicious appetizer or an attractive garnish on a dinner plate.

1 (8-oz.) jar grape leaves, drained, or	1/2 teaspoon salt
48 fresh grape leaves	1/3 cup pine nuts
6 tablespoons olive oil	3 tablespoons currants
1 large onion, finely chopped	2 cups water
1 cup uncooked short-grain rice	6 tablespoons lemon juice
1/4 cup minced fresh parsley	2 cups beef broth
2 tablespoons chopped fresh dill or	Lemon wedges
1-1/2 teaspoons dried dill weed	

Fill a large saucepan with water. Bring to a boil. Drop grape leaves into boiling water. Using a slotted spoon, immediately remove canned leaves and drain well. If using fresh grape leaves, blanch in boiling water 1 minute. Lift leaves out with a slotted spoon. Drain well. Remove stems from leaves. Pat each leaf dry with paper towel. Heat 1/4 cup oil in a large skillet. Add onion. Sauté over medium heat until lightly browned, 4 to 5 minutes. Add rice, parsley, dill, salt, pine nuts, currants and 1 cup water. Cover and reduce heat. Simmer 10 minutes or until liquid is absorbed. Cool. Place 1 teaspoon rice mixture in center of each leaf, shiny surface down. Fold like an envelope. Roll up loosely to allow space for rice to expand. Arrange rolls in layers in a 3-quart saucepan. Sprinkle with lemon juice and remaining 2 tablespoons oil. Pour broth and 1 cup water over rolls. Weight rolls down with a baking dish to keep in place. Cover. Simmer over low heat 35 minutes or until tender when pierced with a fork. Cool. To serve, arrange on a platter and garnish with lemon wedges. Makes 48 appetizer servings.

Tempura

Frittered fish and vegetables done Japanese-style make a congenial dish for a garden party.

Tempura Batter, see below
Peanut oil or corn oil for deep-frying
6 large shrimp, peeled with tails left on,
   deveined
6 Chinese pea pods, trimmed
6 medium mushrooms

2 small carrots, thinly sliced diagonally
1 yellow crookneck squash, ends trimmed,
   cut in 1/4-inch slices
1/2 medium eggplant, cut in 1/4-inch slices
6 large scallops
Grated gingerroot and daikon

Tempura Batter:
2 eggs
1 cup ice water

3/4 cup all-purpose flour

Prepare Tempura Batter. Using a deep-fat fryer, electric frying pan, wok or heavy saucepan, pour oil to 3-inch depth. Heat to 375F (190C). At this temperature a 1-inch cube of bread will turn golden brown in 50 seconds. When oil is ready, dip a few whole vegetables or slices and several shrimp and scallops in batter. Immediately place batter-coated vegetables and seafood in hot oil. With chopsticks, swirl each vegetable slightly so batter cooks into a lacy design. Cook each item until golden brown. Repeat with remaining vegetables and seafood. Avoid crowding. Drain well on paper towel before serving. Serve with grated gingerroot and daikon for dipping. Makes 6 appetizer servings.

Tempura Batter:
Whisk eggs in a medium bowl until blended. Beat in water and flour until smooth. Place bowl of batter inside a bowl lined with ice to keep batter cold while cooking vegetables.

Chile con Queso   Photo on page 97.

Double this popular Mexican appetizer recipe for a large group.

2 tablespoons butter
1 large onion, finely chopped
2 large tomatoes, peeled, chopped
2 canned green chili peppers
1/4 teaspoon salt

1/4 teaspoon freshly ground pepper
3/4 lb. teleme cheese, sliced, or
   3/4 lb. Monterey Jack or Cheddar cheese,
   shredded (3 cups)
Small hot deep-fried tortillas or tortilla chips

Melt butter in a combination cooking-serving dish over medium heat. Add onion. Sauté until lightly browned, 4 to 5 minutes. Add tomatoes. Sauté 1 minute. Split chili peppers and remove seeds. Chop peppers. Add chopped peppers, salt and pepper to tomato mixture. Sauté 1 minute. Add cheese. Heat until cheese melts, 3 to 4 minutes. Place dish over a warming candle or on a warming tray. Serve with hot tortillas or tortilla chips. Makes 3 cups.

 Avoid overheating cheese or it can become stringy, rather than sauce-like in consistency.

Stuffed-Vegetable Platter

This decorative platter is fast to assemble.

Oyster-Stuffed Tomatoes:
1-1/2 cups cherry tomatoes
1 (3-3/4-oz.) can smoked oysters

Parsley sprigs

Chive-Stuffed Pea Pods:
24 Chinese pea pods, trimmed
1 (3-oz.) pkg. cream cheese,
   room temperature

2 tablespoons whipping cream
2 tablespoons chopped chives

Cheese-Tipped Fennel:
1 bunch fennel or celery
3 oz. blue cheese, room temperature

Endive with Curried Shrimp:
3 medium Belgian endive
1/4 cup mayonnaise

1/2 teaspoon curry powder
24 small cooked shrimp

Prepare Oyster-Stuffed Tomatoes, Chive-Stuffed Pea Pods, Cheese-Tipped Fennel and Endive with Curried Shrimp. Arrange 4 types of appetizers on a platter. Cover and refrigerate up to 2 hours. Makes 12 to 16 appetizer servings.

Oyster-Stuffed Tomatoes:
Cut a slash in each tomato. Insert an oyster in each tomato. Skewer closed with a wooden pick if desired. Garnish with a parsley sprig.

Chive-Stuffed Pea Pods:
Blanch Chinese pea pods in boiling salted water 30 seconds. Drain well. Refresh in cold water. Drain well. Carefully slit open 1 side of each pea pod. In a small bowl, blend cream cheese, cream and chives. Spread cheese filling inside each pod. Use a piping bag, if desired.

Cheese-Tipped Fennel:
Cut fennel bulb or celery stalks into 1-1/2-inch pieces. Spread ends of pieces with blue cheese. Garnish as desired.

Endive with Curried Shrimp:
Separate endive leaves. In a small bowl, combine mayonnaise and curry powder. Place a dollop of mayonnaise mixture on the bottom end of each leaf. Place a shrimp on top of mayonnaise mixture. Garnish as desired.

Stuffed-Vegetable Platter, featuring Oyster-Stuffed Tomatoes, Chive-Stuffed Pea Pods, Cheese-Tipped Celery and Endive with Curried Shrimp.

How to Prepare Baby Artichokes

1/Pull off lower outer leaves from artichokes. Trim stem ends. Cut each artichoke in half.

2/Using the tip of a peeler or paring knife, scrape or scoop out the fuzzy choke center.

Italian Antipasto

A tangy tomato sauce coats this array of vegetables, surrounded by tuna and anchovies.

1 cup chili sauce
1 cup ketchup
1/2 cup water
1/2 cup white-wine vinegar
1/2 cup lemon juice
1/3 cup olive oil
2 garlic cloves, minced
1 tablespoon brown sugar
1 tablespoon Worcestershire sauce
1 tablespoon Dijon-style mustard
1/2 teaspoon salt

1/2 teaspoon freshly ground pepper
1 (9-oz.) pkg. frozen artichoke hearts, thawed, or 12 fresh baby artichokes or artichoke hearts
12 small boiling onions, peeled
3 small carrots, sliced
1 small cauliflower, cut in flowerets
1/2 lb. button mushrooms
2 (7-oz.) cans white albacore tuna
1 (20-oz.) can rolled anchovies with capers
2 tablespoons chopped fresh parsley

In a 3-quart saucepan, combine chili sauce, ketchup, water, vinegar, lemon juice, oil, garlic, brown sugar, Worcestershire sauce, mustard, salt and pepper. Bring to a boil. Reduce heat. Simmer 5 minutes. If using fresh artichokes, pull off lower outer leaves. Trim stem ends. Cut each artichoke in half. Using the tip of a peeler or paring knife, scrape or scoop out the fuzzy choke center. Add artichokes and onions to tomato sauce. Simmer 10 minutes. Add carrots and cauliflower. Simmer 7 minutes. Add mushrooms. Simmer 3 minutes or until vegetables are crisp-tender. Spoon onto a platter. Cover and refrigerate. To serve, place tuna in center of platter. Top with rolled anchovies and parsley. Makes 12 appetizer servings.

Florentine Meatballs

Spinach, Parmesan cheese, sausage and ground turkey give an added flavor dimension to meatballs.

1 (12-oz.) bunch spinach or 1 (10-oz.) pkg.
   frozen chopped spinach, thawed
3 tablespoons butter
1 small onion, chopped
3 eggs
2 slices sourdough French bread, crumbled
2 tablespoons chopped fresh parsley
1/3 cup freshly grated Parmesan cheese
   (1 oz.)

1 teaspoon salt
1/2 teaspoon freshly ground pepper
1/2 teaspoon dried leaf oregano
2 garlic cloves, minced
1 lb. ground turkey
1/2 lb. ground pork
1/2 lb. bulk Italian sausage
All-purpose flour
2 tablespoons red-wine vinegar

Wash fresh spinach thoroughly in several changes of cold water. Discard stems and bruised or tough leaves. Chop washed spinach. Place chopped spinach and a small amount of water in a medium saucepan. Cook over medium heat until spinach is limp, 3 to 4 minutes. Drain well. Squeeze fresh cooked or thawed frozen spinach to remove as much moisture as possible; set aside. Melt 1 tablespoon butter in a large skillet over medium heat. Add onion. Sauté until soft, 1 to 2 minutes. Beat eggs in a large bowl. Mix in breadcrumbs, parsley, cheese, salt, pepper, oregano and garlic. Add turkey, pork, sausage, spinach and onion. Mix well to blend. Shape into 1-inch balls. Roll meatballs in flour. Melt 2 tablespoons butter in a large skillet over medium heat. Add meatballs. Sauté until browned on all sides and cooked through, 4 to 5 minutes. Add vinegar and cook until liquid is reduced to a glaze, shaking pan to coat meatballs. Serve in a warming dish or fondue pot. Makes 48 appetizer servings.

Grilled Shiitake Mushrooms with Cheese

This almost-instant appetizer presents the meaty shiitake mushroom in a cloak of goat cheese.

4 large shiitake mushrooms
1/4 cup unsalted butter, melted
3 tablespoons minced fresh parsley
2 garlic cloves, minced

1 teaspoon chopped fresh basil or tarragon, or
   1/4 teaspoon dried leaf basil or tarragon
2 oz. chèvre cheese

Preheat oven to 400F (205C). Butter a 9-inch pie dish or 4 individual ramekins. Remove stems from mushrooms. Slice mushrooms and stems 1/3-inch thick. Arrange in pie dish or ramekins. In a small saucepan, heat melted butter, parsley, garlic and basil or tarragon over low heat until blended, 1 minute. Pour butter mixture over mushrooms. Bake 5 minutes. Cut cheese in 4 slices. Place 1 slice in each ramekin or over mushrooms in pie dish. Change oven temperature to broil. Place mushroom mixture under broiler. Broil until cheese melts, about 1 minute. Makes 4 appetizer servings.

 The regular large mushrooms, about 1-3/4 inches in diameter, make a suitable stand-in for shiitake mushrooms.

Hot Mushroom & Sausage Triangles

Filo encases these succulent appetizer morsels in a crispy wrapper. Freeze them for a spontaneous party.

1 lb. mild Italian sausage
2 tablespoons butter
1/2 lb. mushrooms, chopped
2 green onions, chopped
2 tablespoons chopped fresh parsley
2 tablespoons fine dry breadcrumbs

1 egg, lightly beaten
1 cup shredded Gruyère or Jarlsberg cheese
  (4 oz.)
8 sheets filo dough (18" x 12")
1/4 cup butter, melted

Place sausages in a medium saucepan. Cover with cold water. Bring to a boil. Remove from heat. Let stand 15 minutes. Drain well. Remove casings and chop sausage. Preheat oven to 375F (190C). Butter 2 baking sheets. Melt 2 tablespoons butter in a large skillet over medium-high heat. Add mushrooms and green onions. Sauté until glazed, about 2 minutes. Cool. In a medium bowl, combine sausage, mushrooms and green onions, parsley, breadcrumbs, egg and cheese. Mix lightly. Lay out 1 filo sheet. Brush lightly with melted butter. Cover remaining sheets with plastic wrap or a slightly damp towel to prevent drying. Cut filo sheet in 3-inch strips across short side, making 6 strips. Place a generous teaspoon of filling at 1 end of each strip. Fold like a flag into triangles. Place on buttered baking sheet. Repeat with remaining filo sheets and sausage mixture. Bake 15 minutes or until golden brown. Serve hot. Makes 48 appetizer servings.

Tiny Mushroom Pastries

Cream-cheese pastry forms a flaky container for a creamy mushroom filling.

Cream-Cheese Pastry, see below
2 tablespoons butter
1 small onion, finely chopped
1/2 lb. mushrooms, chopped
1 teaspoon chopped fresh tarragon or
  1/4 teaspoon dried leaf tarragon

1/4 teaspoon salt
1/4 teaspoon freshly ground pepper
2 egg yolks
1/2 cup dairy sour cream

Cream-Cheese Pastry:
3-oz. pkg. cream cheese, room temperature
1/2 cup butter, room temperature
2 tablespoons whipping cream

1-1/4 cups all-purpose flour
1/2 teaspoon salt

Prepare dough for Cream-Cheese Pastry. Preheat oven to 350F (175C). Melt butter in a large skillet over medium heat. Add onion. Sauté until lightly browned, 4 to 5 minutes. Add mushrooms. Sauté until mushrooms are glazed, about 2 minutes. Remove from heat. Add tarragon, salt and pepper. In a small bowl, beat egg yolks until blended. Stir in sour cream. Stir sour-cream mixture into mushroom mixture. Spoon mushroom filling into dough-lined tart shells. Bake 15 to 20 minutes or until pastry is golden brown and filling is set. Makes 24 appetizer servings.

Cream-Cheese Pastry:
Place cream cheese and butter in a medium bowl. Beat until creamy. Add whipping cream. Mix until blended. Stir in flour and salt. Mix until dough clings together in a ball. Wrap in plastic wrap. Refrigerate until firm, about 30 minutes. Roll pastry on a lightly floured board to 1/8-inch thickness. Line 24 (1-1/2- to 2-inch) tart pans with pastry dough, pressing with fingertips to make an even layer about 1/8-inch thick. Refrigerate 15 minutes or until dough is firm.

Stuffed Mushrooms

Large mushroom caps form edible containers for this meaty Italian stuffing.

Wine Sauce, see below
12 (2-inch) mushrooms, about 1 lb.
2 tablespoons butter
1 small onion, chopped
1/2 lb. ground veal, ground turkey or
   ground pork
1/4 teaspoon salt
1/4 teaspoon freshly ground pepper

1 tablespoon chopped fresh parsley
1 teaspoon chopped fresh basil or
   1/4 teaspoon dried leaf basil
1/4 cup freshly grated Parmesan or
   Romano cheese (3/4 oz.)
1/4 cup finely chopped prosciutto
   or cooked ham
1 egg

Wine Sauce:
1 tablespoon butter
1/4 cup chopped onion
1/4 cup chopped tomato
1/2 teaspoon chopped fresh basil or
   1/8 teaspoon dried leaf basil

1/4 cup dry white wine
1/2 cup chicken broth

Prepare Wine Sauce. Preheat oven to 375F (190C). Remove mushroom stems and reserve. Melt butter in a large skillet over medium-high heat. Add mushroom caps. Sauté until glazed, about 2 minutes. Remove from skillet; set aside. Finely chop stems Place mushroom stems and onion in large skillet. Sauté mushroom stems and onion until soft, about 2 minutes. Add ground meat. Sauté until meat is browned and crumbly, 4 to 5 minutes. Add salt, pepper, parsley and basil. Mix in 2 tablespoons cheese, prosciutto or cooked ham and egg. Pack 1 rounded tablespoon meat mixture into each mushroom cap. Place stuffed mushroom caps in an 8-inch square baking dish. Pour Wine Sauce over mushrooms. Sprinkle remaining cheese over mushrooms. Cover with foil. Bake 15 minutes. Remove foil and continue baking 10 minutes. Makes 12 appetizer servings.

Wine Sauce:
Melt butter in a small saucepan over medium heat. Add onion and tomato. Sauté until soft, about 2 minutes. Add basil, wine and broth. Bring to a boil. Cook over high heat until liquid is reduced slightly. Set aside until ready to use.

French-Fried Potato Skins

Use left-over potatoes for making Potatoes Anna, page 135, or Bacon & Potato Squares, page 86.

6 large baking potatoes, scrubbed
Oil for deep-frying
Salt to taste

Seasonings: seasoned salt, garlic salt,
   celery salt, grated Parmesan cheese,
   toasted sesame seeds

Using a vegetable peeler, cut long thin strips or spirals of potato skin. Reserve potatoes for later use. Place potato skins in a bowl of ice water. Let stand 30 minutes. Drain well. Pat dry with paper towel. Using a deep-fat fryer, electric frying pan, wok or heavy saucepan, pour oil to 3-inch depth. Heat to 390F (200C). At this temperature a 1-inch cube of bread will turn golden brown in 20 seconds. When oil is ready, drop in chilled potato skins, a few at a time. Fry until skins are golden brown and crisp, about 1 minute. Repeat with remaining potato skins. Drain well on paper towel. Sprinkle skins with salt or choice of seasoning. Serve immediately. Makes 6 to 8 appetizer servings.

HOT & COLD SOUPS

Vegetables from the garden or marketplace are the basis for tantalizing soups. Whether cold or hot, soups are nutritious, easy and thrifty. They add endless variety, great charm and even sophistication to a menu. Their personality range is boundless. Consider frosty summer Gazpacho Monterey, garnished with avocado, sunflower seeds and cooling ice cubes, or a whimsical pumpkin shell bearing an earthy soup.

The blender and food processor have revolutionized the soup kitchen. These handy machines quickly turn combinations of stock and assorted vegetables into smooth puree, intertwining flavors into exotic new tastes. Often these soups are low-calorie because the vegetable purees provide rich body and thickening power without the necessity for whipping cream or a bechamel sauce.

With fresh stock from the pot or freezer or by utilizing instant bouillon, soups are fast to assemble. Plus they have that handy asset of being flexible and expandable. The soup pot can always be enriched and stretched to feed an impromptu guest.

These international soups come from many lands. Cheese-crusted Les Halles Onion Soup comes from the old bustling Parisian marketplace, where once homebound revelers and hardworking merchants rubbed elbows.

Yellow Split-Pea Soup was a favorite childhood soup, a carryover from mother's Swedish heritage. After marrying into a Greek family, I added Lentil Soup to our midwinter soup repertoire.

Superb soups are a part of fine dining. Cold or hot, first course or full meal, soups are a delight for all seasons.

Soup's On
Beef & Barley Soup, page 56
French Vegetable Soup, page 50
Green Goddess Dip with
Vegetable Dippers, page 32
Cheeses with Crusty Bread
Assorted Crackers
Fresh Pear Tarts

Vichyssoise

A classic French soup, perfect to begin a summer meal.

4 medium leeks
2 tablespoons butter
1 medium onion, chopped
5 medium potatoes, peeled, sliced
1 qt. chicken broth
1/2 teaspoon dried leaf tarragon

1/2 teaspoon salt
1/4 teaspoon freshly ground pepper
2 cups milk
1 cup whipping cream
1/4 cup dry sherry
2 tablespoons finely chopped chives

Trim leeks discarding green tops. Quarter lengthwise, cutting almost to the root. Wash under cold running water, pulling layers apart so grit is removed. Finely chop washed leeks. Melt butter in a 3-quart saucepan over medium heat. Add leeks and onion. Sauté until barely golden, 2 to 3 minutes. Add potatoes, broth, tarragon, salt and pepper. Cover and reduce heat. Simmer 30 minutes or until potatoes are soft. Cool slightly. Puree in 2 to 3 batches in a blender or food processor fitted with a steel blade. Add milk. Process just to combine milk. Cover and refrigerate. Immediately before serving, stir in cream and sherry. Ladle chilled soup into bowls, mugs or large-bowled wine glasses. Sprinkle with chives. Makes 10 servings.

Gazpacho Monterey

This Spanish soup makes a cool first course or luncheon entree.

1 medium cucumber, peeled, finely chopped
1 small red onion, finely chopped
5 large tomatoes, peeled, finely chopped
2 garlic cloves, minced
1 cup beef broth
1 cup vegetable-juice cocktail
2 tablespoons lime juice
Toppings: toasted slivered almonds, diced avocado,
    garlic-buttered croutons, diced cream cheese,
    roasted pumpkin seeds, crumbled crisp bacon

2 tablespoons olive oil
1/2 teaspoon salt
1/2 teaspoon freshly ground pepper
1 tablespoon chopped fresh basil or
    3/4 teaspoon dried leaf basil
6 ice cubes

In a medium bowl, combine cucumber, onion, tomatoes, garlic, broth, vegetable juice, lime juice, oil, salt, pepper and basil. Cover and refrigerate. Ladle chilled soup into bowls. Add an ice cube to each bowl. Serve with toppings listed above. Makes 6 servings.

If cucumbers are large, cut them in half. Then scoop out large seeds before chopping.

Dilled Cucumber Soup

This refreshing soup makes a perfect addition to a fish dinner.

2 large cucumbers, peeled
1 qt. chicken broth
2 tablespoons dry white wine
2 tablespoons white-wine vinegar
2 teaspoons chopped fresh dill or
   1/2 teaspoon dried dill weed
2 tablespoons cornstarch

2 tablespoons cold water
1/2 cup plain yogurt
1/2 cup dairy sour cream
1/4 teaspoon salt
1/8 teaspoon white pepper
2 tablespoons chopped chives
   or green-onion tops

Cut cucumbers in half lengthwise. Remove seeds with a spoon. Dice cucumbers. Puree diced cucumbers and 1 cup broth in a blender or food processsor fitted with a steel blade. Place cucumber puree and 3 cups broth in a 3-quart saucepan. Bring to a boil over medium heat. Add wine, vinegar and dill. Cover and reduce heat. Simmer 10 minutes. In a small bowl, combine cornstarch and cold water. Stir cornstarch paste into soup. Stir over medium heat until thickened, about 2 minutes. Cool slightly. Process a few seconds in 2 to 3 batches in a blender or food processor fitted with a steel blade. Add yogurt and sour cream. Process until smooth. Add salt and white pepper. Refrigerate 2 hours. Ladle chilled soup into bowls or mugs. Garnish with chives or green-onion tops. Makes 6 servings.

Tomato Fantasy Soup

Melon balls give this quick and easy soup a fruity overtone.

1 qt. fresh or canned tomato puree, chilled
1/4 cup dry white wine
1/2 teaspoon salt
1/4 teaspoon freshly ground pepper
Few drops hot-pepper sauce
1 teaspoon grated lime peel
1 teaspoon grated orange peel

3 tablespoons plain yogurt
1/3 cup dairy sour cream
6 small cantaloupe balls
6 small honeydew or casaba melon balls
6 small watermelon balls
6 sprigs mint or basil

In a large bowl, stir together tomato puree, wine, salt, pepper, hot-pepper sauce, lime peel and orange peel. Cover and refrigerate. In a small bowl, stir together yogurt and sour cream. Divide chilled soup among 6 bowls. Top each serving with a dollop of yogurt mixture. Add 3 different kinds of melon balls and mint or basil to each bowl of soup. Makes 6 servings.

Use a melon-baller to shape the melon balls evenly for garnish.

Cream of Broccoli Soup

A beautiful green winter soup to begin a meal.

1 large bunch broccoli	3 tablespoons butter
1/3 cup chopped onion	3 tablespoons all-purpose flour
2 cups water	1/4 teaspoon white pepper
4 teaspoons chicken bouillon granules or	1-1/2 cups half and half
4 bouillon cubes	1/4 cup dairy sour cream
1 garlic clove, minced	2 tablespoons chopped chives
1/2 teaspoon dried leaf thyme	

Cut flowerets from broccoli. Peel broccoli stems. Dice stems. In a 3-quart saucepan, place broccoli flowerets and stems, onion, water, bouillon granules or cubes, garlic and thyme. Cover. Bring to a boil. Reduce heat and simmer 15 minutes or until broccoli is tender. Cool slightly. Puree broccoli mixture in 2 to 3 batches in a blender or food processor fitted with a steel blade. Set pureed mixture aside. Melt butter in large saucepan over medium heat. Stir in flour. Cook 2 minutes, stirring constantly. Add white pepper and half and half. Cook until thickened, stirring constantly, about 2 minutes. Stir in broccoli puree. Heat through. Ladle soup into bowls. Top each serving with a dollop of sour cream. Sprinkle with chives. Makes 4 to 5 servings.

Carrot Soup

Sweet tender carrots turn into a tantalizing golden puree.

1 large onion, quartered	1/2 teaspoon dried leaf thyme
6 large carrots, cut in 1-inch pieces	1/4 teaspoon salt
1 medium turnip, cut in wedges	1/4 teaspoon freshly ground pepper
2 garlic cloves	Hot-pepper sauce to taste
1 qt. chicken broth	
Toppings: toasted sunflower seeds,	
toasted slivered almonds,	
chopped pistachios, diced red-skinned apples	

In a 3-quart saucepan, place onion, carrots, turnip, garlic, broth, thyme, salt and pepper. Cover. Simmer over low heat until vegetables are soft, 15 to 20 minutes. Cool slightly. Puree in 2 to 3 batches in a blender or food processor fitted with a steel blade. Season with hot-pepper sauce to taste. Ladle soup into bowls. Serve with toppings listed above. Soup may also be served chilled. Makes 6 servings.

 When chives are unavailable, chopped green-onion tops make a good substitute.

Wild Rice & Mushroom Soup

This is an elegant starter for a party meal.

2 cups water
1/2 teaspoon salt
1/2 cup uncooked wild rice
2 tablespoons butter
1 medium onion, finely chopped
1/2 cup finely chopped celery
1/4 lb. mushrooms, chopped
1/2 teaspoon curry powder

1/2 teaspoon dry mustard
1/4 teaspoon white pepper
1 qt. chicken broth
3 tablespoons cornstarch
3 tablespoons cold water
1 cup half and half
1/2 cup dry sherry
2 tablespoons chopped chives or fresh parsley

Place water and salt in a 2-quart saucepan. Bring to a boil. Add wild rice. Cover and reduce heat. Simmer 25 to 30 minutes or until rice is tender; set aside. Melt butter in a 3-quart saucepan over medium-high heat. Add onion. Sauté until soft, 1 to 2 minutes. Add celery and mushrooms. Sauté 1 minute. Stir in curry powder, mustard and white pepper. Add broth. Cover and reduce heat. Simmer 10 minutes. In a small bowl, combine cornstarch and cold water. Stir cornstarch paste into soup. Stir over medium heat until thickened, about 2 minutes. Add cooked rice, half and half and sherry. Heat through. Ladle soup into bowls. Garnish with chives or parsley. Makes 8 servings.

Artichoke & Filbert Soup

An elegant soup for a gala dinner starring duckling or lamb.

4 medium artichokes
1/2 teaspoon salt
1/3 cup filberts
1 qt. chicken broth
2 tablespoons cornstarch

2 tablespoons cold water
1/2 cup whipping cream
1/4 teaspoon white pepper
1/8 teaspoon freshly grated nutmeg
2 tablespoons dry sherry

Remove all leaves and stems from artichokes. Using a spoon or melon-baller, scrape or scoop out the fuzzy choke center. Trim well to retain only artichoke bottoms. In a 2-quart saucepan, combine artichoke bottoms and salt. Cover with water. Bring to a boil. Cook 35 minutes or until very tender. Drain well. Cool and dice. Preheat oven to 300F (150C). Spread filberts in a 9-inch pie dish. Bake 10 minutes or until lightly browned. Cool. Place 5 to 6 filberts on a cutting board. Chop coarsely with a sharp knife; set aside. In a 3-quart saucepan place diced artichokes, broth and remaining toasted whole filberts. Cover. Simmer over low heat 20 minutes. Cool slightly. Puree mixture in 2 to 3 batches in a blender or food processor fitted with a steel blade. Return artichoke mixture to saucepan. In a small bowl, combine cornstarch and cold water. Stir cornstarch paste into soup. Stir over medium heat until thickened, about 2 minutes. Stir in cream, white pepper, nutmeg and sherry. Heat through. Ladle soup into bowls. Garnish with chopped toasted filberts. Makes 6 scrvings.

 Toasting nuts until golden brown brings out their nutty flavor.

Les Halles Onion Soup

A classic from the original bustling Parisian food market.

1-1/2 qts. Rich Beef Stock, see below
3 tablespoons butter
5 large yellow onions, thinly sliced
6 slices buttered toasted French bread,
   1/2-inch thick

1/2 cup freshly grated Parmesan cheese
   (1-1/2 oz.)
1/2 cup shredded Gruyère cheese (2 oz.)

Rich Beef Stock:
1-1/2 lbs. meaty beef shank bones
1-1/2 lbs. meaty veal shank bones
2 qts. water
1 medium carrot, diced

1 medium onion, coarsely chopped
2 teaspoons salt
1 bay leaf
2 garlic cloves, minced

Prepare Rich Beef Stock. Melt butter in a 3-quart saucepan over low heat. Add onions. Sauté until golden brown, about 20 minutes, stirring occasionally. Add Rich Beef Stock. Cover and simmer 30 minutes. Ladle soup into ovenproof bowls. Top each serving with a slice of French bread. In a small bowl, combine cheeses. Sprinkle cheese mixture over each slice of bread. Place filled soup bowls under broiler. Broil until cheese melts and lightly browns, about 2 minutes. Makes 6 servings.

Rich Beef Stock:
Preheat oven to 425F (220C). Place beef and veal shank bones in a roasting or broiler pan. Bake 30 minutes or until browned. Place bones and drippings in a large pot. Add water, carrot, onion, salt, bay leaf and garlic. Cover. Bring to a boil. Skim off foam. Cover and reduce heat. Simmer 2 hours. Strain off stock. Discard vegetables and bones. Cover and refrigerate. Lift fat from chilled stock. Discard fat. Makes about 2 quarts.

French Vegetable Soup

A variety of 6 vegetables blend in this pale-green soup.

2 large or 3 small leeks
2 tablespoons butter
1 bunch green onions, chopped,
   white part only
2 celery stalks, chopped
2 medium carrots, shredded
1 medium turnip, shredded
1 (1-lb.) can butter beans, drained

1 qt. chicken broth
1/2 teaspoon dried leaf thyme
1/4 teaspoon salt
1/4 teaspoon white pepper
1/4 cup dairy sour cream or
   Crème Fraîche, page 166
2 tablespoons chopped fresh parsley

Trim leeks discarding green tops. Quarter lengthwise, cutting almost to the root. Wash under cold running water, pulling layers apart so grit is removed. Chop washed leeks. Melt butter in a 3-quart saucepan over medium heat. Add leeks, green onions, celery, carrots and turnip. Sauté vegetables until glazed, 5 to 7 minutes. Add beans, broth, thyme, salt and white pepper. Cover and reduce heat. Simmer 25 minutes or until vegetables are soft. Cool slightly. Puree soup in 2 to 3 batches in a blender or food processor fitted with a steel blade. Return soup to saucepan. Heat through. Ladle soup into bowls. Top each serving with a dollop of sour cream or Crème Fraîche. Garnish with parsley. Makes 6 servings.

How To Make Les Halles Onion Soup

1/Cook beef and veal shank bones in oven until well browned.

2/Strain stock, discarding vegetables and bones.

3/Sauté onions until golden brown, about 20 minutes.

4/Top each serving with toasted French bread and sprinkle with cheese mixture.

How To Make Jerusalem Artichoke & Leek Bisque

1/Peel Jerusalem artichokes using a small paring knife. Place in a bowl of lemon juice and cold water to prevent discoloration.

2/Trim leeks discarding green tops. Quarter lengthwise. Wash thoroughly under cold water.

Jerusalem Artichoke & Leek Bisque

Nutty-flavored Jerusalem artichokes, known as sunchokes, combine with leeks to make a flavorful soup.

1 lb. Jerusalem artichokes
2 tablespoons lemon juice
2 large leeks
2 tablespoons butter
1 garlic clove, minced
3 cups chicken broth
1/2 teaspoon dried leaf tarragon

1/4 teaspoon white pepper
3/4 cup whipping cream or half and half
1/4 cup dry white wine
3 tablespoons toasted chopped filberts or
   slivered blanched almonds
2 tablespoons chopped fresh parsley

Peel and dice Jerusalem artichokes. Place in a bowl of cold water with lemon juice to prevent discoloration. Trim leeks discarding green tops. Quarter lengthwise, cutting almost to the root. Wash under cold running water, pulling layers apart so grit is removed. Chop leeks. Melt butter in a 3-quart saucepan over medium heat. Add leeks. Sauté until soft but not browned, about 5 minutes. Drain Jerusalem artichokes. Add Jerusalem artichokes and garlic to saucepan. Cook 2 minutes. Add broth. Cover and reduce heat. Simmer 20 minutes or until Jerusalem artichokes are tender. Cool slightly. Puree mixture in 2 to 3 batches in a blender or food processor fitted with a steel blade. Return Jerusalem artichoke mixture to saucepan. Add tarragon and white pepper. Stir in whipping cream or half and half and wine. Heat through. Ladle soup into bowls. Sprinkle with nuts and parsley. Makes 6 servings.

Sherried Mushroom Soup

Sherry gives a mellow warmth to this creamy mushroom soup.

3 tablespoons butter
1 small onion, finely chopped
3/4 lb. mushrooms, chopped
2 tablespoons chopped celery leaves
3 cups chicken broth
1 garlic clove, minced
1/2 teaspoon salt

1/4 teaspoon freshly ground pepper
1/4 teaspoon dried leaf tarragon
2 cups half and half or milk
1/4 cup dry sherry
1/4 cup dairy sour cream or plain yogurt
1 tablespoon chopped chives or fresh parsley

Melt butter in a 3-quart saucepan over medium heat. Add onion. Sauté until glazed, 2 to 3 minutes. Add mushrooms and celery leaves. Sauté 2 minutes. Add broth, garlic, salt, pepper and tarragon. Cover and reduce heat. Simmer 10 minutes. Cool slightly. Puree mixture in 2 to 3 batches in a blender or a food processor fitted with the steel blade. Return soup to saucepan. Add half and half or milk. Heat through. Stir in sherry. Ladle soup into bowls. Top each serving with a dollop of sour cream or yogurt. Sprinkle with chives or parsley. Makes 6 servings.

Variation

Substitute 3/4 pound tree oyster or abalone mushrooms for regular mushrooms to give an exotic flavor.

Minestrone

Sliced Italian sausage can embellish this wonderful vegetable soup.

2 cups dried cranberry beans or
  Great Northern beans
1 meaty ham bone (about 1 lb.)
1 medium leek
1 tablespoon olive oil
1 large onion, chopped
2 celery stalks, chopped
1/2 head small Savoy cabbage, shredded
1 (1-lb. 12-oz.) can whole Italian tomatoes,
  pureed
1 lb. Italian sausage (about 5 sausages),
  if desired

1 qt. chicken broth
1/2 teaspoon freshly ground pepper
1 medium carrot, diced
3/4 lb. Italian green beans,
  cut in 1/2-inch pieces
1 large potato, peeled, diced
1/4 cup ditalini or other small pasta
1/4 cup freshly grated Parmesan or
  Romano cheese (3/4 oz.)

Wash beans. Place in a 3-quart saucepan. Cover with 1-1/2 quarts water. Soak 6 to 8 hours. Drain well. Cover beans with 1-1/2 quarts water. Add ham bone. Cover and bring to a boil. Simmer over low heat 1 hour or until beans are tender. Drain off liquid and reserve. Trim ends and tough outside leaves from leek. Quarter leek lengthwise, cutting almost to the root. Wash under cold running water, pulling layers apart so grit is removed. Chop washed leek. Heat oil in a large pot over medium heat. Add leek, onion, celery and cabbage. Sauté until vegetables are glazed, 3 to 4 minutes. Add reserved bean liquid and tomatoes. Add sausages, if desired. Cover and reduce heat. Simmer 10 minutes. Add half the cooked beans to soup. Coarsely grind remaining beans in a food processor. Add ground beans, broth, pepper, carrot, green beans and potato to soup. Simmer until vegetables are tender, about 6 minutes. Add pasta. Remove from heat. Let stand 3 minutes to cook pasta. Remove sausages. Thinly slice sausages and return to soup. Ladle soup into bowls. Sprinkle with cheese. Makes 10 to 12 servings.

Lentil Soup

Wine vinegar sparks this often forgotten Middle Eastern soup.

1-1/3 cups lentils
2 tablespoons olive oil
1 medium onion, chopped
1 celery stalk, chopped
1 bay leaf
1/2 teaspoon salt
1/4 teaspoon freshly ground pepper

2 qts. water
1/4 cup tomato paste
1/4 cup red-wine vinegar
1/2 teaspoon dried leaf oregano
1/4 cup dairy sour cream or plain yogurt
8 sprigs cilantro or parsley

Wash lentils. Cover with cold water. Soak 2 hours. Drain well. Heat oil in a 3-quart saucepan over medium heat. Add onion and celery. Sauté until glazed, 2 to 3 minutes. Add soaked lentils, bay leaf, salt, pepper and water. Cover and reduce heat. Simmer 1-1/2 hours. Add tomato paste, vinegar and oregano. Simmer 30 minutes. Lentils should be tender. Ladle soup into bowls. Top each serving with a dollop of sour cream or yogurt and a sprig of cilantro or parsley. Makes 8 servings.

Yellow Split-Pea Soup

A Swedish tradition calls for yellow pea soup, pancakes and lingonberries for Thursday's dinner.

1 cup yellow split peas
1 meaty ham bone (about 1 lb.)
2 qts. water
1/2 teaspoon dry mustard
1/2 teaspoon ground ginger

1/2 teaspoon freshly ground pepper
2 large carrots, cut in 1-inch pieces
1 large onion, chopped
Salt to taste

Wash split peas. In a 4-quart saucepan, combine split peas, ham bone, water, mustard, ginger, pepper, carrots and onion. Cover. Bring to a boil. Reduce heat and simmer 2 hours. Cool slightly. Remove ham bone. Separate meat from bone. Discard bone. Dice cooked ham. Puree vegetables and broth in 2 to 3 batches in a blender or food processor fitted with a steel blade. Return soup to saucepan. Add diced ham. Heat through. If necessary, add additional water to thin soup to desired consistency. Season with salt. Makes 8 servings.

Variation

Green split peas, small white beans or pea beans, are equally good in this recipe. Substitute 1 pound sausage for ham, if desired.

 Freeze soups in straight-sided containers with a wide-mouth opening for easy thawing and reheating.

1/Place a pastry round over each soup bowl. Press edges against outside of bowl to seal tightly.

2/Bake Tomato Soup Under a Pastry Cap until pastry is puffed and golden.

Tomato Soup Under a Pastry Cap

A billowy balloon of puff pastry caps this fresh-tasting soup.

2 (10-oz.) pkgs. frozen puff-pastry shells,
  thawed
1 tablespoon butter
1 large onion, chopped
1 (6-oz.) can tomato paste
1 qt. chicken broth
3 large tomatoes, peeled, quartered
1 garlic clove, minced
1 tablespoon chopped fresh basil or
  3/4 teaspoon dried leaf basil

1 tablespoon chopped fresh parsley
1/2 teaspoon freshly ground pepper
3/4 cup half and half or milk
2 tablespoons fine julienned carrots
2 tablespoons fine julienned leeks or
  green onions
1 egg white, slightly beaten

Place pastry shells on a board. Cover with plastic wrap. Bring to room temperature, about 1 hour. Melt butter in a 3-quart saucepan over medium heat. Add onion. Sauté until lightly browned, 3 to 4 minutes. Add tomato paste and broth. Bring to a boil. Cover and reduce heat. Simmer 30 minutes. Cool slightly. Puree mixture in 2 to 3 batches in a blender or food processor fitted with a steel blade. To a small amount of puree, add tomatoes, garlic, basil, parsley and pepper. Process again. Return pureed mixture to saucepan. Stir in half and half or milk. Heat through. Cool. Stack pastry shells in pairs. On a lightly floured board, roll each pair into an 8-inch round. Ladle soup into 6 ovenproof bowls, each about 6 inches in diameter. Top each serving with 1 teaspoon each of carrots and leeks or green onions. Brush rim and outside edge of each bowl with egg white in a 1-inch band. Place a pastry round over top of each soup bowl. Press pastry edges against outside of bowl to seal tightly. Soup can be prepared in advance up to this point and refrigerated. Preheat oven to 425F (220C). Bake 15 minutes or until pastry is puffed and golden brown. Serve immediately. Makes 6 servings.

Beef & Barley Soup

An old-fashioned soup makes a perfect lunch for a cool winter day.

1 tablespoon olive oil	1 cup chopped tomatoes
2 slices meaty beef shank (about 1-1/2 lbs.)	3 tablespoons barley
1 qt. water	1/4 teaspoon dried leaf thyme
1 onion, chopped	1/4 teaspoon salt
1 carrot, chopped	1/4 teaspoon freshly ground pepper
1 inner celery stalk, chopped	1 qt. beef broth
1 small turnip, chopped	2 tablespoons chopped fresh parsley

Heat oil in a 3-quart saucepan over medium heat. Add beef shanks. Brown on both sides. Add water. Cover. Bring to a boil. Skim off foam. Cover and reduce heat. Simmer 1-3/4 hours or until meat is tender. Remove meat. Cool slightly. Discard bones and fat. Dice meat and return to saucepan. Add onion, carrot, celery, turnip, tomatoes, barley, thyme, salt, pepper and broth. Cover. Simmer 30 minutes or until vegetables are tender. Ladle soup into bowls. Sprinkle with parsley. Makes 6 to 8 servings.

Curried Pea Vichyssoise

Fresh peas give a touch of green to the ever-popular Vichyssoise.

2 large leeks	1/4 teaspoon salt
1 tablespoon butter	1/4 teaspoon white pepper
1 teaspoon curry powder	4 leaves fresh mint, chopped
2 medium potatoes, peeled, diced	1/2 cup whipping cream
3 cups chicken broth	1/4 cup dairy sour cream or plain yogurt
1-1/4 cups fresh shelled peas or	6 sprigs mint
1 (10-oz.) pkg. frozen baby peas	

Trim ends and tough outside leaves from leeks. Quarter lengthwise, cutting almost to the root. Wash under cold running water, pulling layers apart so grit is removed. Chop leeks. Melt butter in a 3-quart saucepan over medium heat. Add curry powder. Cook 1 minute, stirring constantly. Add leeks. Sauté until soft and glazed, 2 to 3 minutes. Add potatoes and broth. Cover and reduce heat. Simmer 15 minutes or until potatoes are soft. Add peas, salt, white pepper and chopped mint. Simmer uncovered 2 minutes. Cool slightly. Puree in 2 to 3 batches in a blender or food processor fitted with a steel blade. Return soup to saucepan. Stir in whipping cream. Heat through. Ladle soup into bowls. Top each serving with a dollop of sour cream or yogurt and a mint sprig. Soup may also be served chilled. Makes 6 servings.

 Celery leaves add flavor to any soup stock.

How To Make Borscht

1/Use a hand shredder to prepare vegetables for Borscht.

2/Or, use a food processor fitted with shredding blade to prepare vegetables.

Borscht

Sausages make a choice accompaniment to this ruby-red beet soup.

3 tablespoons butter
1 bunch beets (4 beets or 1 lb.),
   finely shredded
2 small carrots, finely shredded
1 medium onion, finely shredded
1 medium turnip, finely shredded
2 cups finely shredded red cabbage
1-1/2 qts. beef broth
1/4 cup red-wine vinegar

2 teaspoons brown sugar
1/2 teaspoon salt
1/4 teaspoon freshly ground pepper
2 tablespoons cornstarch
2 tablespoons cold water
1/4 cup dairy sour cream or plain yogurt
2 tablespoons chopped chives
8 thin lemon slices

Melt butter in a 4-quart saucepan over medium heat. Add beets, carrots, onion, turnip and cabbage. Sauté until glazed, 4 to 5 minutes. Add broth, vinegar, brown sugar, salt and pepper. Cover and reduce heat. Simmer 45 minutes or until vegetables are soft. In a small bowl, combine cornstarch and cold water. Stir cornstarch paste into soup. Stir over medium heat until thickened, about 2 minutes. Ladle soup into bowls. Top each serving with a dollop of sour cream or yogurt. Sprinkle with chives. Float a lemon slice in each bowl. Makes 8 servings.

German Beef & Celery-Root Soup

Accompany this hearty soup with hot buttered dark-rye bread and finish off with fruit and cheese.

1 tablespoon olive oil
4 slices meaty beef shank (about 2-1/2 lbs.)
1 large onion, chopped
2-1/2 qts. beef broth
1 bunch leeks, 2 large or 3 small
1 large celery root, peeled,
   cut in 1/2-inch pieces

1/2 teaspoon freshly ground pepper
Salt to taste
1/2 cup freshly grated Parmesan or
   Romano cheese (1-1/2 oz.)

Heat oil in a 4-quart saucepan over medium heat. Add beef shanks and onion. Brown well. Add broth. Bring to a boil. Skim off foam. Cover and reduce heat. Simmer 2 hours or until meat is tender. Remove shanks from broth. Cool slightly. Discard bones and fat. Dice meat. Skim off fat from broth. Trim ends and tough outside leaves from leeks. Quarter lengthwise, cutting almost to the root. Wash under cold running water, pulling layers apart so grit is removed. Chop leeks. Add celery root to broth. Simmer 10 minutes. Add leeks, diced meat and pepper to broth. Simmer until celery root is tender, about 5 minutes. Season with salt. Ladle soup into bowls. Sprinkle with cheese. Makes 8 servings.

Pot-au-Feu

Serve this French stew with a medley of condiments.

1 medium onion, peeled
4 whole cloves
1 lb. meaty veal or beef shank bones
1 (2- to 2-1/2-lb.) beef sirloin-tip roast
   or beef rump roast
1 bay leaf
2 garlic cloves, peeled
1 teaspoon salt
6 peppercorns
1/2 teaspoon dried leaf thyme

3 qts. water
3 medium leeks
6 small carrots, split in half lengthwise
3 small turnips, halved
6 small new potatoes, scrubbed
6 sprigs parsley
Condiments: Dijon-style mustard,
   coarse salt, cornichons,
   freshly grated or prepared horseradish

Stud onion with cloves. In a large pot, combine onion, shank bones, beef roast, bay leaf, garlic, salt, peppercorns and thyme. Add water almost to cover meat. Bring to a boil. Skim off foam. Cover and reduce heat. Simmer 2 hours. Trim ends and tough outside leaves from leeks. Split lengthwise, cutting almost to the root. Wash under cold running water, pulling layers apart so grit is removed. Add leeks, carrots, turnips and potatoes. Simmer 15 minutes or until vegetables are tender. Place meat on a large platter. Surround with vegetables. Strain broth. Discard bay leaf and peppercorns. Skim off fat from broth. Serve broth as a first course. Slice meat. Garnish with parsley. Serve with condiments listed above. Makes 6 servings.

 Inserting whole cloves in an onion makes it easy to remove the spice after cooking.

The Farmer's Soup

What fun to lace this French country soup with cream and cheese at the table.

3 medium leeks
2 tablespoons butter
1 large onion, finely chopped
1-1/2 qts. chicken broth
2 large potatoes, peeled, diced

2 teaspoons chopped fresh tarragon or
   1/2 teaspoon dried leaf tarragon
1/4 teaspoon salt
1/4 teaspoon freshly ground pepper
3 tablespoons chopped fresh parsley

Toppings:
1 cup whipping cream
1 cup shredded Gruyère, samso, Jarlsberg,
   Parmesan or Romano cheese (4 oz.)

Trim leeks discarding green tops. Quarter lengthwise, cutting almost to the root. Wash under cold running water, pulling layers apart so grit is removed. Finely chop washed leeks. Melt butter in a 4-quart saucepan over medium heat. Add onion. Sauté until soft, 1 to 2 minutes. Add broth and potatoes. Cover and reduce heat. Simmer 15 minutes. Add leeks, tarragon, salt and pepper. Cover. Simmer 10 minutes or until vegetables are soft. Coarsely mash vegetables with a potato masher. Stir to combine well. Ladle soup into bowls. Sprinkle with parsley. Serve with cream and choice of cheese as listed above. Makes 8 servings.

Pistou Soup

From Italy and Southern France comes this appealing mixed vegetable soup.

Pesto Sauce, page 168
1 small leek or 2 green onions
1 qt. chicken broth
1 medium potato, peeled, diced
1 medium carrot, thinly sliced
1/4 lb. green beans, cut in 1-inch pieces
1 medium zucchini, ends trimmed,
   thinly sliced
1 medium yellow crookneck squash,
   ends trimmed, thinly sliced

1/4 cup shelled fresh peas or
   frozen baby peas, thawed
1 medium tomato, peeled, chopped
1 tablespoon chopped fresh parsley
Salt and pepper to taste
1/4 cup freshly grated Parmesan or
   Romano cheese (3/4 oz.)

Prepare Pesto Sauce. Trim ends and tough outside leaves from leek. Quarter lengthwise, cutting almost to the root. Wash under cold running water, pulling layers apart so grit is removed. Thinly slice leek or chop green onions. In a 3-quart saucepan, heat broth. Add potato and carrot. Cover and reduce heat. Simmer 10 minutes. Add green beans, zucchini, crookneck squash and leek or green onions. Cover. Simmer 10 minutes or until vegetables are crisp-tender. Add peas, tomato and parsley. Simmer 2 minutes. Season with salt and pepper. Ladle soup into bowls. Serve with Pesto Sauce and cheese. Makes 4 servings.

Early California Soup in a Pumpkin Tureen

This soup from the gold-rush days is a great way to greet Halloween.

1 (3-lb.) frying chicken
1-1/2 qts. water
1 onion, peeled, quartered
1 celery stalk, chopped
1-1/2 teaspoons salt
1/2 teaspoon freshly ground pepper
1 medium pumpkin (about 8 lbs.)
1 garlic clove, minced
1/2 teaspoon dried leaf oregano
1/2 teaspoon ground cumin

1/8 teaspoon hot-pepper sauce
2 ears yellow corn, grated
2 yellow crookneck squash, ends trimmed, sliced
2 cups diced steamed banana squash or Hubbard squash
Toppings: chopped cilantro, roasted pumpkin seeds, diced avocado, diced red pepper, grated Monterey Jack cheese

In a 3-quart saucepan, combine chicken, water, onion, celery, salt and pepper. Cover. Simmer 1 hour. Preheat oven to 375F (190C). While chicken is cooking, cut off top of pumpkin. Scoop out seeds. Place pumpkin on an ovenproof platter. Bake 15 minutes or until heated through. Lift chicken from broth. Cool slightly. Remove meat from bones. Discard skin and bones. Pull meat into strips with fingers or 2 forks. Skim off fat from broth. Strain broth. Cook broth over medium heat until reduced to 1-1/2 quarts. Add garlic, oregano, cumin, hot-pepper sauce, corn and crookneck squash. Simmer 2 minutes. Add chicken and banana squash or Hubbard squash. Heat through. Pour hot soup in hot pumpkin shell. Serve with toppings listed above. Makes 6 servings.

Cheese Soup with Pumpkin

A pumpkin shell makes an attractive container for serving this cheese and wine soup.

1 small to medium pumpkin or Hubbard squash (about 8 lbs.)
2 tablespoons butter, melted
2 tablespoons butter
1 large onion, finely chopped
2 large carrots, shredded
2 celery stalks, finely chopped
1 qt. chicken broth
1 garlic clove, minced

1/4 teaspoon salt
1/4 teaspoon freshly ground pepper
1/4 teaspoon ground nutmeg
3/4 cup milk or half and half
1 cup shredded Cheddar or Gruyère cheese (4 oz.)
1/3 cup dry white wine
2 tablespoons minced fresh parsley

Preheat oven to 375F (205C). Butter a baking sheet. To prepare pumpkin or squash tureen, cut off top of pumpkin or squash. Scoop out seeds. Brush inside with 2 tablespoons melted butter. Replace lid. Place pumpkin or squash on buttered baking sheet. Bake 45 minutes or until tender when pierced with a fork but still firm. While pumpkin or squash is baking, melt 2 tablespoons butter in a 3-quart saucepan. Add onion, carrots and celery. Sauté over medium heat until soft, about 10 minutes. Add broth, garlic, salt, pepper and nutmeg. Cover. Simmer 20 minutes or until vegetables are tender. Cool slightly. Puree vegetable mixture in 2 to 3 batches in a blender or food processor fitted with a steel blade. Place vegetable puree in saucepan. Stir in milk or half and half. Heat through. Add cheese and wine. Heat until cheese melts. Place hot pumpkin or squash tureen on a serving platter. Pour in soup. Sprinkle with parsley. Ladle soup into bowls, spooning some cooked pumpkin or squash into each, if desired. Makes 5 to 6 servings.

Chestnut Soup

This Italian-style soup goes admirably with pork or duck.

1 lb. fresh chestnuts or
   1 (8-oz.) can unsweetened chestnut puree
2 tablespoons butter
1 large onion, finely chopped
1-1/3 cups chopped carrot
1 cup chopped celery

1 qt. chicken broth
1/4 teaspoon salt
1/2 teaspoon freshly ground pepper
1/8 teaspoon ground cloves
1/4 cup half and half
2 tablespoons chopped fresh parsley

To peel fresh chestnuts, pierce tops with a pointed knife and place in a 2-quart saucepan. Cover with cold water. Bring to a boil and immediately remove from heat. Drain and peel a few at a time, leaving remaining chestnuts in hot water. If they cool and become difficult to peel, reheat quickly; don't cook chestnuts or they will be impossible to peel. Melt butter in a 3-quart saucepan over medium heat. Add onion, carrots and celery. Sauté 10 minutes or until vegetables are glazed. Add broth, salt, pepper and cloves. Bring to a boil. Cover and reduce heat. Simmer 20 minutes or until vegetables are tender. Add chestnuts or chestnut puree. Simmer 10 minutes to blend flavors. Cool slightly. Puree mixture in 2 to 3 batches in a blender or food processor fitted with a steel blade. Add half and half. Process just to mix in. Ladle soup into bowls. Sprinkle with parsley. Makes 4 servings.

Fruited Vegetable Soup

Apples and wine spark this pale-orange soup with a fruity flavor.

1 tablespoon butter
1 large red or yellow onion, chopped
2 celery stalks, finely chopped
2 medium, tart apples, peeled, cored, diced
1 large tomato, peeled, chopped
3-1/2 cups chicken broth

1/2 teaspoon dried leaf tarragon
1/4 teaspoon freshly ground pepper
1/4 cup dry white wine
1/4 cup dairy sour cream or whipping cream
2 tablespoons chopped chives or
   fresh parsley

Melt butter in a 3-quart saucepan over medium heat. Add onion and celery. Sauté until vegetables are soft, 4 to 5 minutes. Add apples and tomato. Sauté 2 to 3 minutes. Add broth, tarragon and pepper. Cover and reduce heat. Simmer 30 minutes or until vegetables are soft. Cool slightly. Puree mixture in 2 to 3 batches in a blender or food processor fitted with a steel blade. Return pureed soup to saucepan. Add wine. Heat through. Ladle soup into bowls. Top each serving with a dollop of sour cream or whipping cream. Sprinkle with chives or parsley. Makes 6 servings.

Whenever available, fresh herbs are preferable to bottled dried herbs. A good ratio of equivalents is to use 1/4 the amount of dried as fresh.

SALADS

Salads play a versatile role in menu planning. They can be light and refreshing as a first course, hearty for a bounteous luncheon or warm-weather entree, or a classic finale served with fruit and cheese.

The essentials for a delightful salad arrangement are the freshest-possible vegetables and a perfectly blended dressing, carefully applied. Salads can be showpieces. Beauty is found in the simple elegance of hearts of butter lettuce dotted with colorful nasturtium blossoms. Served in a footed glass bowl, Garden Greens with Nasturtium Blossoms is a treat for the eye as well as the palate. Italian Salad offers a colorful combination of sliced bright red tomatoes adorned with creamy white mozzarella cheese and vibrant green fresh basil.

Salads span decades and continents. Western Cobb Salad, with its attractive spoke-like design, was first created at the Brown Derby Restaurant in Los Angeles. Swedish-Style Cucumbers in Dill are a treat that accompanies every smorgasbord table.

Greek Country Salad with its feta cheese and glistening ripe olives will be a hit whenever you serve it. Chinese Chicken Salad with Sesame-Soy Dressing makes a flavor-packed main dish. Looking through this chapter you will find a salad to suit every occasion.

Remember, when creating salads, small touches add charm. That feathery wisp of dill, the pungent leaves of fresh basil or spicy sprigs of cilantro add extra flavor. Colorful flower blossoms lend a fresh surprise to the salad bowl. These seemingly small touches create salads with a very personal note.

Summer Salad Buffet

Chinese Chicken Salad, page 73
Green Bean & Mushroom Salad, page 67
Washington Square Deli Salad, page 67
Scandinavian Vegetable & Cheese Salad, page 77
Vintners' Herb Braided Bread, page 177
Chocolate Potato Cake, page 186

Multi-Layered Gazpacho Salad   Photo on pages 74 and 7

A wide-mouth spring-closed canning jar is an ideal container for this colorful picnic salad.

Garlic-Wine Dressing, see below
3 large tomatoes, peeled, thinly sliced
2 medium cucumbers, peeled, thinly sliced
2 red or green bell peppers, seeded,
    julienned
1/2 lb. mushrooms, sliced

1 large red onion, sliced
Salt to taste
Freshly ground pepper to taste
12 whole black oil-cured olives or
    pitted black olives
2 green onions, chopped

Garlic-Wine Dressing:
1/3 cup olive oil
2 tablespoons tarragon-flavored white-wine
    vinegar
2 tablespoons dry white wine
1 garlic clove, minced

1/4 teaspoon salt
1/4 teaspoon freshly ground pepper
1 tablespoon chopped fresh parsley
1 tablespoon chopped fresh basil or
    3/4 teaspoon dried leaf basil

Prepare Garlic-Wine Dressing. In a 2-quart wide-mouth jar or glass bowl, alternate layers of tomatoes, cucumbers, red or green peppers, mushrooms and red onion. Sprinkle each layer lightly with salt and pepper. Place olives and green onions in circles on top of salad. Pour Garlic-Wine Dressing over salad. Cover and refrigerate at least 1 hour. For a different appearance, line glass bowl with lettuce leaves. Arrange salad ingredients in circles or rows rather than a layered pattern. Makes 6 servings.

Garlic-Wine Dressing:
Combine all ingredients in a small bowl or jar. Mix well. Cover. Refrigerate until ready to use.

Continental Salad

This decorative salad keeps its fresh appeal during buffet service.

Citrus Dressing, see below
2-1/2 cups diced celery
5 medium tomatoes, sliced
1/2 cup finely chopped watercress

1/2 cup whole black oil-cured olives or
    pitted black olives
3 tablespoons chopped fresh parsley
2 Belgian endive, separated into leaves

Citrus Dressing:
2/3 cup olive oil
2 tablespoons orange juice
3 tablespoons lemon juice
1 garlic clove, minced

1-1/2 teaspoons grated orange peel
1/2 teaspoon salt
1/4 teaspoon freshly ground pepper

Prepare Citrus Dressing. In a large bowl, place celery, tomatoes, watercress, olives and parsley. Pour Citrus Dressing over vegetable mixture. Toss lightly. Line a large salad bowl with endive leaves. Place salad in lined bowl. Makes 6 to 8 servings.

Citrus Dressing:
Combine all ingredients in a small bowl or jar. Mix well. Cover. Refrigerate until ready to use.

Western Cobb Salad

This old-time salad is in vogue today, updated with mushrooms and sprouts.

Parsley-Vinaigrette Dressing, see below
2 split chicken breasts, cooked,
    chilled (about 2/3 lb.)
1 small head butter lettuce
1/2 lb. mushrooms, sliced
2 medium tomatoes, peeled, diced, or
    1-1/2 cups cherry tomatoes

1 large avocado, peeled, diced
8 slices bacon, cooked crisp, crumbled
2 hard-cooked eggs, shredded
1/2 cup alfalfa sprouts
1/2 cup crumbled blue cheese (2 oz.)

Parsley-Vinaigrette Dressing:
1/2 cup safflower oil
3 tablespoons white-wine vinegar
1 teaspoon Dijon-style mustard
1 teaspoon chopped fresh tarragon or
    1/4 teaspoon dried leaf tarragon

1 tablespoon minced fresh parsley
1/2 teaspoon salt
1/4 teaspoon freshly ground pepper

Prepare Parsley-Vinaigrette Dressing. Remove and discard skin and bones from chicken. Pull meat into strips using fingers or 2 forks. Arrange butter-lettuce leaves on 4 salad plates. Place an attractive arrangement of chicken, mushrooms, tomatoes, avocado, bacon, eggs, sprouts and blue cheese on each plate. Serve with Parsley-Vinaigrette dressing. Makes 4 servings.

Parsley-Vinaigrette Dressing:
Combine all ingredients in a small bowl or jar. Mix well. Cover. Refrigerate until ready to use.

Salade Niçoise

This hearty salad makes an ideal summer supper with French bread, sweet butter and fruit.

2 (6-oz.) jars marinated artichoke hearts
2 teaspoons Dijon-style mustard
1 tablespoon chopped shallots or
    green onions
3 tablespoons white-wine vinegar
1/4 cup olive oil
Salt and pepper to taste
1 medium head butter lettuce
1 lb. Italian-style green beans, cooked,
    cut in 2-inch pieces or 2 (10-oz.) pkgs.
    frozen Italian green beans, cooked
4 to 6 small new potatoes, cooked,
    peeled, sliced

1-1/2 cups cherry tomatoes, halved
2 (7-oz.) cans white albacore tuna, drained
12 whole black oil-cured olives or
    pitted black olives
1 (2-oz.) can rolled anchovy fillets with
    capers
1 medium red onion, sliced,
    separated into rings
4 hard-cooked eggs, quartered
1/4 cup minced fresh parsley

In a small bowl, drain marinade from artichoke hearts. Set artichoke hearts aside. Add mustard, shallots or green onions, vinegar and oil to marinade. Season with salt and pepper. Mix well. Cover and refrigerate dressing until ready to use. Line a salad bowl with butter-lettuce leaves. On lettuce, arrange green beans, potatoes, cherry tomatoes and artichoke hearts. Using a fork, flake tuna in large chunks. Spoon tuna over salad. Top with olives, anchovy fillets, onion rings and eggs. Sprinkle with parsley. Cover and refrigerate, if desired. Serve with dressing. Makes 4 servings.

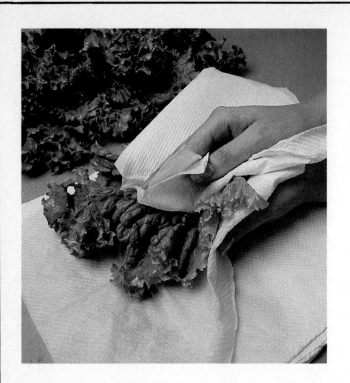

How to Dry Salad Greens

Wash salad greens thoroughly in several changes of cold water. Shake greens dry or use a salad spinner. Place greens between layers of paper towel and pat to remove excess water.

Watercress & Endive Salad

A spicy, refreshing salad to follow lamb, pork or seafood.

Tarragon-Vinaigrette Dressing, see below
1 large bunch watercress

1 small Belgian endive
1 small head Boston lettuce

Tarragon-Vinaigrette Dressing:
2 tablespoons olive oil
1/4 cup safflower oil
2 tablespoons white-wine vinegar
1/2 teaspoon chopped fresh tarragon or
   1/8 teaspoon dried leaf tarragon

1/4 teaspoon salt
1/8 teaspoon freshly ground pepper

Prepare Tarragon-Vinaigrette Dressing. Trim stems from watercress. Cut endive into 1/8-inch-thick julienne strips. Tear lettuce into bite-size pieces. In a large salad bowl, combine watercress, endive and lettuce. Pour Tarragon-Vinaigrette Dressing over greens. Toss lightly. Makes 4 servings.

Tarragon-Vinaigrette Dressing:
Combine all ingredients in a small bowl or jar. Mix well. Cover. Refrigerate until ready to use.

Green Bean & Mushroom Salad   Photo on page 90.

Fresh tarragon gives a zesty flavor to this French salad.

Herb Vinaigrette, see below
1 lb. small young, slender green beans
1/2 lb. mushrooms, sliced

12 cherry tomatoes, halved
1 medium head butter or leaf lettuce

Herb Vinaigrette:
6 tablespoons olive oil
2 tablespoons white-wine vinegar
4 teaspoons Dijon-style mustard
1/2 teaspoon salt

1/2 teaspoon freshly ground pepper
2 teaspoons minced fresh tarragon or
    1/2 teaspoon dried leaf tarragon

Prepare Herb Vinaigrette. Trim ends from green beans. Cut beans lengthwise. In a 3-quart saucepan, bring salted water to a boil. Add beans and boil, uncovered, 5 to 7 minutes or until crisp-tender. Drain well. Rinse under cold water. Drain well. Place in a large bowl. Pour Herb Vinaigrette over beans. Cover and refrigerate 1 hour. Add mushrooms and tomatoes. Mix lightly. Arrange lettuce leaves on salad plates. Spoon marinated vegetables on greens. Makes 6 servings.

Herb Vinaigrette:
Combine all ingredients in a small bowl or jar. Mix well. Cover. Refrigerate until ready to use.

Washington Square Deli Salad

A fresh basil vinaigrette flavors this favorite salad from a San Francisco North Beach restaurant.

Basil Vinaigrette, see below
1 medium head romaine lettuce
1/3 cup slivered fontina or provolone cheese
    (1-1/2 oz.)
1/3 cup julienned salami (1-1/2 oz.)
1/3 cup julienned mortadella or
    Italian sausage (1-1/2 oz.)

1/2 cup whole black oil-cured olives or
    pitted black olives
1 (6-oz.) jar marinated artichoke hearts,
    drained
1/3 cup slivered red bell pepper

Basil Vinaigrette:
1/3 cup olive oil
2 tablespoons red-wine vinegar
1/2 teaspoon salt
1/4 teaspoon freshly ground pepper
2 tablespoons chopped fresh basil or
    1/2 teaspoon dried leaf basil

1 tablespoon chopped fresh parsley
2 tablespoons freshly grated Parmesan or
    Romano cheese
1/2 teaspoon dry mustard

Prepare Basil Vinaigrette. Tear inner leaves of romaine lettuce into bite-size pieces. Arrange romaine in a large shallow salad bowl. Top with cheese, salami, sausage, olives, artichoke hearts and red bell pepper. Serve with Basil Vinaigrette. Makes 4 servings.

Basil Vinaigrette:
Combine all ingredients in a small bowl or jar. Mix well. Cover. Refrigerate until ready to use.

Mushroom-Gruyère Salad   Photo on pages 74 and 75.

A tasty salad, ideal for a picnic or buffet because it stays fresh.

Lemon Dressing, see below
1 lb. mushrooms, thinly sliced
3 inner celery stalks,
  thinly sliced diagonally (about 2 cups)
6 to 8 large leaves butter lettuce or
  curly endive

1/2 lb. Gruyère, Jarlsberg or samso cheese,
  julienned
2 cups cherry tomatoes, halved
2 tablespoons chopped chives or fresh parsley

Lemon Dressing:
1/4 cup safflower oil
1/4 cup olive oil
3 tablespoons lemon juice
1/2 teaspoon salt
1/2 teaspoon dried leaf tarragon

1/4 teaspoon dry mustard
1-1/2 teaspoons Dijon-style mustard
1/2 teaspoon grated lemon peel
1 garlic clove, minced
1/4 teaspoon freshly ground pepper

Prepare Lemon Dressing. Place mushrooms and celery in a large bowl. Pour Lemon Dressing over mushroom mixture. Mix well. Cover and refrigerate 1 hour. Line serving bowl with butter lettuce or curly endive. Spoon mushroom mixture into lined bowl. Sprinkle with cheese. Place tomatoes in a circle around top of salad. Sprinkle with chives or parsley. Makes 8 servings.

Lemon Dressing:
Combine all ingredients in a small bowl or jar. Mix well. Cover. Refrigerate until ready to use.

Gingered Cucumber Salad

An ideal salad to begin an Oriental dinner.

Gingered Soy Dressing, see below
2 medium cucumbers, peeled, thinly sliced
4 green onions

4 radishes, thinly sliced
2 tablespoons sesame seeds

Gingered Soy Dressing:
1 teaspoon grated gingerroot or
  1/2 teaspoon ground ginger
1/2 teaspoon dry mustard
1/2 teaspoon grated lemon peel

2 teaspoons honey
2 tablespoons soy sauce
2 tablespoons sesame oil
2 tablespoons lemon juice

Prepare Gingered Soy Dressing. Place cucumber slices in a medium bowl. Add Gingered Soy Dressing. Mix lightly. Cover and refrigerate 30 minutes. Cut green onions into 1-1/2-inch pieces. Cut ends of each piece lengthwise, making several 1/4-inch slashes. Place onions in a bowl of ice water. Let stand 5 to 10 minutes. Onion ends will fan out like a party snapper. Spoon cucumbers and dressing into individual bowls. Top each salad with 2 or 3 onion pieces. Sprinkle radishes and sesame seeds over each salad. Makes 4 servings.

Gingered Soy Dressing:
Combine all ingredients in a small bowl or jar. Mix well. Cover. Refrigerate until ready to use.

How to Clean Spinach

Wash spinach thoroughly in several changes of cold water. Discard stem ends by breaking off. Remove any bruised or tough leaves. Drain or dry well with paper towel.

Vegetable Platter Salad   Photo on pages 74 and 75.

A handsome make-ahead salad to accompany any meal.

Italian Dressing, see below
2 (1-lb.) bunches spinach
1/4 lb. mushrooms, thinly sliced
1-1/2 cups cherry tomatoes, halved
1 cup alfalfa sprouts

1 fennel, diced, or 1 cup diced celery
1 medium cucumber, peeled, sliced
2 medium carrots, sliced, or 1/2 head
    medium cauliflower, cut in flowerets
1 small red onion, cut in thin strips

Italian Dressing:
1/2 cup olive oil
1/2 cup safflower oil
3 tablespoons red-wine vinegar
3 tablespoons lemon juice
3/4 teaspoon salt

3/4 teaspoon dry mustard
1/2 teaspoon Worcestershire sauce
2 garlic cloves, minced
1/2 cup freshly grated Parmesan or
    Romano cheese (1-1/2 oz.)

Prepare Italian Dressing. Wash spinach thoroughly in several changes of cold water. Discard stems and bruised or tough leaves. Drain well. Tear spinach into bite-size pieces. Arrange spinach on a 14-inch platter. On spinach, arrange mushrooms, tomatoes, sprouts, fennel or celery, cucumber, carrots or cauliflower and onion in a spoke pattern. Cover salad and refrigerate until ready to serve. Serve with Italian Dressing. Makes 8 servings.

Italian Dressing:
Combine all ingredients in a small bowl or jar. Mix well. Cover. Refrigerate until ready to use.

Sprouted Spinach Salad

A spicy dressing adds great flavor to this colorful spinach salad.

Curry Dressing, see below
2 (1-lb.) bunches spinach
8 slices bacon, cooked crisp, crumbled

2 hard-cooked eggs, shredded
1/4 lb. alfalfa sprouts or bean sprouts
1-1/2 cups cherry tomatoes, halved

Curry Dressing:
3 tablespoons white-wine vinegar
2 tablespoons dry white wine
1/2 cup safflower oil
2 teaspoons soy sauce
3/4 teaspoon salt

1/2 teaspoon freshly ground pepper
1 teaspoon brown sugar
1 teaspoon dry mustard
1 teaspoon curry powder

Prepare Curry Dressing. Wash fresh spinach thoroughly in several changes of cold water. Discard stems and bruised or tough leaves. Drain well. Tear spinach into bite-size pieces. Place spinach in a large salad bowl. Pour Curry Dressing over spinach. Toss lightly. On top of salad, place concentric circles of bacon, egg, sprouts and tomatoes. Makes 6 to 8 servings.

Curry Dressing:
Combine all ingredients in a small bowl or jar. Mix well. Cover. Refrigerate until ready to use.

Hot Spinach & Bacon Salad Flambé

For drama, this showy salad gets a fast flambé at the table.

1 (1-lb.) bunch spinach
4 slices bacon, diced
1-1/2 tablespoons red-wine vinegar
1/4 teaspoon sugar
1/4 teaspoon salt

1/4 teaspoon freshly ground pepper
1/2 teaspoon Dijon-style mustard
1-1/2 tablespoons brandy, Cognac or Pernod
1-1/2 tablespoons toasted pine nuts or
  pistachios

Wash fresh spinach thoroughly in several changes of cold water. Discard stems and bruised or tough leaves. Drain well. Tear spinach into bite-size pieces. Place in a plastic bag. Refrigerate until needed. Using a large skillet or electric skillet, cook bacon until crisp. Remove with a slotted spoon. Drain on paper towel. Pour off all bacon drippings, reserving 3 tablespoons. Place 3 tablespoons drippings and half of spinach in skillet. Cook over medium heat, continually lifting leaves from bottom of skillet until wilted. Continue to add remaining spinach until all leaves are evenly wilted. In a small bowl or jar, combine vinegar, sugar, salt, pepper and mustard. Mix well. Add vinegar mixture to spinach. Mix well. In a small saucepan, heat liquor until warm, about 150F (65C). Using a long match, carefully ignite liquor. Spoon flaming liquor over salad. After the flame goes out, sprinkle salad with pine nuts or pistachios. Makes 2 to 3 servings.

 Select a liquor with a high alcohol proof. This will aid in the flambé step.

French Potato Salad

For a complete meal, serve this salad with cold meats.

Mustard-Tarragon Dressing, see below
6 medium boiling potatoes (about 1-1/2 lbs.)
1/4 cup dry white wine
3 tablespoons chopped red onion
3 tablespoons chopped fresh parsley

2 medium tomatoes, cut in wedges
12 whole black oil-cured olives or
   pitted black olives
2 hard-cooked eggs, quartered
6 cornichons or gherkins

Mustard-Tarragon Dressing:
2 tablespoons white-wine vinegar
6 tablespoons safflower oil or olive oil
2 teaspoons Dijon-style mustard

1/2 teaspoon dried leaf tarragon
1/2 teaspoon salt
1/4 teaspoon freshly ground pepper

Prepare Mustard-Tarragon Dressing. In a medium saucepan, bring salted water to a boil. Add whole unpeeled potatoes and cook 15 to 20 minutes. Potatoes should be tender when pierced with a knife. Drain well. Cool slightly. Peel, quarter and slice potatoes 1/4-inch thick. Place slices in a large bowl. Pour wine over potato slices. Mix gently. Cool 10 minutes. Pour Mustard-Tarragon Dressing over potatoes. Mix lightly. Gently stir in onion. Sprinkle salad with parsley. Serve chilled or at room temperature. Serve on a platter garnished with tomato wedges, olives, eggs and cornichons or gherkins. Makes 6 servings.

Mustard-Tarragon Dressing:
Combine all ingredients in a small bowl or jar. Mix well. Cover. Refrigerate until ready to serve.

Garden Greens with Nasturtium Blossoms

Color a salad with brilliant nasturtiums for a bit of drama.

Oil & Lime Dressing, see below
1 bunch watercress
1 large head butter lettuce

6 to 8 nasturtium blossoms
3 tablespoons toasted chopped filberts or
   walnuts

Oil & Lime Dressing:
2 tablespoons walnut oil and
   2 tablespoons safflower oil or
   1/4 cup safflower oil
1-1/2 tablespoons lime juice

1-1/2 teaspoons Dijon-style mustard
1/2 teaspoon dried leaf tarragon
1/4 teaspoon salt
1/4 teaspoon freshly ground pepper

Prepare Oil & Lime Dressing. Trim stems from watercress. Tear lettuce leaves and watercress into bite-size pieces. Combine greens in a salad bowl. Pour Oil & Lime Dressing over greens. Toss lightly. Garnish with nasturtium blossoms. Sprinkle nuts over salad. Makes 4 servings.

Oil & Lime Dressing:
Combine all ingredients in a small bowl or jar. Mix well. Cover. Refrigerate until ready to use.

Variation
Substitute violet or chive blossoms for nasturtium blossoms.

Italian Salad

An attractive salad, blending the red, white and green colors of the Italian flag.

1 tablespoon chopped fresh basil
3 tablespoons olive oil
3 large tomatoes, peeled, sliced
2 teaspoons white-wine vinegar
1/4 teaspoon salt

1/4 teaspoon freshly ground pepper
1/4 lb. Italian mozzarella or
    soft teleme cheese, thinly sliced
4 sprigs basil

In a small bowl, marinate chopped basil in oil 15 minutes. Arrange tomatoes on a large platter with a slightly raised edge. Add vinegar to basil and oil. Spoon basil mixture over tomatoes. Sprinkle salt and pepper over tomatoes. Arrange cheese over tomatoes. Garnish with basil sprigs. Makes 4 servings.

Pasta Salad Provençal

Salami and garbanzo beans make this pasta salad a hearty entree for any picnic.

Lemon-Basil Dressing, see below
4 cups cooked small shell-shaped or
    spiral pasta
1 (16-oz.) can garbanzo beans, drained
1 large green bell pepper, julienned
1 large red bell pepper, julienned
3/4 cup whole black oil-cured olives or
    pitted black olives

1/4 cup capers
1/2 cup chopped fresh parsley
1 head curly endive or escarole
1/4 lb. thinly sliced salami,
    Italian sausage or mortadella

Lemon-Basil Dressing:
2/3 cup olive oil
3 tablespoons lemon juice
2 garlic cloves, minced
1 tablespoon minced fresh basil or
    3/4 teaspoon dried leaf basil

1 teaspoon salt
1/4 teaspoon freshly ground pepper

Prepare Lemon-Basil Dressing. In a large bowl, combine cooked pasta, garbanzo beans, green pepper, red pepper, olives, capers and parsley. Mix lightly. Pour Lemon-Basil Dressing over vegetables. Mix lightly. Line a large platter with endive or escarole. Place pasta salad in center of platter. Surround salad with salami or sausage slices. Makes 8 servings.

Lemon-Basil Dressing:
Combine all ingredients in a small bowl or jar. Mix well. Cover. Refrigerate until ready to use.

Sweet & Sour Hot Slaw

This colorful slaw is quick and easy to assemble, especially when using a food processor.

2-1/2 cups shredded green cabbage
1-1/2 cups shredded red cabbage
1 carrot, shredded
2 green onions, chopped
1/3 cup cider vinegar

3 tablespoons brown sugar
1/2 teaspoon salt
1/4 teaspoon freshly ground pepper
1/3 cup dairy sour cream
1 teaspoon Dijon-style mustard

In a medium bowl, combine green and red cabbage, carrot and green onions. In a small saucepan, combine vinegar, sugar, salt and pepper. Stir over medium heat until sugar dissolves. Pour hot vinegar sauce over vegetables. Mix well. In a small bowl, stir together sour cream and mustard. Stir sour-cream mixture into vegetables. Serve immediately. Makes 6 servings.

Chinese Chicken Salad   Photo on pages 74 and 75.

This is a delicious salad entree for a luncheon or summer supper.

Sesame-Soy Dressing, see below
4 split chicken breasts, cooked, chilled
    (about 1-1/3 lbs.)
2 cups shredded iceberg lettuce or
    Chinese cabbage
1 medium bunch cilantro, stems removed,
    leaves chopped

1/3 cup diced celery
2 green onions, cut in 1-inch slivers
1/4 cup toasted slivered almonds
2 tablespoons toasted sesame seeds
8 spears fresh pineapple, papaya or
    cantaloupe

Sesame-Soy Dressing:
1/2 teaspoon dry mustard
1/2 teaspoon grated lemon peel
1 tablespoon honey

2 tablespoons soy sauce
2 tablespoons sesame oil
2 tablespoons lime juice

Prepare Sesame-Soy Dressing. Remove and discard skin and bones from chicken. Pull meat into strips using fingers or 2 forks. Place chicken in a large bowl. Pour Sesame-Soy Dressing over chicken strips. Mix well. Add lettuce or cabbage, cilantro, celery, green onions and almonds. Mix lightly. Spoon onto plates. Garnish with pineapple, papaya or cantaloupe spears. Sprinkle with sesame seeds. Makes 4 servings.

Sesame-Soy Dressing:
Combine all ingredients in a small bowl or jar. Mix well. Cover. Refrigerate until ready to use.

Chinese cabbage may be called Napa cabbage in your market.

Shown on the following pages, front row, left to right: Mushroom-Gruyère Salad, page 68; Chinese Chicken Salad, page 73. Back row, left to right: Raw vegetable tray with Herb Cream Cheese, page 35; Multi-Layered Gazpacho Salad, page 64; and Vegetable Platter Salad, page 69.

How To Make Mexican Jícama & Orange Salad

1/Peel jícama by pulling outer skin starting at the root end.

2/Cut off stem end of bell pepper. Remove seeds and inner pith. Slice pepper in rings.

Mexican Jícama & Orange Salad

The brown-skinned tuber, jícama, pronounced HEE-kah-mah, tastes like water chestnuts.

Mexican Dressing, see below
1 large head romaine lettuce or curly endive
3 navel oranges, peeled, diced
1 small red onion, diced

1 cup peeled, diced jícama
1 red or green bell pepper, cut in rings
3 tablespoons roasted sunflower seeds

Mexican Dressing:
6 tablespoons safflower oil or olive oil
3 tablespoons white-wine vinegar
1/4 teaspoon ground cumin

1/4 teaspoon dried leaf oregano
1/4 teaspoon salt
1/4 teaspoon freshly ground pepper

Prepare Mexican Dressing. Tear romaine lettuce or curly endive into bite-size pieces. Place in a salad bowl. Arrange oranges, onion, jícama and red or green bell pepper on romaine lettuce or endive. Pour Mexican Dressing over salad. Sprinkle sunflower seeds over salad. Makes 6 servings.

Mexican Dressing:
Combine all ingredients in a small bowl or jar. Mix well. Cover. Refrigerate until ready to use.

Jícama does not discolor so this salad can be made ahead and still look fresh and colorful.

Scandinavian Vegetable & Cheese Salad

Dill adds its distinctive flavor to this multi-colored salad.

Dill Dressing, see below
1 cup thinly sliced carrots
1 cup cauliflowerets
1 cup sliced fennel or celery
1 cup sliced mushrooms
1/2 cup diced red or green bell pepper

1 cup halved cherry tomatoes
1 cup sliced zucchini
1/3 cup sliced green onions
3 tablespoons chopped fresh parsley
1/2 lb. Jarlsberg cheese, julienned

Dill Dressing:
6 tablespoons safflower oil
2 tablespoons white-wine vinegar
1/2 teaspoon salt
1/4 teaspoon freshly ground pepper

1 garlic clove, minced
1/2 teaspoon dried dill weed
1 teaspoon Dijon-style mustard

Prepare Dill Dressing. In a large bowl, combine carrots, cauliflowerets, fennel or celery, mushrooms, red or green bell pepper, tomatoes, zucchini, green onions and parsley. Pour Dill Dressing over vegetables. Mix well. Cover and refrigerate several hours. At serving time mix salad again and sprinkle with cheese. Makes 6 to 8 servings.

Dill Dressing:
Combine all ingredients in a small bowl or jar. Mix well. Cover. Refrigerate until ready to use.

Greek Country Salad

This cheese salad, known as Salata Horiatiki, appears with wide variation throughout Greece.

Oil & Vinegar Dressing, see below
1 head curly endive
1 small head romaine lettuce
1 cucumber, peeled, sliced
2 medium tomatoes, cut in wedges, or
    1 cup cherry tomatoes, halved

1/2 cup whole black oil-cured olives or
    pitted black olives
2 green onions, chopped, or
    1/4 cup chopped red onion
1/4 lb. feta cheese, cut in 1/2-inch pieces

Oil & Vinegar Dressing:
6 tablespoons olive oil
2 tablespoons red-wine vinegar
1 teaspoon chopped fresh oregano or
    1/4 teaspoon dried leaf oregano

1/2 teaspoon salt
1/4 teaspoon freshly ground pepper

Prepare Oil & Vinegar Dressing. Tear curly endive and romaine lettuce into bite-size pieces. Place in a large salad bowl. Add cucumber, tomatoes, olives and onions. Pour Oil & Vinegar Dressing over salad. Toss lightly. Top with cheese. Makes 6 servings.

Oil & Vinegar Dressing:
Combine all ingredients in a small bowl or jar. Mix well. Cover. Refrigerate until ready to use.

Pickled Beets

Young beets from the garden are perfect for this Scandinavian vegetable relish.

2 cups sliced cooked or drained canned beets
1 small red onion, sliced,
   separated into rings
1 tablespoon sugar
1/2 teaspoon dry mustard

1/2 teaspoon salt
8 whole cloves
1 garlic clove
1/3 cup cider vinegar
1/4 cup water

Layer beets and onion in a wide-mouth pint jar. In a small saucepan, combine sugar, mustard, salt, cloves, garlic, vinegar and water. Bring mixture to a boil. Pour hot liquid over beets and onion rings. Cover and refrigerate 24 to 48 hours. Makes 1 pint.

Swedish-Style Cucumbers in Dill

A classic Scandinavian accompaniment to seafood.

1/2 cup white-wine vinegar
2 tablespoons water
1/4 cup sugar
1/2 teaspoon salt
1/4 teaspoon freshly ground pepper

1 tablespoon chopped fresh dill or
   3/4 teaspoon dried dill weed
3 tablespoons minced fresh parsley
3 large cucumbers, peeled, thinly sliced

In a medium bowl, combine vinegar, water, sugar, salt, pepper, dill and parsley. Add cucumbers. Mix lightly. Cover. Refrigerate 2 hours, stirring occasionally. Makes 6 servings.

Jerusalem Artichoke & Seafood Salad

This marinated salad makes an enticing first course.

Shallot-Mustard Vinaigrette Dressing,
   see below
1/2 lb. Jerusalem artichokes
1/2 lb. mushrooms, thinly sliced
3 tablespoons chopped fresh parsley

1 medium head butter lettuce
12 medium, cooked shrimp, peeled, deveined,
   or 1 cup small cooked shrimp
12 cherry tomatoes, halved
4 to 6 sprigs watercress

Shallot-Mustard Vinaigrette Dressing:
6 tablespoons safflower oil
2 tablespoons white-wine vinegar
1/4 teaspoon salt

1/4 teaspoon freshly ground pepper
1 shallot, chopped
2 teaspoons Dijon-style mustard

Prepare Shallot-Mustard Vinaigrette Dressing. Cook Jerusalem artichokes whole in boiling salted water until tender, about 15 minutes. Drain well. Cool slightly. Peel and slice Jerusalem artichokes 1/4-inch thick. In a medium bowl, combine Jerusalem artichokes, mushrooms and parsley. Pour dressing over vegetables. Mix lightly. Cover and refrigerate 1 hour. Line salad plates with butter lettuce. Spoon salad onto lettuce. Top with shrimp and tomatoes. Garnish with watercress. Makes 6 servings.
Shallot-Mustard Vinaigrette Dressing:
Combine all ingredients in a small bowl or jar. Mix well. Cover. Refrigerate until ready to use.

1/Tear romaine and butter lettuce into bite-size pieces.

2/Peel shallots, removing only the dry outer skin.

Shallot Salad

Set a salad-bar buffet for a festive course at a dinner party or garden lunch.

Shallot Dressing, see below
1 large head romaine lettuce
1 large head butter lettuce
Toppings: 1/2 cup roasted sunflower seeds
   3 hard-cooked egg yolks, shredded
   1/4 lb. bacon, cooked crisp, crumbled
   1 avocado, peeled, diced
   1 cup alfalfa sprouts

Shallot Dressing:
2/3 cup safflower oil
1/4 cup red-wine vinegar
1 tablespoon Dijon-style mustard
2 tablespoons chopped shallots or
   green onions, white part only

1/2 teaspoon salt
1/4 teaspoon freshly ground pepper

Prepare Shallot Dressing. Tear romaine and butter lettuce into bite-size pieces. Place in a large salad bowl. Pour Shallot Dressing over greens. Toss lightly. Serve with toppings listed above. Makes 8 servings.

Shallot Dressing:
Combine all ingredients in a small bowl or jar. Mix well. Cover. Refrigerate until ready to use.

Prepare avocado just before serving. If prepared in advance, sprinkle avocado with lemon juice to prevent browning.

Tabbouleh

This Lebanese wheat salad carries well on a picnic outing.

Spicy Dressing, see below
1 cup bulgur (precooked cracked wheat)
1 cup boiling water
1 bunch green onions, chopped
1 cup chopped fresh parsley
1/3 cup lightly packed chopped fresh
   mint leaves

1 medium head romaine lettuce
2 medium tomatoes, cut in wedges
1/2 cup whole black oil-cured olives or
   pitted black olives
3 to 4 sprigs mint

Spicy Dressing:
1/3 cup olive oil
3 tablespoons lemon juice
1 teaspoon ground allspice
1 teaspoon grated lemon peel

1/2 teaspoon ground cumin
1 teaspoon salt
1/4 teaspoon freshly ground pepper

Prepare Spicy Dressing. Place bulgur in a heatproof bowl. Add boiling water. Cover and let stand 2 hours. Drain bulgur, squeezing out any excess water. In a medium bowl, combine green onions, parsley, mint and soaked bulgur. Mix lightly. Pour Spicy Dressing over bulgur mixture. Mix lightly. Line a salad bowl or platter with romaine leaves. Place salad in center. Garnish with tomato wedges, olives and mint sprigs. Makes 6 servings.

Spicy Dressing:
Combine all ingredients in a small bowl or jar. Mix well. Cover. Refrigerate until ready to use.

Shredded Egg & Radish Salad

A quick and easy salad, ideal for all seasons.

6 hard-cooked eggs, shredded
2 tablespoons mayonnaise
2 tablespoons dairy sour cream
1 teaspoon Dijon-style mustard
1/4 teaspoon salt

1/4 teaspoon white pepper
1 green onion, finely chopped
3 tablespoons chopped fresh parsley
6 leaves butter lettuce
1 large bunch radishes, thinly sliced

In a small bowl, combine eggs, mayonnaise, sour cream, mustard, salt and white pepper. Mix lightly. Stir in green onion and parsley. Arrange lettuce leaves on a platter. Spoon egg-salad mixture over lettuce. Place a circle of radish slices around egg salad. Cover and refrigerate until serving time. Makes 6 servings.

Escarole & Sausage Bistro Salad

Polish kielbasa, German knackwurst or strings of cocktail sausages are all good sausage choices.

Red-Wine Vinaigrette Dressing, see below
3 mild Italian sausages (about 10 oz.)
2 tablespoons butter
2 garlic cloves, minced
3 slices sourdough French bread,
   cut in 1/2-inch cubes

4 slices thick-sliced bacon, diced
1/2 bunch escarole or curly endive
1 small head romaine lettuce
1 cup cherry tomatoes, halved

Red-Wine Vinaigrette Dressing:
1/3 cup olive oil
2 tablespoons red-wine vinegar
1/2 teaspoon salt

1/4 teaspoon freshly ground pepper
1 teaspoon Dijon-style mustard

Prepare Red-Wine Vinaigrette Dressing. Place sausages in a small saucepan. Cover with cold water. Cover and bring to a boil. Remove pan from heat. Let stand 15 minutes. Drain well. Slice sausages diagonally; set aside. Melt butter in a small skillet over medium heat. Add garlic and French-bread cubes. Sauté over low heat until bread cubes are golden brown, 3 to 4 minutes. Place bacon in a small skillet. Cook over medium heat until crisp. With a slotted spoon, lift out bacon pieces. Drain on paper towel. Reserve drippings. Tear escarole or curly endive and romaine into bite-size pieces. Place greens in a large salad bowl. Pour 2 tablespoons hot bacon drippings over salad greens. Toss lightly. Add Red-Wine Vinaigrette Dressing. Toss lightly. Scatter sausage slices, bacon, bread cubes and tomatoes over salad. Makes 6 servings.

Red-Wine Vinaigrette Dressing:
Combine all ingredients in a small bowl or jar. Mix well. Cover. Refrigerate until ready to use.

Marinated Four-Bean Salad

A medley of fresh-cooked or canned beans, steeped in dressing, makes a great picnic or barbecue dish.

1 (1-lb.) can garbanzo beans, drained
1 (1-lb.) can kidney beans, drained
1 (1-lb.) can Italian-style green beans,
   drained
1 (1-lb.) can wax beans, drained
3 tablespoons sugar
1/2 cup white-wine vinegar
1/2 cup olive oil

1/2 teaspoon salt
1/4 teaspoon freshly ground pepper
1/2 teaspoon dry mustard
1/2 teaspoon dried leaf basil
1 small red onion, sliced,
   separated into rings or chopped
3 tablespoons chopped fresh parsley

In a large bowl, mix together 4 kinds of beans. In a small bowl, combine sugar and vinegar. Let stand until dissolved. Stir in oil, salt, pepper, mustard and basil. Pour vinegar mixture over beans. Mix thoroughly. Cover and refrigerate several hours. To serve, add onion and parsley. Mix lightly. Makes 12 servings.

Salads which marinate and intensify in flavor as they are stored are often good choices for picnic outings. Plan to store them in a container with a tight lid which makes for easy carrying.

EGGS & SOUFFLÉS

Vegetables and eggs are natural partners. Interesting combination dishes are created around them such as soufflés, omelets, roulades, frittatas and crepes. Together they offer great diversity.

Egg cookery calls for special care and alertness. Here are some useful egg-cookery tips. Whole raw eggs separate best when cold right from the refrigerator. Room temperature is best for beating to maximum volume. Therefore, separate eggs as soon as you take them from the refrigerator. Then let them stand 30 minutes before beating. A trace of fat, such as a speck of egg yolk or a greasy bowl or beaters, prevents egg whites from expanding to their greatest volume. Avoid overbeating egg whites. Beating egg whites to the point where they lose their glossy sheen and become dry, keeps them from expanding to their fullest potential volume during baking.

Quiches, timbales, and frittatas should be baked only until barely set. They continue to firm up after being removed from the oven. Oven baking these dishes to the point where they puff up will cause them to collapse and squeeze out liquid when the lacy egg network cools and contracts. Then their silken texture turns tough and grainy.

Soufflés are not difficult to master despite their formidable reputation. They can even be totally assembled in advance. Allow the soufflé mixture to stand at room temperature for 1 hour before baking. This convenience makes them excellent choices for party dishes.

This chapter offers festive choices for brunch, lunch, first course or dinner entrees. Try Ham-Filled Spinach Soufflé Roll for an elegant luncheon. Cauliflower or Spinach Soufflés make superb dinner accompaniments. Custard-like entrees including Persian Vegetable Pie are versatile dishes ideal for picnics or appetizers.

Midsummer Luncheon
Ham-Filled Spinach Soufflé Roll, page 91
Mushroom-Gruyère Salad, page 68
Croissants
Summer Fruit Platter

Fresh Mushroom Soufflé

If it helps your timetable, assemble this dish completely and let stand 1 hour before baking.

3/4 cup milk
2 tablespoons cornstarch
2 tablespoons cold water
1/2 teaspoon salt
1/4 teaspoon ground nutmeg
2 tablespoons butter
1 shallot or green onion, chopped

1/4 lb. mushrooms, finely chopped
2 teaspoons lemon juice
1/2 cup shredded Swiss or Gruyère cheese
(2 oz.)
4 eggs, separated
1 egg white

Preheat oven to 375F (190C). Butter a 1-1/2-quart soufflé dish or a round 10-inch baking dish. Scald milk by heating in a small saucepan over low heat until bubbles appear around the edge. In a small bowl, combine cornstarch and cold water. Add cornstarch paste to scalded milk. Cook over medium heat until thickened, stirring constantly. Add salt and nutmeg; set aside. Melt butter in a large skillet over medium heat. Add shallot or green onion. Sauté until soft, 2 to 3 minutes. Add mushrooms and lemon juice. Sauté mushrooms 1 minute or until glazed. Remove from heat. In a large bowl, beat egg yolks until lemon-colored. Stir in milk mixture, mushroom mixture and cheese. In a large bowl, beat 5 egg whites until soft peaks form; do not beat until dry. Gently fold egg whites into mushroom mixture. Turn into buttered dish. Bake 25 to 30 minutes or until center is set. Serve immediately. Makes 4 servings.

Cauliflower Soufflé

A delectable and different soufflé to accompany pork, turkey or duck.

1 medium head cauliflower
3 tablespoons lemon juice
1 (3-oz.) pkg. cream cheese,
  room temperature
5 eggs, separated
3 tablespoons dairy sour cream

1/4 teaspoon salt
1/4 teaspoon white pepper
1/4 teaspoon ground nutmeg
1/4 cup freshly grated Parmesan cheese
  (3/4 oz.)

Preheat oven to 400F (205C). Butter a 1-1/2-quart soufflé dish or a round 10-inch baking dish. Separate cauliflower into flowerets. Place in a large saucepan with 2 inches of boiling salted water and lemon juice. Cover. Simmer over low heat until crisp-tender, about 12 minutes. Cool slightly. Press cauliflower through a ricer or shred in a food processor fitted with a shredding blade. In a medium bowl, beat cream cheese until creamy. Beat in egg yolks, sour cream, salt, white pepper, nutmeg and Parmesan cheese. Mix in riced or shredded cauliflower. In a large bowl, beat egg whites until soft peaks form; do not beat until dry. Gently fold egg whites into cauliflower mixture. Turn into buttered dish. Bake 25 minutes or until center is set. Serve immediately. Makes 4 servings.

 For maximum height during baking, beat egg whites until they retain an upward, but still glossy peak. Egg whites should be at room temperature when beaten.

Spinach Soufflé with Chive Sauce

Fresh spinach colors this soufflé a beautiful green.

Chive Sauce, see below
1 (12-oz.) bunch spinach or 1 (10-oz.) pkg.
   frozen chopped spinach, thawed, drained
1 tablespoon butter
5 eggs, separated
2 tablespoons cornstarch

2 tablespoons cold water
3/4 cup milk
1/2 teaspoon salt
1/4 teaspoon ground nutmeg
1 cup shredded Gruyère or Jarlsberg cheese
   (4 oz.)

Chive Sauce:
1/2 cup whipping cream
1/3 cup dairy sour cream

2 tablespoons chopped chives
   or green-onion tops

Prepare Chive Sauce. Preheat oven to 375F (190C). Butter a 2-quart soufflé dish or a round 11-inch casserole dish. Wash fresh spinach thoroughly in several changes of cold water. Discard stems and bruised or tough leaves. Drain well. Chop spinach. Melt butter in a large skillet over medium-high heat. Add spinach. Cook until slightly wilted but still crisp-tender, about 1 minute. Drain well. Place spinach and egg yolks in a blender or food processor fitted with a steel blade. Process until smooth. Place mixture in a large bowl. In a small saucepan, combine cornstarch and cold water. Add milk to cornstarch paste. Cook over medium heat until thickened, stirring constantly. Stir in salt and nutmeg. Stir cornstarch mixture and 3/4 cup cheese into spinach mixture. In a small bowl, beat egg whites until soft peaks form; do not beat until dry. Gently fold egg whites into spinach mixture. Spoon into buttered dish. Sprinkle remaining 1/4 cup cheese on top. Bake 30 minutes or until center is set. Serve immediately with Chive Sauce. Makes 6 servings.

Chive Sauce:
In small bowl whip cream until stiff. Fold in sour cream and chives or green onions. Refrigerate until ready to use.

Chestnut Soufflé

A superb dish with roast duck or venison.

1 tablespoon butter
1 medium onion, chopped
1 medium carrot, shredded
1 (15-oz.) can unsweetened chestnut puree
4 eggs, separated

1/4 cup dry sherry
1/2 teaspoon salt
1/4 teaspoon freshly ground pepper
1/4 cup toasted pecans or almonds
2 tablespoons freshly grated Parmesan cheese

Preheat oven to 350F (175C). Butter a 1-1/2-quart soufflé dish or a round 10-inch baking dish. Melt butter in a large skillet over medium heat. Add onion and carrot. Sauté until soft, about 10 minutes. Place chestnut puree in a blender or food processor fitted with a steel blade. Process until broken into small pieces. Add egg yolks and sherry. Process until smooth. Add salt, pepper, nuts and sautéed vegetables. Process 2 seconds just to chop nuts finely. Transfer to a large bowl. In a medium bowl, beat egg whites until soft peaks form; do not beat until dry. Fold 1/3 of egg whites into chestnut mixture. Gently fold in remaining egg whites. Turn into buttered dish. Bake 30 to 35 minutes or until center is set. Serve immediately. Makes 6 servings.

How To Make Zucchini Squares

1/Place zucchini in a colander. Salt lightly. Let stand 15 minutes.

2/Squeeze zucchini to remove all excess moisture.

Zucchini Squares

When the garden is abundant with zucchini, bake them into these cheese-streaked squares.

2-1/2 lbs. zucchini (about 6 medium-large zucchini), ends trimmed, shredded
Salt
2 tablespoons butter
4 eggs
1-1/2 cups shredded Jarlsberg, Swiss or samso cheese (6 oz.)

1/4 cup chopped fresh parsley
2 green onions, chopped
2 tablespoons chopped fresh basil or 1 teaspoon dried leaf basil
1 garlic clove, minced
2 tablespoons freshly grated Parmesan cheese

Preheat oven to 350F (175C). Lightly butter an 11" x 7" baking dish. Place zucchini in a colander. Salt lightly. Let stand 15 minutes. Salt draws out bitter juices from zucchini. Squeeze out moisture. Zucchini should be quite dry. Melt butter in a large skillet over medium heat. Add zucchini. Sauté 2 minutes or until crisp-tender. In a medium bowl, beat eggs until blended. Mix in 1-1/2 cups cheese, parsley, green onions, basil, garlic and sautéed zucchini. Place in buttered baking dish. Sprinkle with Parmesan cheese. Bake 30 minutes or until set. Cool slightly. Cut in squares. Serve hot or chilled. Makes 12 servings.

These nutritious squares make great picnic fare or party appetizers.

Spinach & Sunflower Squares

Use this versatile omelet as an appetizer, first course, or entree.

1 (12-oz.) bunch spinach or 1 (10-oz.) pkg.
    frozen chopped spinach, thawed, drained
2 tablespoons butter
1 bunch green onions, chopped
1/4 lb. mushrooms, sliced
1/4 cup chopped fresh parsley
6 eggs
1/4 cup whipping cream

1/2 teaspoon salt
1/4 teaspoon freshly ground pepper
2 teaspoons chopped fresh tarragon or
    1/2 teaspoon dried leaf tarragon
1/2 cup shredded Jarlsberg cheese (2 oz.)
1/4 cup freshly grated Parmesan cheese
    (3/4 oz.)
1/3 cup roasted sunflower seeds

Preheat oven to 350F (175C). Butter a 9-inch square baking dish. Wash fresh spinach thoroughly in several changes of cold water. Discard stems and bruised or tough leaves. Drain well. Chop spinach. Melt butter in a large skillet over medium heat. Add green onions. Sauté until glazed, 2 to 3 minutes. Add mushrooms. Sauté 1 minute. Add spinach. Sauté 2 minutes. Remove from heat. Mix in parsley. In a large bowl, beat eggs until blended. Mix in cream, salt, pepper, tarragon, vegetable mixture and Jarlsberg cheese. Pour into buttered baking dish. Sprinkle with Parmesan cheese and sunflower seeds. Bake 20 minutes or until set. Cut in squares. Serve hot. Makes 6 servings or 36 appetizers.

Variation

Add 6 strips bacon, cooked crisp, crumbled, along with Jarlsberg cheese.

Bacon & Potato Squares

Smoky bacon enriches this shredded-potato casserole for a savory side dish.

1/2 lb. sliced bacon, diced
1 medium onion, chopped
3 eggs
2/3 cup dairy sour cream
1/4 cup all-purpose flour
3/4 teaspoon salt

1/4 teaspoon freshly ground pepper
4 large baking potatoes, peeled,
    coarsely shredded
2 tablespoons chopped chives or fresh parsley
1/4 cup dairy sour cream

Preheat oven to 400F (205C). In a large skillet, cook bacon until crisp. Remove with a slotted spoon. Drain on paper towel. Pour off drippings, reserving 3 tablespoons. Grease 12" x 8" baking dish with 1 tablespoon reserved drippings. Place 2 tablespoons reserved drippings in skillet. Add onion. Sauté over medium heat 2 to 3 minutes or until soft, stirring occasionally. In a large bowl, beat eggs until blended. Mix in 2/3 cup sour cream, flour, salt and pepper. Place potatoes in cheesecloth or kitchen towel. Squeeze out moisture. Add shredded potatoes, chives or parsley and half the bacon to egg batter. Pour into greased baking dish. Sprinkle remaining bacon over top. Bake 10 minutes. Reduce oven temperature to 325F (165C). Continue baking 45 to 50 minutes or until lightly browned. Cut in squares. Top each serving with additional sour cream. Serve hot. Makes 8 servings.

Carrot-Fontina Squares

A quick luncheon dish that is excellent hot or chilled.

2 tablespoons butter
6 large carrots, shredded
3 green onions, chopped
6 eggs
1-1/4 cups half and half
1/4 teaspoon ground nutmeg
1/4 teaspoon salt

1/2 teaspoon freshly ground pepper
1/3 cup chopped fresh parsley
3/4 cup alfalfa sprouts
1 cup shredded fontina or
  Gruyère cheese (4 oz.)
3 tablespoons roasted sunflower seeds

Preheat oven to 350F (175C). Lightly butter an 11'' x 7'' baking dish. Melt butter in a large skillet over medium heat. Add carrots and green onions. Sauté 3 to 4 minutes, or until vegetables are soft. In a large bowl, beat eggs until blended. Stir in half and half, nutmeg, salt, pepper, parsley, sprouts, sautéed vegetables and cheese. Spoon into buttered baking dish. Sprinkle with sunflower seeds. Bake 25 to 30 minutes or until set and lightly browned on edges. Cut in squares. Serve hot or chilled. Makes 8 to 10 servings.

Dutch Babie with Mushroom Center

A billowy oven pancake forms the backdrop for a cheesy mushroom sauce.

2 tablespoons butter
2 eggs
1/2 cup milk

1/2 cup all-purpose flour
Mushroom Sauce, see below
2 tablespoons chopped fresh parsley

Mushroom Sauce:
2 tablespoons butter
3/4 lb. mushrooms, sliced
2 tablespoons dry sherry

1/2 cup dairy sour cream
1 cup shredded Jarlsberg, Gruyère or
  fontina cheese (4 oz.)

Preheat oven to 425F (220C). Place butter in a 9-inch pie dish. Heat in oven until butter melts, 2 minutes. In a blender or food processor fitted with a steel blade, combine eggs, milk and flour. Process until smooth. Pour batter into hot buttered pie dish. Bake 18 to 20 minutes or until puffed and golden brown. While pancake bakes, prepare Mushroom Sauce. Cut pancake into 6 wedges. Spoon Mushroom Sauce in center. Sprinkle with parsley. Serve hot. Makes 6 servings.

Mushroom Sauce:
Melt butter in a large skillet over medium-high heat. Add mushrooms. Sauté until glazed, 1 to 2 minutes. Add sherry and bring to a boil. Cook until liquid is slightly reduced. Reduce heat to low. Add sour cream and cheese. Heat, stirring constantly until cheese melts. Set aside until ready to use.

Asparagus & Eggs Milanese

During asparagus season, this is a favored Milanese business lunch.

1-1/2 lbs. large asparagus spears
1/4 cup butter
4 eggs
1/4 teaspoon salt
1/4 teaspoon freshly ground pepper

1/4 teaspoon dried leaf tarragon
1/3 cup diced prosciutto or cooked ham
1/2 cup freshly grated Romano cheese
  (1-1/2 oz.)
2 tablespoons minced fresh parsley

Preheat oven to 375F (190C). Cook asparagus spears in boiling salted water 5 to 7 minutes or steam until barely tender, 10 to 15 minutes. Drain well. Place 1 tablespoon butter in each of 4 individual oval or rectangular baking dishes. Heat in oven until butter melts, 2 minutes. Break 1 egg in center of each dish. Sprinkle egg with salt, pepper and tarragon. Return to oven. Bake until whites are just set, 5 minutes. Remove from oven. Arrange asparagus alongside eggs. Top with diced prosciutto or cooked ham. Sprinkle cheese and parsley over top. Bake 1 minute or until cheese melts. Makes 4 servings.

Mushroom-Filled Soufflé Roll

A light-as-air soufflé is wrapped around a creamy mushroom filling.

Mushroom Filling, see below
1/4 cup butter
1/2 cup all-purpose flour
1 pint (2 cups) milk, heated
1/2 teaspoon salt

1 tablespoon dry sherry or vermouth
4 eggs, separated
6 cherry tomatoes
6 sprigs parsley

Mushroom Filling:
1 (3-oz.) pkg. cream cheese,
  room temperature
1/2 cup dairy sour cream
1 chopped green onion

2 tablespoons minced fresh parsley
1/8 teaspoon salt
1/8 teaspoon white pepper
1/4 lb. mushrooms, finely minced

Prepare Mushroom Filling. Preheat oven to 350F (175C). Butter a 15" x 10" jelly-roll pan. Line with waxed paper. Butter paper generously to prevent soufflé from sticking. Melt butter in a medium saucepan over medium heat. Blend in flour. Cook, stirring constantly 2 minutes. Remove from heat. Gradually whisk in hot milk. Return to heat. Cook until thickened, stirring constantly. Remove from heat. Stir in salt, sherry or vermouth and egg yolks. In a large bowl, beat egg whites until soft peaks form; do not beat until dry. Gently fold egg whites into yolk mixture. Pour soufflé mixture into buttered baking pan. Bake 30 to 35 minutes or until top springs back when lightly touched. Invert immediately on a kitchen towel. Remove baking pan and peel off waxed paper. Cool 5 minutes. Spread soufflé with filling. Roll up jelly-roll fashion from long side. Place on a platter. Slice. Serve hot or at room temperature. Garnish with cherry tomatoes and parsley sprigs. Makes 8 servings.

Mushroom Filling:
In a small bowl, beat together cream cheese, sour cream, green onion, parsley, salt and white pepper. Add mushrooms. Mix lightly. Set aside until ready to use.

Artichoke & Sausage Frittata

This Italian-style open-faced omelet makes a simple entree for brunch, lunch or supper.

1 (9-oz.) pkg. frozen artichoke hearts, thawed or 1 lb. fresh baby artichokes or artichoke hearts, see page 40
3 tablespoons butter
2 shallots or green onions, chopped
6 eggs
1/4 teaspoon salt
1/4 teaspoon freshly ground pepper

1 teaspoon chopped fresh basil or 1/4 teaspoon dried leaf basil
2 tablespoons chopped fresh parsley
2 mild Italian sausages, cooked, thinly sliced
1/3 cup freshly grated Parmesan cheese (1 oz.)

If using fresh artichokes, pull off lower outer leaves. Trim stem ends. Cut each artichoke in half. Using the tip of a peeler or paring knife, scrape or scoop out the fuzzy choke center. Place artichoke hearts in a medium saucepan with boiling salted water to cover. Cook, covered, over medium heat until tender. Allow 7 minutes for frozen artichoke hearts and 10 to 15 minutes for fresh artichoke hearts. Drain well. Melt 1 tablespoon butter in a large skillet over medium heat. Add artichokes and shallots or green onions. Sauté until glazed, 3 to 4 minutes, stirring lightly; set aside. In a large bowl, beat eggs until blended. Mix in salt, pepper, basil, parsley, sausage and cheese. Stir in artichoke mixture. Place remaining 2 tablespoons butter in a large heavy skillet with ovenproof handle. Melt butter over medium heat. Add artichoke mixture. Cook over medium-high heat without stirring until edges are lightly browned. Place a large plate on top of skillet. Turn frittata onto plate. Slide uncooked side of frittata back into skillet. Or place the large skillet under broiler. Brown frittata lightly. Cut in wedges. Serve hot or chilled. Makes 4 servings.

Swiss Potato Omelet

Here's a fast, hearty brunch dish.

2 medium boiling potatoes
3 tablespoons butter
1 small onion, finely chopped
1/2 cup diced cooked ham
4 eggs

1 tablespoon half and half
2 tablespoons chopped fresh parsley
1/4 teaspoon salt
1/4 teaspoon freshly ground pepper
1/2 cup shredded Gruyère cheese (2 oz.)

In a medium saucepan, cook whole, unpeeled potatoes in boiling salted water, until barely tender, 15 to 20 minutes. Drain well. Peel and slice potatoes 1/4-inch thick. Melt butter in a large skillet with ovenproof handle over medium heat. Add onion. Sauté until glazed, 2 to 3 minutes. Add ham and sliced potatoes. Sauté until potatoes are lightly browned. In small bowl, beat eggs until light. Stir in half and half, parsley, salt and pepper. Pour egg mixture over potato mixture. Cook until set. Shake skillet occasionally slipping a spatula around edge to allow egg mixture to run underneath. Sprinkle cheese on top. Place under broiler to melt cheese. Serve hot. Makes 4 servings.

Ham-Filled Spinach Soufflé Roll

This savory luncheon roll could also be filled with seafood.

2 (1-lb.) bunches spinach or
  2 (10-oz.) pkgs. frozen chopped spinach,
  thawed, drained
2 tablespoons butter
2 green onions, chopped
5 eggs, separated
1/4 teaspoon salt
1/4 teaspoon ground nutmeg
1 cup dairy sour cream

3/4 cup freshly grated Parmesan cheese
  (2-1/4 oz.)
1 cup ground ham, flaked smoked trout
  or salmon
1 shallot or green onion, chopped
3 tablespoons chopped fresh parsley
2 tablespoons sour cream, if desired
1 teaspoon chopped chives, if desired

Preheat oven to 350F (175C). Butter a 15'' x 10'' jelly-roll pan. Line with waxed paper. Butter paper generously. Wash fresh spinach thoroughly in several changes of cold water. Discard stems and bruised or tough leaves. Drain well. Chop spinach. Melt butter in a large skillet over medium heat. Add spinach and 2 chopped green onions. Cook until vegetables are slightly wilted, 2 to 3 minutes for frozen, 5 to 6 minutes for fresh. Drain off liquid. In a large bowl, beat egg whites until foamy. Add salt and continue beating until soft peaks form; do not beat until dry. In a large bowl, beat egg yolks until thick and pale. Beat in nutmeg, 1/3 cup sour cream and 1/2 cup cheese. Stir spinach mixture into egg yolk mixture. Gently fold in egg whites. Pour soufflé mixture into buttered baking pan. Sprinkle with remaining 1/4 cup cheese. Bake 30 to 35 minutes or until top springs back when lightly touched. Invert immediately on a kitchen towel. Remove baking pan and peel off waxed paper. Cool 5 minutes. Combine remaining 2/3 cup sour cream, ham, shallot or green onion and parsley. Spread sour-cream mixture over spinach soufflé. Roll up jelly-roll fashion from long side. Place on a platter. Garnish with sour cream and chopped chives, if desired. Slice. Serve hot or at room temperature. Makes 8 servings.

Persian Vegetable Pie

Toasted pistachios are a crunchy delight in this oven omelet.

1 (12-oz.) bunch spinach or 1 (10-oz.) pkg.
  frozen chopped spinach, thawed, drained
2 tablespoons butter
1 large bunch green onions, chopped
1-1/3 cups chopped iceberg lettuce
1 bunch parsley, chopped
2 garlic cloves, minced
5 eggs

1/2 teaspoon salt
1/4 teaspoon freshly ground pepper
1/4 cup toasted chopped pistachios or walnuts
6 cherry tomatoes, halved
3 tablespoons grated dry Monterey Jack or
  Romano cheese
Plain yogurt, if desired

Preheat oven to 350F (175C). Lightly butter a 9-inch pie dish. Wash fresh spinach thoroughly in several changes of cold water. Discard stems and bruised or tough leaves. Drain well. Chop spinach. Melt butter in a large skillet over medium heat. Add green onions. Sauté until glazed, 2 to 3 minutes. Add spinach, lettuce, parsley and garlic. Stir until limp, 2 to 3 minutes. In a large bowl, beat eggs until blended. Add salt, pepper, sautéed vegetables and half the nuts. Place in buttered pie dish. Arrange cherry tomatoes, cut-side down, around top. Sprinkle with remaining nuts and grated cheese. Bake 25 minutes or until set. Cool slightly. Cut in wedges. Serve hot or chilled. Serve with yogurt, if desired. Makes 6 servings.

Ham-Filled Spinach Soufflé Roll served with Green Bean & Mushroom Salad, page 67.

How To Make Southern Corn Pudding

1/Using a sharp knife, cut kernels from cob. Scrape cob to obtain milk-like juice.

2/Stir pudding well to mix in corn, bacon and chives. Then pour into buttered baking dish.

Southern Corn Pudding

Bacon and chives add color to this flavorful side dish.

About 6 large ears fresh corn
3 eggs
1 pint (2 cups) milk
2 teaspoons sugar
1/2 teaspoon salt

1/4 teaspoon freshly ground pepper
1/8 teaspoon hot-pepper sauce
2 tablespoons butter, melted
4 slices bacon, cooked crisp, crumbled
2 tablespoons chopped chives

Preheat oven to 350F (175C). Butter a 1-1/2-quart baking dish. Using a sharp knife, cut kernels from cobs. Scrape cobs with a sharp spoon or knife to remove milk. Discard cobs. Should make about 2 cups corn and milk. In a medium bowl, beat eggs until blended. Stir in milk, sugar, salt, pepper, hot-pepper sauce and melted butter. Mix in corn, bacon and chives. Pour into buttered baking dish. Bake 30 to 40 minutes or until center is set. Makes 6 servings.

Zucchini-Prosciutto Timbales

An eye-catching make-ahead vegetable accompaniment.

3 medium zucchini, ends trimmed, shredded
   (about 4 cups)
Salt
1 tablespoon butter
1/4 cup chopped red or white onion
3 eggs
1/4 cup whipping cream

1/4 teaspoon salt
1/8 teaspoon freshly ground pepper
1/4 teaspoon dried leaf tarragon
1/4 cup minced fresh parsley
1/3 cup chopped prosciutto or cooked ham
1 cup shredded Gruyère, Jarlsberg or
   fontina cheese (4 oz.)

Preheat oven to 350F (175C). Lightly butter 4 individual soufflé dishes, small timbale molds or custard cups. Place zucchini in a colander. Salt lightly. Let stand 15 minutes. Salt draws out bitter juices from zucchini. Squeeze out moisture. Zucchini should be quite dry. Melt butter in a large skillet over medium-high heat. Add zucchini and onion. Sauté 2 to 3 minutes, stirring, until crisp-tender. In a medium bowl, beat eggs until blended. Mix in cream, 1/4 teaspoon salt, pepper, tarragon, parsley, prosciutto or cooked ham, cheese and sautéed vegetables. Spoon zucchini mixture into buttered dishes. Bake 25 to 30 minutes or until set. Unmold or serve in baking dishes. Serve immediately. Makes 4 servings.

Carrot Timbales

This custard-like carrot dish makes a fine complement to lamb, pork or chicken.

6 large carrots, cut in 1-inch pieces
1 tablespoon butter
1/3 cup whipping cream
1/3 cup milk
2 eggs

1/4 teaspoon salt
1/4 teaspoon freshly ground pepper
1/4 teaspoon ground nutmeg
6 sprigs parsley

Preheat oven to 375F (190C). Lightly butter 6 individual soufflé dishes, small timbale molds or custard cups. In a medium saucepan, cook carrots in boiling salted water. Cook, covered, 20 minutes or until very soft. Drain well. Puree carrots in a blender or food processor fitted with a steel blade. Add butter, cream, milk, eggs, salt, pepper and nutmeg. Process until blended, 40 seconds. Place soufflé dishes or timbale molds in a large baking dish. Add hot water to baking dish to 1/2-inch depth. Divide carrot mixture evenly between 6 dishes. Bake 30 minutes or until mixture is set. Remove dishes from water bath. Cool 10 minutes. Run a knife around the edge of each dish. Unmold on a platter or individual serving dishes. Garnish with parsley sprigs. Serve hot. Makes 6 servings.

PASTRIES & PASTA

Pastries and pasta offer limitless opportunities for creativeness in team efforts with vegetables. Various shapes, sizes, textures and colors all lend interest to vegetable cookery. A wide range of pastry wrappers for vegetables is included in this chapter.

Discover the chewy whole-wheat crust under Vegetable-Topped Whole-Wheat Pizza or crispy layers of filo dough in Spanakopita, a Greek favorite. You will find recipes for layered puff pastry dough, tender Butter Pastry with a Spinach & Chèvre Quiche and a flaky Sour-Cream Pastry with various quiche recipes. These doughs are easy to handle and provide a welcome texture contrast with fresh, crunchy vegetables.

Pastry and pasta dishes make delightful entrees for light or daily dining or for entertaining. Provide a meal with character when serving Tortilla Flats, a big flour tortilla cartwheel laden with vegetables. My Vegetable-Stuffed Pocket Sandwiches enlivened with sunflower seeds, offer a fresh, instant meal with character—a satisfying change from the usual sandwich fare. Easy and elegant quiches enriched with vegetables make a perfect choice for a portable entree or picnic any season. Feature them for brunch, guest luncheon, or family supper.

Whatever the choice, enjoy the delightful blending of vegetables in a variety of pastries or with any pasta.

Pizza-Making Party
Vegetable-Topped
Whole-Wheat Pizza, page 95
Italian Sausage & Mushroom Pizza, page 98
Shallot Salad, page 79
Lemon Ice

Vegetable-Topped Whole-Wheat Pizza

Colorful vegetables top this quick and easy pizza.

Whole-Wheat Pizza Crust, see below
2 tablespoons olive oil
3 green onions, chopped
1 medium zucchini, ends trimmed, sliced
1 medium, yellow straightneck squash,
  ends trimmed, thinly sliced
1/3 lb. mushrooms, sliced
1/4 teaspoon salt
1/4 teaspoon freshly ground pepper

1 (6-oz.) can tomato paste
3/4 cup whole black pitted olives
3/4 cup small cherry tomatoes or
  large cherry tomatoes cut in half
1-1/2 teaspoons dried leaf oregano
3/4 cup shredded Cheddar cheese (3 oz.)
3/4 cup shredded Monterey Jack
  cheese (3 oz.)
3 tablespoons freshly grated Parmesan cheese

Whole-Wheat Pizza Crust:
3/4 cup warm water (105F, 40C)
1/2 pkg. (1-1/2 teaspoons) active dry yeast
1/2 teaspoon salt
1 teaspoon sugar

1 teaspoon olive oil
3/4 cup whole-wheat flour
3/4 cup unbleached all-purpose flour

Prepare dough for Whole-Wheat Pizza Crust. Preheat oven to 450F (220C). Heat oil in a large skillet over medium heat. Add green onions, zucchini and yellow squash. Sauté 2 minutes or until crisp-tender. Add mushrooms, salt and pepper. Sauté 1 minute or until glazed. Cool slightly. Spread tomato paste evenly over dough. Spoon vegetable mixture over tomato paste. Scatter olives and cherry tomatoes over vegetables. Sprinkle with oregano and cheeses. Bake 15 minutes or until crust is golden brown on edges. Makes 6 servings.

Whole-Wheat Pizza Crust:
Oil a 14-inch pizza pan. Place warm water in a medium bowl. Sprinkle yeast in water. Let stand until yeast has dissolved, about 5 minutes. Stir in salt, sugar, oil and half of whole-wheat and all-purpose flours. Mix well. Add remaining whole-wheat and all-purpose flours. Mix until dough forms a ball. Turn dough onto a lightly floured board. Knead until smooth and satiny, about 5 minutes. Cover dough with a bowl or plastic wrap. Let rest 15 minutes. Working with hands, shape pizza dough to fit pan. Set aside until ready to use.

Variation
Substitute Basic Pizza Crust, page 98, or Cornmeal Crust, page 96, for Whole-Wheat Pizza Crust.

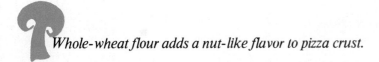

Whole-wheat flour adds a nut-like flavor to pizza crust.

Taco Pizza Pie

An eye-catching pizza for a 30-minute supper entree.

Cornmeal Crust, see below
1 lb. lean ground beef
1 garlic clove, minced
1/4 teaspoon salt
1/4 teaspoon ground cumin
1/2 teaspoon chili powder
1 (4-oz.) can chopped green chilies
1 (8-1/2-oz.) can refried beans

2 medium tomatoes, chopped
3 green onions, chopped
1/3 cup coarsely chopped green bell pepper
1 cup shredded Monterey Jack cheese (4 oz.)
1 cup shredded Cheddar cheese (4 oz.)
Dairy sour cream
Bottled taco sauce or Guacamole, page 171

Cornmeal Crust:
1-1/2 cups all-purpose flour
1/2 cup yellow cornmeal
1 tablespoon baking powder

1 teaspoon salt
1/2 cup shortening or margarine
1/2 cup milk

Prepare dough for Cornmeal Crust. Preheat oven to 400F (205C). In a large skillet, combine ground beef, garlic, salt, cumin and chili powder. Sauté over medium heat until beef is browned, 4 to 5 minutes. Stir in green chilies. Spread refried beans over pizza dough. Spread beef and chili mixture over refried beans. Place tomatoes in a circle around outer edge of pizza. Place green onions in circle inside tomatoes. Place green pepper in center. Sprinkle cheeses over pizza. Bake 20 minutes or until crust is golden brown on edges. Serve with sour cream and taco sauce or Guacamole. Makes 4 to 6 servings.

Cornmeal Crust:

In a large bowl, mix together flour, cornmeal, baking powder and salt. Cut in shortening or margarine until mixture resembles fine crumbs. Stir in milk and mix until dough forms into a ball. Turn dough onto a well-floured board. Knead until smooth, 10 to 12 times. Roll dough into a 13-inch circle. Fold into quarters. Place dough on ungreased cookie sheet or pizza pan. Unfold. Pinch edge of circle to form a 1-inch rim. Set aside until ready to use.

Variation

For a more traditional crust, substitute Basic Pizza Crust, page 98.

Taco Pizza Pie served with Chile con Queso, page 37

Italian Sausage & Mushroom Pizza

This pizza can be baked ahead, then reheated when guests arrive.

Basic Pizza Crust, see below	**2 tablespoons butter**
1 lb. mild Italian sausages	**2 green onions, chopped**
4 eggs	**1/4 lb. mushrooms, sliced**
1 lb. ricotta cheese	**1/4 cup chopped fresh parsley**
1/2 cup freshly grated Romano cheese	**1/4 lb. mozzarella or Monterey Jack cheese,**
(1-1/2 oz.)	**sliced**

Basic Pizza Crust:

1/2 cup very warm water (125F, 50C)	**1 tablespoon sugar**
1/2 pkg. (1-1/2 teaspoons) active dry yeast	**1 tablespoon safflower oil**
1/2 teaspoon salt	**1-1/2 cups unbleached all-purpose flour**

Prepare dough for Basic Pizza Crust. Preheat oven to 425F (220C). Place sausages in a medium saucepan. Add water to cover. Cover and bring to boil. Remove from heat. Let stand 15 minutes. Remove sausages from liquid. Cool slightly. Remove casings, if desired. Thinly slice sausages. In a medium bowl, beat eggs until well blended. Mix in ricotta cheese and 1/4 cup Romano cheese. Melt butter in a large skillet over medium heat. Add green onions. Sauté until glazed, 2 to 3 minutes. Add mushrooms. Sauté 1 minute. Add mushroom mixture to ricotta mixture. Add sausage slices and parsley. Spoon sausage mixture over dough. Top with cheese slices and remaining 1/4 cup Romano cheese. Bake 20 minutes or until crust is lightly browned. Makes 10 to 12 servings.

Basic Pizza Crust:
Oil a 14-inch pizza pan. Place warm water in a medium bowl. Sprinkle yeast in water. Let stand until yeast has dissolved, about 5 minutes. Stir in salt, sugar, oil and half the flour. Mix well. Add remaining flour and mix until dough forms a ball. Turn dough onto a lightly floured board. Knead until smooth and satiny, about 5 minutes. Cover dough with a bowl or plastic wrap. Let rest 15 minutes. Working with hands, shape pizza dough to fit pan. Set aside until ready to use.

Vegetable-Stuffed Pocket Sandwiches

Pita or pocket bread makes a handy container for a healthful sandwich filling.

4 pita breads	**12 cherry tomatoes, halved**
Butter, room temperature	**1 small red onion, sliced**
1/4 lb. Monterey Jack or Jarlsberg cheese,	**1 cup alfalfa sprouts**
thinly sliced (4 oz.)	**1/4 cup plain yogurt**
1/4 lb. fresh mushrooms, sliced	**3 tablespoons roasted sunflower seeds**
1 small avocado, peeled, sliced	

Preheat oven to 350F (175C). Slit open 1 side of pita breads. Spread butter inside each pita bread. Wrap breads in foil. Bake 10 minutes. Fill each bread with cheese, mushrooms, avocado slices, tomatoes, onion, sprouts, yogurt and sunflower seeds. Serve immediately. Makes 4 servings.

Bavarian Onion & Bacon Pie

A great Sunday supper entree to serve with green salad, cheese and fruit.

3/4 cup warm water (105F, 40C)
1 (1/4-oz.) pkg. (1 tablespoon)
   active dry yeast
1/2 teaspoon salt
1/2 teaspoon sugar
2 tablespoons vegetable oil

Onion & Bacon Filling:
1/2 lb. bacon, diced
6 large onions, thinly sliced
3 eggs

About 2 cups all-purpose flour or
   1 cup all-purpose flour and
   1 cup whole-wheat flour
Onion & Bacon Filling, see below
1/4 cup roasted sunflower seeds

3/4 cup dairy sour cream
1/4 teaspoon salt
1/8 teaspoon freshly ground pepper

Place warm water in a large bowl. Sprinkle yeast into water. Let stand until yeast has dissolved, about 5 minutes. Mix in salt, sugar and oil. Gradually add flour to make a soft dough. Turn out dough on a lightly floured board. Knead until smooth and satiny, about 5 minutes. Cover dough with a bowl or plastic wrap. Let rest 30 minutes. Prepare Onion & Bacon Filling. Preheat oven to 425F (220C). Oil a 14-inch pizza pan. Punch down dough by pushing your fist into center. Pull edges of dough over center. With oiled fingers, press dough onto bottom of oiled pan. Spread Onion & Bacon Filling over dough. Sprinkle with sunflower seeds. Bake 25 minutes or until crust is lightly browned and filling set. Cut in wedges. Serve hot. Makes 8 servings.

Onion & Bacon Filling:
In a large skillet, cook bacon until crisp. Remove bacon with a slotted spoon. Drain on paper towel. Pour off bacon drippings, reserving 1/4 cup. Return 1/4 cup bacon drippings to skillet. Add onions. Sauté over medium-low heat until golden. Cool onions. In a small bowl, beat eggs until blended. Mix in sour cream, salt, pepper, onions and bacon. Set aside until ready to use.

Pasta Bolognese

Long, slow cooking creates a distinct flavor for this Italian sauce. Use it with tagliarini or lasagna.

2 tablespoons olive oil
2 large onions, finely chopped
3 medium carrots, shredded
1 celery stalk, chopped
3/4 lb. mild Italian sausage
1 lb. ground pork
1 lb. ground turkey or veal
4 garlic cloves, minced

1 (2-lb.) can tomato puree
1/2 cup dry white wine
2 tablespoons chopped fresh basil or
   2 teaspoons dried leaf basil
2 tablespoons chopped fresh parsley
About 1-1/2 lbs. tagliarini,
   spaghetti or other thin pasta
Freshly grated Parmesan or Romano cheese

Heat oil in a large saucepan over medium heat. Add onions, carrots and celery. Sauté until glazed. Remove casing from sausage. Crumble sausage. Add sausage to vegetables. Sauté 2 to 3 minutes. Add ground pork and turkey or veal. Sauté until lightly browned and crumbled. Add garlic, tomato puree and wine. Cover and reduce heat. Simmer 2 hours. Stir occasionally. Skim off fat. Add basil and parsley. Cook tagliarini or spaghetti in a large pot of boiling salted water until al dente. Drain well. Place cooked pasta on a heated platter. Spoon sauce over pasta. Serve with grated cheese. If desired, make sauce in advance. Refrigerate or freeze until ready to use. Makes 8 to 10 servings.

How To Make Milanese Torta Rustica

1/Spread spinach mixture over prosciutto. Cover with ricotta cheese.

2/Sprinkle shredded egg yolk over pimientos.

Tortilla Flats

Plate-size flour tortillas make a fast and fun-to-serve pizza.

1 tablespoon olive oil
1 large onion, chopped
2 medium zucchini, ends trimmed,
    thinly sliced
1 tablespoon butter
1/4 lb. mushrooms, sliced
1 garlic clove, minced
1/2 cup sliced pitted ripe olives

8 slices salami, julienned
4 (8-inch) flour tortillas
1/4 cup tomato paste
3/4 teaspoon dried leaf oregano
1 cup shredded Monterey Jack cheese (4 oz.)
1/4 cup freshly grated Parmesan or
    Romano cheese (3/4 oz.)

Preheat oven to 400F (205C). Heat oil in a large skillet over medium-high heat. Add onion. Sauté until glazed, 2 to 3 minutes. Add zucchini. Sauté 2 minutes. Place onion and zucchini in a medium bowl. Melt butter in a medium skillet over medium-high heat. Add mushrooms and garlic. Sauté 1 minute, or until mushrooms are glazed. Add mushroom mixture, olives and salami to vegetables. Mix well. Place tortillas in single layer on ungreased baking sheets. Spread with tomato paste. Sprinkle with oregano. Divide vegetable mixture evenly over each tortilla. Sprinkle with cheeses. Bake 5 minutes to melt cheese and lightly brown edges of tortillas. Serve immediately. Makes 4 servings.

Milanese Torta Rustica

The translation for this Italian dish is country pie.

Sour-Cream Pastry, see below
1/3 lb. thinly sliced prosciutto or
  cooked ham
2 (12-oz.) bunches spinach or
  2 (10-oz.) pkgs. frozen chopped spinach,
  thawed, drained
3 tablespoons minced fresh parsley
2 green onions, finely chopped

2 garlic cloves, minced
1/2 teaspoon salt
1/4 teaspoon freshly ground pepper
2 cups ricotta cheese (1 lb.)
1 (4-oz.) jar whole pimientos
4 hard-cooked egg yolks, shredded
1 tablespoon whipping cream

Sour-Cream Pastry:
2 cups all-purpose flour
2/3 cup butter

1 egg
1/3 cup dairy sour cream

Prepare dough for Sour-Cream Pastry. Preheat oven to 425F (220C). Cover bottom of dough-lined springform pan with half the prosciutto or cooked ham. Wash fresh spinach thoroughly in several changes of cold water. Discard stems and bruised or tough leaves. Chop spinach. Blanch spinach in boiling salted water 3 minutes. Drain well. In a medium bowl combine drained spinach, parsley, green onions, garlic, salt and pepper. Spread over prosciutto or cooked ham. Cover with ricotta cheese. Slit pimientos and open flat. Arrange on ricotta cheese. Sprinkle shredded egg yolk over pimientos. Arrange remaining prosciutto or cooked ham on top. Place second circle of pastry over prosciutto or cooked ham. Pinch edges of dough together. Cut a slit in the top for steam to escape. Brush top of dough with cream. Bake 10 minutes. Reduce temperature to 375F (190C). Continue baking 25 minutes or until golden brown. Cool slightly. Remove pan sides. Cut in wedges and serve at desired temperature. Makes 8 to 10 servings.

Sour-Cream Pastry:
Place flour in a medium bowl. Add butter. Cut in butter until mixture is coarse and crumbly. In a small bowl, beat egg with sour cream. Stir sour-cream mixture into flour mixture. Shape into a ball. Wrap dough in plastic wrap. Refrigerate 30 to 40 minutes to firm dough. Roll out 2/3 of the pastry into a 15-inch circle. Roll remaining dough into a 10-inch circle. Arrange 15-inch circle in bottom and up sides of a 9-inch springform pan. Set 10-inch pastry circle aside.

Pasta with Fresh Tomato & Basil

The simplicity of this pasta dish makes it a joy to prepare.

4 large ripe tomatoes, peeled, seeded,
  chopped (2 cups)
2 garlic cloves, minced
1/3 cup chopped fresh basil
2 green onions, chopped

1/4 teaspoon salt
1/2 teaspoon freshly ground pepper
1/2 lb. large macaroni, shells,
  rigatoni or other desired pasta

In a medium bowl, combine tomatoes, garlic, basil, green onions, salt and pepper. Cover. Refrigerate 4 hours. Cook pasta in a large pot of boiling salted water until al dente, about 10 minutes. Drain well. Place pasta in a large bowl. Pour chilled sauce over pasta. Mix lightly. Makes 4 servings.

Spinach & Chèvre Quiche

This quiche is excellent with lamb or fish.

Butter Pastry, see below
1 tablespoon Dijon-style mustard
2 (12-oz.) bunches spinach or
   2 (10-oz.) pkgs. frozen chopped spinach,
   thawed, drained
2 tablespoons butter
2 green onions, chopped
3 eggs
1/2 cup whipping cream or half and half

1/4 teaspoon ground nutmeg
1/2 teaspoon salt
1/4 teaspoon freshly ground pepper
2 tablespoons minced fresh parsley
3/4 cup crumbled chèvre or
   feta cheese (3 oz.)
6 cherry tomatoes, halved, or
   1 medium tomato, sliced
3 tablespoons freshly grated Parmesan cheese

Butter Pastry:
1-1/4 cups all-purpose flour
1/2 cup unsalted butter

1 egg yolk
1-1/2 to 2 tablespoons ice water

Prepare dough for Butter Pastry. Spread dough-lined pan with mustard. Refrigerate 15 minutes to firm dough. Preheat oven to 400F (220C). Wash fresh spinach thoroughly in several changes of cold water. Discard stems and bruised or tough leaves. Drain well. Chop spinach. Melt butter in large skillet over medium heat. Add green onions. Sauté until glazed, 1 to 2 minutes. Add spinach. Cook until fresh spinach is slightly wilted or frozen spinach heated through. Squeeze out excess moisture. In a medium bowl, beat eggs until light. Mix in cream, nutmeg, salt, pepper, parsley, spinach mixture and 3/4 cup crumbled cheese. Pour cheese mixture into chilled dough-lined pan. Place cherry tomatoes cut-side down or tomato slices in a circle around top of cheese mixture. Sprinkle with Parmesan cheese. Bake 10 minutes. Reduce temperature to 350F (175C). Continue baking 25 minutes or until a knife inserted in center comes out clean. Serve warm. Makes 8 servings.

Butter Pastry:

Place flour in a medium bowl. Cut butter into small pieces. Add butter to flour. Cut in with a pastry blender until mixture resembles fine crumbs. Add egg yolk. Combine lightly with a fork. Add ice water. Mix until dough clings together in a ball. On a lightly floured board, roll out dough to a 13-inch circle. Fit into an 11-inch flan pan with a removable bottom or a 9- or 10-inch quiche dish or pie dish. If using a flan pan, roll a rolling pin across the top to trim edge of dough even with top of pan. If using a quiche dish, fold dough edge under so it is even with rim of dish; press dough into scalloped sides of dish. If using a pie dish, fold dough under for a raised edge; use thumb and fingers to form a high fluted edge. Set aside until ready to use.

Variation

Substitute 2 (10-oz.) packages frozen chopped asparagus or broccoli, or baby peas for frozen spinach.

Overbaking a quiche or frittata until it puffs will cause it to contract and fall when cool.

Zucchini & Walnut Quiche

Vary the cheese and nuts for a totally different flavor combination.

Butter Pastry, page 102
1 tablespoon Dijon-style mustard
1 lb. zucchini, ends trimmed,
    shredded (3 to 4 medium zucchini)
Salt
4 eggs
1 pint (2 cups) whipping cream
1/4 teaspoon salt

1/4 teaspoon freshly ground pepper
1/8 teaspoon ground nutmeg
Red (cayenne) pepper
1 cup shredded white Cheddar,
    Asiago or Gruyère cheese (4 oz.)
1/3 cup toasted chopped walnuts or
    filberts, or toasted slivered almonds

Prepare dough for Butter Pastry. Spread dough-lined pan with mustard. Refrigerate 15 minutes to firm dough. Place shredded zucchini in a colander. Salt lightly. Let stand 15 minutes. Salt draws out bitter juices from zucchini. Squeeze out moisture. Zucchini should be quite dry. Preheat oven to 425F (220C). In a medium bowl, beat eggs until blended. Mix in cream, 1/4 teaspoon salt, pepper, nutmeg and red pepper. Add zucchini, cheese and half the nuts. Pour zucchini mixture into chilled dough-lined pan. Sprinkle remaining nuts over filling. Bake 15 minutes. Reduce temperature to 350F (175C). Continue baking 20 to 30 minutes or until a knife inserted in center comes out clean. Cool 10 minutes. Serve warm. Makes 8 servings.

Leek & Italian-Sausage Quiche

Fennel-spiced sausage paired with sweet leeks makes a winner.

Butter Pastry, page 102
1 tablespoon Dijon-style mustard
1 bunch leeks, 2 large or 3 small
4 mild Italian sausages (about 3/4 lb.)
1 cup shredded Jarlsberg, Gruyère or
    samso cheese (4 oz.)
4 eggs

1-1/2 cups whipping cream or
    half and half
1/2 teaspoon salt
1/4 teaspoon white pepper
1/4 teaspoon ground nutmeg
2 teaspoons butter

Prepare dough for Butter Pastry. Preheat oven to 425F (220C). Spread dough-lined pan with mustard. Refrigerate 15 minutes to firm dough. Trim ends and tough outer leaves from leeks. Quarter leeks lengthwise, cutting almost to the root. Wash under cold running water, pulling layers apart so grit is removed. Thinly slice leeks. Remove sausage from casings. Crumble sausage. In a large skillet, sauté sausage over medium heat until lightly browned. Pour off sausage drippings, except 2 tablespoons. Add leeks to sausage and 2 tablespoons drippings. Sauté 3 minutes or until leeks are glazed. Remove from heat. Mix in 1/2 cup cheese. Spoon into chilled dough-lined pan. In a medium bowl, beat eggs until blended. Mix in cream or half and half, salt, white pepper and nutmeg. Stir in remaining cheese. Pour egg mixture over sausage mixture. Dot with butter. Bake 15 minutes. Reduce temperature to 350F (175C). Continue baking 20 to 30 minutes or until a knife inserted in center comes out clean. Cool 10 minutes. Serve warm. Makes 8 servings.

Whipping cream gives a velvet-like texture to the custard in this quiche. If watching calories, substitute milk.

Sour-Cream Vegetable Pancakes

A variety of shredded vegetables enhance these tender pancakes.

1/4 cup butter
2 cups shredded carrots, zucchini,
   yellow crookneck squash or
   mushrooms
2 egg yolks

1/2 cup dairy sour cream
3 tablespoons cornstarch
1/4 teaspoon salt
1/4 teaspoon freshly ground pepper

Melt 2 tablespoons butter in a large skillet over medium heat. Add carrots, zucchini, yellow squash or mushrooms, or desired combination. Sauté 1 to 2 minutes or until crisp-tender, stirring constantly. Remove from heat. Cool slightly. Beat egg yolks in a medium bowl. Add sour cream, cornstarch, salt and pepper. Mix well. Stir in sautéed vegetables. Melt 1 tablespoon butter in a large skillet over medium-high heat. Spoon pancake batter into 1-3/4-inch rounds on skillet. Cook until lightly browned on 1 side. Turn and lightly brown other side. Repeat with remaining butter and batter. Serve hot with sausage or bacon and fresh fruit, if desired. Makes about 10 pancakes.

Spanakopita

This Greek mixed-greens pie is splendid served hot, warm or cold.

3 (1-lb.) bunches spinach
6 eggs
1/3 cup olive oil
1 teaspoon salt
1/2 teaspoon freshly ground pepper
1/2 teaspoon dried leaf oregano
1/2 lb. feta cheese, crumbled
1 cup freshly grated Parmesan or
   Romano cheese (3 oz.)

1 small bunch Swiss chard or curly endive,
   finely chopped
1 bunch parsley, finely chopped
1 bunch green onions, finely chopped
12 sheets filo dough (18" x 12")
6 tablespoons butter, melted

Preheat oven to 375F (190C). Butter a 13" x 9" baking dish. Wash spinach thoroughly in several changes of cold water. Discard stems and bruised or tough leaves. Drain well. Finely chop spinach. Beat eggs in a medium bowl. Mix in oil, salt, pepper, oregano and cheeses. Mix lightly. Place spinach, Swiss chard or curly endive, parsley and green onions in a large bowl. Pour cheese mixture over greens. Mix well. Line buttered baking dish with 1 filo sheet. Brush with melted butter. Cover remaining sheets with plastic wrap or a damp towel to prevent drying. Layer 5 more filo sheets in baking dish, brushing each with melted butter. Allow filo sheets to overlap sides of dish. Place greens mixture in filo-lined baking dish. Smooth top. Fold any overlapping filo over greens. Arrange 6 more buttered filo sheets over top, folding to fit top. Brush top filo sheet with butter. With a sharp knife, cut through top layers of filo making 3 lengthwise cuts. Make 5 crosswise cuts, forming squares across top surface. Bake 50 minutes or until greens are tender and pastry is golden brown. Cool slightly. Finish cutting into squares. Serve at desired temperature. Makes 24 pieces.

Galettes Sarasin

A French buckwheat crepe holds a savory spinach, Gruyère and ham filling.

Buckwheat Crepes, see below
2 (1-lb.) bunches spinach or
  2 (10-oz.) pkgs. frozen chopped spinach,
  thawed, drained
1 tablespoon butter, melted
3 tablespoons whipping cream

1/4 teaspoon ground nutmeg
1/4 teaspoon white pepper
8 (6'' x 4'') slices boiled ham
8 slices Gruyère or
  Jarlsberg cheese (about 6 oz.)

Buckwheat Crepes:
2 eggs
1-1/2 cups milk
1 cup buckwheat-pancake mix
1 tablespoon cassis syrup or
  crème de cassis

2 tablespoons vegetable oil
3 tablespoons butter

Prepare Buckwheat Crepes. Preheat oven to 400F (220C). Lightly butter a baking sheet. Wash fresh spinach thoroughly in several changes of cold water. Discard stems and bruised or tough leaves. Chop spinach. Blanch in boiling water 3 minutes. Drain fresh blanched or frozen thawed spinach well. In a small bowl, mix together spinach, butter, cream, nutmeg and white pepper. To fill each crepe, place unbrowned side up. Cover with a slice of ham. Add a slice of cheese. Top with a spoonful of spinach mixture. Fold crepe like an envelope. Place on a buttered baking sheet. Repeat with remaining crepes and filling. Bake 5 minutes or until heated through. Serve immediately. Makes 8 servings.

Buckwheat Crepes:
In a blender, combine eggs, milk, pancake mix, cassis syrup or crème de cassis and oil. Process until smooth. Heat a 12-inch crepe pan, skillet or griddle over medium heat. Add 1 teaspoon butter. Tilt pan to coat surface. Place 1/4 cup batter in pan. Cook until crepe is golden brown on edges and dry on top. Turn out onto a plate. It is not necessary to cook both sides. Repeat with remaining batter, preparing pan with 1 teaspoon butter for each crepe and using 1/4 cup batter each time. Cover cooked crepes and refrigerate until ready to fill, if desired. Makes 8 crepes.

Variation

Substitute for spinach 2 (10-ounce) packages frozen chopped broccoli or artichoke hearts, thawed, drained.

The Buckwheat Crepes can be made in advance and stored in the refrigerator 2 to 3 days. For longer storage, seal crepes in an air-tight container. Place crepes in freezer. Bring crepes to room temperature before using.

1/Pierce chestnut tops with a pointed knife. Place in a medium saucepan.

2/Drain and peel a few chestnuts at a time. Don't allow to cool too long as they will become difficult to peel.

Chestnut & Vegetable Stuffing

The Greeks place this hearty chestnut stuffing in the holiday bird. Leftovers reheat beautifully.

1 lb. chestnuts
3 medium onions, chopped
1/2 cup butter
1/2 lb. lean ground beef or veal
1/2 lb. chicken livers, chopped
3 medium carrots, shredded
2 celery stalks, finely chopped
1/3 cup raisins, chopped

1-1/2 teaspoons poultry seasoning
1-1/2 teaspoons ground cinnamon
1/2 teaspoon ground nutmeg
1/4 teaspoon ground cloves
1/2 cup toasted chopped walnuts
1 (6-oz.) pkg. zwieback
6 eggs

Butter a 13'' x 9'' baking dish. To peel fresh chestnuts, pierce tops with a pointed knife and place in a medium saucepan. Cover with cold water. Bring to a boil and immediately remove from heat. Drain and peel a few at a time, leaving remaining chestnuts in hot water. If they cool and become difficult to peel, reheat quickly; don't cook chestnuts or they will be impossible to peel. Chop peeled chestnuts. Place onions and water to cover in a small saucepan. Bring to a boil. Reduce heat and simmer 10 minutes. Drain well. Melt butter in a large skillet over medium-high heat. Add ground beef or veal, chicken livers and cooked onions. Sauté until meats are lightly browned. Add carrots, celery, chopped chestnuts and raisins. Cover and reduce heat. Simmer 2-1/2 hours or until very mushy. Add a small amount of water if necessary just to moisten. Add poultry seasoning, cinnamon, nutmeg, cloves and walnuts. Simmer 30 minutes. With a potato masher, mash well. Cool slightly. Crush zwieback into fine crumbs. Mix into stuffing mixture. Beat eggs until light in a large bowl. Stir in stuffing. Preheat oven to 350F (175C). Spoon stuffing into buttered baking dish. Cover with foil. Bake 1 hour. Stuffing can also be placed in an 18-pound turkey. Serve hot. Makes 12 to 14 servings.

How To Make California-Style Böreks

1/Fold larger piece of dough over meat patty, nearly covering it.

2/Fold each filo corner in, meeting at the center. This makes a square packet filled with meat.

Decorative Caviar Tart

Choose a different caviar to vary this open-face tart.

Lemon-Butter Crust, see below
6 oz. cream cheese, room temperature
1/4 cup dairy sour cream
2 tablespoons chopped green onions
2 tablespoons chopped fresh parsley
Dash hot-pepper sauce
3 oz. golden natural, red or
   black lumpfish caviar

3 tablespoons finely chopped shallots or
   green onions
3 hard-cooked eggs
1/4 lb. mushrooms, sliced
1-1/2 cups cherry tomatoes, halved

Lemon-Butter Crust:
1 cup all-purpose flour
1 teaspoon grated lemon peel

1/2 cup butter
1 egg yolk

Prepare Lemon-Butter Crust. In a small bowl, beat together cream cheese, sour cream, green onions, parsley and hot-pepper sauce. Spread mixture in baked crust. Spoon caviar in a circle in the center. Surround with a ring of shallots or green onions. Separate egg yolks from egg whites. Put yolks and whites separately through a sieve. Surround shallots or green onions with a circle of egg yolk, then a circle of egg white. Circle with mushroom slices and place cherry tomatoes around outer edge. Cover. Refrigerate until ready to serve. Makes 8 servings.

Lemon-Butter Crust:
Place flour and lemon peel in a medium bowl. Cut butter into small pieces. Add butter to flour. Cut in with a pastry blender until mixture resembles fine crumbs. Add egg yolk. Mix until dough clings together in a ball. With hands, press dough into bottom and up sides of an 11-inch fluted flan pan with removable bottom. Refrigerate 15 minutes to firm dough. Preheat oven to 425F (220C). Bake 8 to 10 minutes or until lightly browned. Cool. Set aside until ready to use.

California-Style Böreks

These decorative filo pastries can be assembled in advance, then baked when needed.

2 medium zucchini, ends trimmed,
   shredded
Salt
5 tablespoons butter
1 large onion, chopped
2 large carrots, shredded
2 garlic cloves, minced
1/2 teaspoon freshly ground pepper
1/2 teaspoon ground allspice
1/2 teaspoon dried leaf oregano
1 lb. ground turkey
1/2 lb. ground pork

1 egg
1 tablespoon chopped fresh parsley
1 teaspoon salt
2 slices sweet or sourdough French bread,
   crumbled
3 tablespoons pine nuts, pistachios or
   roasted sunflower seeds
1 cup shredded Jarlsberg or
   Swiss cheese (4 oz.)
1/3 cup freshly grated Parmesan or
   Romano cheese (1 oz.)
8 sheets filo dough (18" x 12")

Preheat oven to 425F (220C). Butter a large baking sheet. Place zucchini in a colander. Salt lightly. Let stand 15 minutes. Salt draws out bitter juices from zucchini. Squeeze out moisture. Zucchini should be quite dry. Melt 2 tablespoons butter in a large skillet over medium-high heat. Add onion and carrots. Sauté until glazed, 2 to 3 minutes. Add zucchini, garlic, pepper, allspice and oregano. Sauté 2 minutes. Cool slightly. In a large bowl, combine ground turkey, ground pork, egg, parsley, 1 teaspoon salt, breadcrumbs, nuts or sunflower seeds, cheeses and sautéed vegetables. Melt remaining 3 tablespoons butter in a small saucepan. Lay out 1 filo sheet. Cover remaining sheets with plastic wrap or slightly damp towel to prevent drying. Brush short half of filo sheet lightly with melted butter. Fold in half crosswise, making a 9" x 6" rectangle. Divide meat mixture into 8 portions. Place 1 portion on lower 1/3 of filo sheet. Shape meat mixture into a round 1/2-inch thick patty. Fold larger piece of dough over meat patty, nearly covering it completely. This makes a square base. Brush filo edges lightly with butter. Fold each corner in, meeting at the center. This makes a square packet of filled pastry with a 4-triangle design on top. Repeat with remaining sheets of filo and filling. Lightly brush tops of pastry with butter. Place on buttered baking sheet. Bake 15 to 20 minutes or until pastry is golden brown. Serve hot. Makes 8 servings.

Pasta with Pesto Primavera

Vary the vegetables to suit local availability.

1 tablespoon Pesto Sauce, page 168
12 Chinese pea pods, trimmed
1 medium zucchini, ends trimmed, julienned
1 yellow crookneck squash,
   ends trimmed, julienned
1/2 lb. fresh fettuccine or tagliarini

2 tablespoons butter
1 tablespoon pine nuts or pistachios
1/4 cup whipping cream
8 cherry tomatoes, halved
3 tablespoons freshly grated Romano cheese

Prepare Pesto Sauce. Separately blanch pea pods, zucchini and crookneck squash in boiling salted water. Blanch until crisp-tender, about 1 minute each. Drain well. Cook fettuccine or tagliarini in a large pot of boiling salted water until al dente, 2 to 3 minutes. Drain well. Place cooked pasta in a large heated bowl. Melt butter in a large skillet over medium heat. Add blanched vegetables, pine nuts or pistachios, Pesto Sauce and cream. Heat, shaking skillet and stirring, 1 to 2 minutes or until sauce reduces slightly. Add tomatoes. Heat 1 minute. Pour mixture over pasta. Mix lightly. Sprinkle with cheese. Serve immediately. Makes 2 servings.

Italian Swiss-Chard Stuffing

Fresh herbs and cheese add a special touch to this succulent chard and pork stuffing.

1/2 loaf sourdough French or
   Italian-style bread (about 12 slices)
2 eggs
1 cup rich turkey or chicken broth
3 tablespoons butter
1 large onion, chopped
1 large bunch Swiss chard, chopped
1 celery stalk, finely chopped
1 lb. ground pork, or
   1/2 lb. ground pork and
   1/2 lb. ground turkey

3/4 teapoon salt
3 tablespoons chopped fresh basil or
   1 teaspoon dried leaf basil
1/2 teaspoon ground sage
1/2 teaspoon dried leaf rosemary
1/2 cup chopped fresh parsley
1 cup freshly grated Romano cheese (3 oz.)

Preheat oven to 375F (190C). Butter a 13" x 9" baking dish. Slice bread 1/2-inch thick. Cut in 1/2-inch cubes. Beat eggs in a large bowl until blended. Mix in broth. Add bread cubes. Toss lightly. Melt 2 tablespoons butter in a large skillet over medium heat. Add onion. Sauté until glazed. Add chard and celery. Sauté until limp. Add sautéed vegetables to bread mixture. Melt remaining 1 tablespoon butter in a large skillet over medium heat. Add ground meat. Sauté until meat is browned. Add salt, basil, sage and rosemary. Combine meat with vegetables. Add parsley and 3/4 cup cheese. Spoon into buttered dish. Sprinkle remaining cheese over top. Bake 30 to 40 minutes or until lightly browned. Serve hot. Makes 10 to 12 servings.

Mushroom Puff Pastry

Using prepared pastry shells makes this a quick, easy entree for the busy cook.

6 frozen puff-pastry shells, thawed
2 tablespoons butter
1/2 lb. mushrooms, sliced
4 oz. cream cheese
1 cup small-curd cottage cheese (8 oz.)
2 egg yolks

1/4 cup minced fresh parsley
1/4 teaspoon dried leaf tarragon
1 cup shredded Gruyère or
   Jarlsberg cheese (4 oz.)
1 egg white, slightly beaten

Place pastry shells on a board. Cover with a slightly damp towel or plastic wrap. Bring to room temperature, about 1 hour. Melt butter in a large skillet over medium-high heat. Add mushrooms. Sauté until glazed, about 1 minute. Remove to a medium bowl. Cool. In a food processor fitted with a steel blade, place cream cheese, cottage cheese, egg yolks, parsley and tarragon. Process until smooth. Add cheese mixture to mushrooms. Mix in shredded cheese. Stack 3 pastry shells. On a lightly floured board, roll pastry into a 14-inch circle. Repeat with remaining pastry shells. Place one 14-inch circle on a 12-inch pizza pan. Allow pastry to overlap on sides. Spread mushroom filling evenly over pastry, just to edge of pan. Place remaining 14-inch pastry circle on top of mushroom filling. Brush overlapping edges of pastry with water. Pinch to seal. Crimp edges. Refrigerate 30 minutes to firm pastry. Preheat oven to 425F (220C). Brush pastry top with egg white. Bake 20 to 25 minutes or until puffed and golden brown. Cut in wedges. Serve warm. Makes 8 servings.

Pissaladière Pastry

Cheese pastry adds an interesting flavor to this onion-tomato tart.

Cheese Crust, see below
1 teaspoon Herbs of Provence, see below
1/4 cup olive oil
2 lbs. sweet Spanish onions, peeled,
    finely chopped
2 large ripe tomatoes, peeled, seeded,
    chopped

3 tablespoons tomato paste
2 (2-oz.) cans flat anchovy fillets, drained
24 small whole pitted black oil-cured olives
    or pitted black olives

Cheese Crust:
1/2 pkg. (1-1/2 teaspoons) active dry yeast
2 teaspoons sugar
1/2 teaspoon salt
1-1/2 cups unbleached all-purpose flour
1/2 cup very warm water (125F, 50C)

2 tablespoons butter, room temperature
1 egg
1-1/2 cups shredded Gruyère or
    Jarlsberg cheese (6 oz.)

Herbs of Provence:
1 tablespoon dried leaf thyme
1 teaspoon dried leaf basil

1 teaspoon dried leaf savory
1 teaspoon dried rosemary or fennel seed

Prepare dough for Cheese Crust. Prepare Herbs of Provence. Preheat oven to 400F (205C). Heat oil in a large skillet over medium heat. Add onions. Sauté over low heat, 30 to 40 minutes or until very soft and caramelized. Add tomatoes, tomato paste and herbs. Cook over low heat until mixture is thick. Cool. Spread tomato mixture on cheese dough. Arrange anchovies over tomato mixture in lattice design. Place an olive in each square formed by lattice. Bake 20 to 25 minutes or until crust is golden brown on edges. Makes 8 servings.

Cheese Crust:
Oil a large baking sheet. In a medium bowl, combine yeast, sugar, salt and flour. Add water, butter and egg. Beat until smooth. Turn onto a lightly floured board. Sprinkle cheese over dough. Knead dough, working in cheese evenly. Cover dough with a bowl or plastic wrap. Let rest 30 minutes. Place Cheese Crust dough on oiled baking sheet. With hands, press dough into a 14'' x 10'' rectangle. Pinch edges to make border. Set aside until ready to use.

Herbs of Provence:
In a small bowl, combine herbs. Store in an airtight container.

Variation
Divide Cheese Crust dough into 8 equal pieces. Press dough into 8 (3-inch) tart pans. Pinch edges to make border. Divide tomato filling, anchovies and olives between tarts. Proceed with recipe.

MAIN DISHES

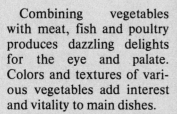

Combining vegetables with meat, fish and poultry produces dazzling delights for the eye and palate. Colors and textures of various vegetables add interest and vitality to main dishes.

This ethnic collection comes from creative cooks around the world. In Turkey, cooks slash eggplant, hollow it and then fill the vegetable boats with a meaty stuffing. Stuffed Eggplant Boats are my adaptation of this Mediterranean favorite. Give an Italian touch to your next dinner party with Spinach Gnocchi Balls.

Cassoulet is a hearty dried-bean dish from the South of France. Farther north in Alsace, you can enjoy Sauerkraut & Sausage, a superb regional dish. Both are great company fare. Shabu Shabu, a Japanese dish, is an excellent dish for parties as guests cook their own meat and vegetable combination in simmering broth.

Cashew Chicken & Vegetables is another choice entree to savor with family or friends. Prepare everything in advance. Then stir-fry just before dining. The rapid cooking has an added bonus because it minimizes nutrient loss.

Spaghetti squash is a new popular vegetable. Lower in calories than pasta, it offers a delightful crunchy texture. Try serving Spaghetti Squash with Greek Meat Sauce. With this wide collection of international recipes, your dining table offers a cooks' tour of the world.

A whimsical party entree certain to create an informal atmosphere is Spuds & Sausages Bandit-Style. Brown lunch bags filled with a hearty surprise greet guests at the table. When opened, steam spills out revealing tasty contents of sliced potatoes and spicy sausage.

Many new dining opportunities are provided in this chapter. Especially popular will be quick dishes for after-five cooks and make-ahead entrees for easy entertaining.

Greek Night at Home

Mushroom Moussaka, page 113
Eggplant Caviar, page 33
Greek Country Salad, page 77
Melon Wedges & Grapes
Baklava

Mushroom Moussaka

Here is a great make-ahead casserole.

Meat Sauce, see below
Custard Sauce, see below
1/3 cup butter
2 lbs. mushrooms, sliced

2 garlic cloves, minced
1/3 cup fine dry breadcrumbs
1 cup freshly grated Parmesan or
   Romano cheese (3 oz.)

Meat Sauce:
1 tablespoon oil
2 medium onions, chopped
2 lbs. lean ground beef or
  1 lb. lean ground beef and
  1 lb. ground turkey
1 (6-oz.) can tomato paste
1 cup red wine

2 garlic cloves, minced
1 teaspoon salt
1/2 teaspoon freshly ground pepper
1-1/2 teaspoons mixed pickling spice
1 cinnamon stick
1 tablespoon minced fresh parsley

Custard Sauce:
1/4 cup butter
1/4 cup all-purpose flour
3 cups milk
3/4 teaspoon salt

1/8 teaspoon freshly ground pepper
1/8 teaspoon ground nutmeg
5 eggs

Prepare Meat Sauce and Custard Sauce. Preheat oven to 350F (175C). Butter a 13" x 9" baking dish. Melt 2 tablespoons butter in a large skillet over medium heat. Add about 1/4 of the mushrooms and garlic. Sauté until glazed, about 1 minute. Do not crowd skillet. Sauté in several batches, using part of the butter each time. Arrange half the mushrooms in buttered baking dish. In a medium bowl, mix Meat Sauce with breadcrumbs. Spread half the Meat Sauce over mushrooms. Sprinkle with half the cheese. Cover with remaining mushrooms and remaining Meat Sauce. Spoon Custard Sauce over top. Sprinkle remaining cheese over top. Bake 50 minutes or until set and lightly browned. Let stand 10 to 15 minutes. Cut in squares. Serve immediately. Makes 12 servings.

Meat Sauce:
Heat oil in a large skillet or Dutch oven over medium heat. Add onions. Sauté until golden. Add ground meat. Cook until browned and crumbly. Add tomato paste, wine, garlic, salt and pepper. Tie pickling spice and cinnamon stick in a cheesecloth bag or place in a tea ball. Add spice bag or tea ball and parsley to meat mixture. Cover and reduce heat. Simmer 1 hour or until sauce is thick and flavors are blended. Remove spice bag and discard. Skim off fat. Set aside until ready to use.

Custard Sauce:
Melt butter in a medium saucepan over medium heat. Blend in flour. Cook 2 minutes. Gradually stir in milk. Add salt, pepper and nutmeg. Cook until thickened, stirring constantly. Beat eggs until light. Stir hot mixture into eggs. Set aside until ready to use.

Although this recipe may seem long and complicated, it can easily be made in parts. Then assemble completed dish at a later time.

Shabu Shabu

The Japanese cook this meat-and-vegetable combination in boiling broth at the table.

Sesame Sauce, see below
1 lb. boneless beef top sirloin steak or
    beef flank steak
1 (12-oz.) bunch spinach
1/2 lb. mushrooms, thinly sliced
1/3 lb. Chinese pea pods, trimmed or
    1 (6-oz.) pkg. frozen pea pods
2 medium carrots, sliced diagonally

2 celery stalks, sliced diagonally
1/2 cup water chestnuts or
    bamboo shoots, sliced
2 qts. beef broth
1/2 cup finely chopped green onion
1/4 cup finely grated gingerroot

Sesame Sauce:
1/3 cup sesame seeds
3 tablespoons sesame oil
2 tablespoons soy sauce

2 teaspoons white-wine vinegar
Dash hot-pepper sauce
1/3 cup beef broth

Prepare Sesame Sauce. Place sirloin or flank steak in a shallow baking dish. Place in freezer 10 minutes to firm. Remove steak from freezer and thinly slice diagonally. Wash spinach thoroughly in several changes of cold water. Discard stems and bruised or tough leaves. Drain well. On a platter, arrange mushrooms, pea pods, carrots, celery, water chestnuts or bamboo shoots and spinach. If using a Japanese cooking pot, pour broth into pot. Place hot charcoal under pot to heat broth. If using an electric saucepan or fondue pot, pour in broth. Bring broth to a slow boil. Using 1/4 of the ingredients at a time, add carrots and celery to simmering stock. Simmer 5 minutes. Add beef strips. Simmer 2 minutes. Add pea pods, water chestnuts or bamboo shoots, mushrooms and spinach. Cook until heated through, about 1 minute. With a skimmer, slotted spoon or chopsticks, remove cooked items to individual serving bowls. Repeat with remaining ingredients in 3 batches. When cooking has been completed, ladle broth into individual bowls. Serve as soup. Serve with green onion, gingerroot and Sesame Sauce. Makes 4 servings.

Sesame Sauce:
Preheat oven to 325F (165C). Place sesame seeds in a 9-inch pie dish. Toast seeds in oven 10 minutes or until lightly browned. Cool. Place sesame seeds in a blender or food processor fitted with a steel blade. Process until fine and pasty. Add sesame oil, soy sauce, vinegar, hot-pepper sauce and broth. Process until smooth. Set aside until ready to serve.

For a true Japanese setting, arrange the meat and vegetables attractively on the platter. In Japan, food presentation is an art form.

Shabu Shabu

Tofu & Vegetable Stir-Fry

Tofu enriches this stir-fry dish for the vegetarian.

1 teaspoon soy sauce
1 teaspoon Worcestershire sauce
1/2 teaspoon grated gingerroot or
   1/4 teaspoon ground ginger
1 garlic clove, minced
1/2 lb. tofu,
   cut in 1/2-inch cubes (8 oz.)
1-1/2 teaspoons cornstarch
1/2 cup water

2 tablespoons vegetable oil
2 inner celery stalks, sliced
2 small zucchini, ends trimmed,
   thinly sliced
1 small red or green bell pepper,
   cut in 3/4-inch squares
1/4 lb. mushrooms, sliced
1 large tomato, cut in wedges

In a small bowl, combine soy sauce, Worcestershire sauce, ginger and garlic. Add tofu. Toss lightly. Let stand 5 minutes. Remove tofu from soy mixture with a slotted spoon. Drain on paper towel. Stir cornstarch and water into soy mixture; set aside. Heat oil in a large skillet or wok over medium heat. Add celery, zucchini and bell pepper. Stir-fry 2 minutes. Add mushrooms. Stir-fry 1 minute. Stir in reserved soy mixture. Cook until thickened, stirring occasionally. Add tofu and tomato. Heat through and serve immediately. Makes 3 to 4 servings.

Spinach-Turkey Stir-Fry

This is a contemporary version of famous old-time spinach and ground beef dish.

1 (1-lb.) bunch spinach or
   1 (10-oz.) pkg. frozen chopped spinach,
   thawed, drained
1 tablespoon butter
3 green onions, chopped
1/4 lb. mushrooms, sliced
1 lb. ground turkey
2 garlic cloves, minced

3/4 teaspoon salt
1/4 teaspoon freshly ground pepper
1/4 teaspoon dried leaf oregano
2 eggs
1/3 cup freshly grated Parmesan cheese
   (1 oz.)
8 cherry tomatoes, halved

Wash fresh spinach thoroughly in several changes of cold water. Discard stems and bruised or tough leaves. Drain well. Chop spinach; set aside. Melt butter in a large skillet over medium heat. Add onions. Sauté until glazed. Add mushrooms. Sauté 1 minute. Push onions and mushrooms to side of skillet. Add ground turkey, garlic, salt, pepper and oregano. Cook until turkey is browned, about 5 minutes. Place spinach over turkey. Cover. Cook until fresh spinach wilts, about 2 minutes or until frozen spinach is heated through. Break eggs over spinach. Stir with a fork to mix. Cook through, about 1 minute. Sprinkle cheese over top. Garnish with cherry tomatoes. Serve immediately. Makes 4 servings.

Serve this spinach mixture in pita or pocket bread for a quick sandwich.

Moo Shu Pork

A wonderfully fast, fun Oriental dish.

1/3 cup dried tree ear mushrooms
2 large dried shiitake mushrooms
3 green onions
8 medium flour tortillas
3 pork chops (about 3/4 lb.)
2 tablespoons safflower oil or peanut oil
1 teaspoon sesame oil
1/2 teaspoon grated gingerroot or
   1/4 teaspoon ground ginger

1 garlic clove, minced
1 inner celery stalk,
   thinly sliced diagonally
1/2 cup sliced bamboo shoots
1 tablespoon soy sauce
1 teaspoon brown sugar
2 eggs, lightly beaten

Place tree ear mushrooms in a small bowl. Cover with water. Let stand 15 minutes. Place shiitake mushrooms in a small bowl. Cover with water. Let stand 15 minutes. Cut green onions into 1-1/2-inch pieces. Cut 1 end of each onion piece lengthwise, making several 1/4-inch slashes. Place onions in a bowl of ice water. Let stand 5 to 10 minutes. Onion ends will spread out like a fan. Preheat oven to 350F (175C). Wrap tortillas in foil. Heat tortillas in oven 10 minutes. Slice pork chops into 1/8-inch-thick strips, discarding bones. Heat 1 tablespoon safflower oil or peanut oil and 1 teaspoon sesame oil in a wok or large skillet over medium-high heat. Add pork and ginger. Stir-fry 2 minutes. Add garlic, celery and bamboo shoots. Stir-fry 1 minute. Add soy sauce and brown sugar. Heat, stirring until blended. Drain mushrooms well. Chop coarsely. Stir mushrooms into pork mixture. Remove from heat. Heat 1 tablespoon safflower oil or peanut oil in a small skillet over medium-high heat. Pour in beaten eggs. Scramble until eggs are barely set. Place scrambled eggs on a hot platter. Cover with pork mixture. Surround with green-onion fans. Serve with hot tortillas. Makes 4 servings.

Variation

Substitute 1/4 lb. fresh cultivated mushrooms, thinly sliced, for tree ear and shiitake mushrooms. Sauté mushrooms with celery in oil.

Danish Hash

A Copenhagen restaurant makes leftover meats special in this hearty dish.

6 tablespoons butter
2 medium onions, thinly sliced
4 potatoes, peeled, parboiled, sliced
1/2 lb. cooked Danish ham,
   cut in 1/2-inch cubes
1/2 lb. cooked roast beef,
   cut in 1/2-inch cubes

1/4 teaspoon salt
1/4 teaspoon freshly ground pepper
4 eggs
2 medium tomatoes, cut in wedges
4 to 5 sprigs parsley

Melt 1 tablespoon butter in a large skillet over medium-high heat. Add onions. Sauté until golden brown. Add 2 tablespoons butter and potatoes to skillet. Sauté until potatoes are golden, turning to brown both sides. Add 1 tablespoon butter, ham cubes and beef cubes to skillet. Sauté until heated through. Add salt and pepper. Spoon onto a large platter. Keep warm. Melt 2 tablespoons butter in large skillet over medium heat. Fry eggs in melted butter until firm. Carefully place fried eggs over hash. Add tomato wedges to remaining drippings and heat through. Spoon tomatoes around hash. Garnish with parsley. Serve immediately. Makes 4 servings.

1/ Lightly oil the bottom of paper bags.

2/Place sliced potatoes, green onions, seasonings and sausages into bags. Clip each bag closed.

Spuds & Sausages Bandit-Style

Brown bags hold this steaming potato dish—a neat and novel way to get dinner on the table.

4 lunch-size brown paper bags
4 medium baking potatoes, peeled,
   sliced 1/4-inch thick
2 green onions, chopped
1/2 teaspoon salt

1/2 teaspoon freshly ground pepper
1/2 teaspoon dried leaf oregano
2 tablespoons butter, melted
4 mild Italian sausages or smoked bratwurst
   (about 1 lb.)

Preheat oven to 375F (190C). Lightly oil inside bottom of paper bags. Place bags on a 15'' x 10'' jelly-roll pan. Divide potatoes and onions equally between bags. Sprinkle salt, pepper and oregano in each bag. Pour melted butter over potatoes. Place 1 sausage in each bag. Fold down bag tops. Secure each with 2 paper clips. Bake 1 hour. Serve immediately on large individual plates. Makes 4 servings.

Don't be concerned—the bags do not scorch during baking.

Paella with Seafood

A medley of colorful vegetables enhances this classic Spanish entree.

1/4 cup olive oil
1 medium onion, finely chopped
2 garlic cloves, minced
1-1/2 cups uncooked short- or
  long-grain white rice
1 large tomato, peeled, chopped
1/2 teaspoon saffron threads
1 (8-oz.) bottle clam juice
1-1/2 cups hot water
1/2 cup dry white wine
1/2 lb. slender asparagus spears

16 large prawns, unshelled
16 small butter, rock or steamer clams,
  unshucked
1 crab, cooked, cracked or
  8 very small lobster tails or
  scampi with shell, cooked
1 (10-oz.) pkg. frozen baby peas, thawed
1 (2-oz.) jar sliced pimiento
Lemon wedges
Cilantro sprigs

Heat oil in a 4-1/2-quart saucepan over medium heat. Add onion and garlic. Sauté until onion is glazed. Add rice. Sauté until rice is glazed. Add tomato, saffron and clam juice. In a small saucepan, bring water and wine to a boil. Pour over rice mixture. Cover and reduce heat. Simmer 20 minutes or until liquid has been absorbed. Fill a medium saucepan 2/3 full of water; bring water to a boil. Add asparagus spears and boil 3 to 4 minutes. Drain well; set aside. Arrange prawns and clams on top of rice mixture. Cover. Steam until clam shells open, 5 to 8 minutes. Discard any shells which do not open. Preheat oven to 375F (190C). Transfer rice mixture and seafood to a large paella pan or ovenproof serving dish. Place crab, lobster tails or scampi, peas, asparagus and pimiento over rice. Cover and heat through in oven, 10 to 15 minutes. Garnish with lemon wedges and cilantro. Serve immediately. Makes 8 servings.

Spinach & Clams Hiely

The Hiely restaurant in Avignon serves this elegant dish in copper ramekins.

2 (12-oz.) bunches spinach or
  2 (10-oz.) pkgs. frozen chopped spinach,
  thawed, drained
1/4 cup butter
3 shallots or green onions, chopped
2 (7-1/2-oz.) cans minced clams,
  drained, juice reserved
1/3 cup dry vermouth or white wine

1/2 cup whipping cream
2 tablespoons cornstarch
2 tablespoons cold water
1/2 teaspoon salt
1/2 teaspoon dried leaf marjoram
1/4 cup freshly grated Parmesan cheese
  (3/4 oz.)
1/4 cup shredded Gruyère cheese (1 oz.)

Preheat oven to 400F (205C). Butter 6 small ramekins or scallop shells. Wash fresh spinach thoroughly in several changes of cold water. Discard stems and bruised or tough leaves. Drain well. Chop spinach. In a large skillet, cook spinach over medium-high heat just until limp. Drain well. Squeeze spinach dry. Melt butter in a medium saucepan over medium heat. Add shallots or green onions. Sauté until glazed. Stir in reserved clam juice, vermouth or wine and cream. Boil until liquid is reduced by 1/3. In a small bowl, combine cornstarch and cold water. Stir cornstarch paste into hot liquid. Stir over medium heat until thickened. Add salt, marjoram, spinach and clams. Combine well. Spoon spinach mixture into buttered ramekins or shells. Combine cheeses in a small bowl. Top each serving with 1/4 of cheese mixture. Bake 10 to 15 minutes or until cheese melts. Serve immediately. Makes 6 servings.

Baked Fish & Vegetables Piraeus

Fish steaks and vegetables combine for a succulent entree named after the Greek port.

1 (1-lb.) bunch spinach
1/4 cup olive oil
1 large onion, finely chopped
2 celery stalks, finely chopped
3 small carrots, thinly sliced
1 bunch green onions, chopped
1/3 cup chopped fresh parsley
1 (8-oz.) can tomato sauce

2 garlic cloves, minced
2 teaspoons chopped fresh basil or
   1/2 teaspoon dried leaf basil
1/2 teaspoon salt
1/2 teaspoon freshly ground pepper
2 lbs. (1-inch-thick) halibut or
   sea-bass steaks
1 lemon, cut in wedges

Butter a 13" x 9" baking dish. Wash spinach thoroughly in several changes of cold water. Discard stems and bruised or tough leaves. Drain well. Chop spinach. Heat oil in a large skillet over medium heat. Add onion. Sauté until soft. Add celery, carrots and green onions. Sauté until glazed. Add spinach, parsley, tomato sauce, garlic, basil, salt and pepper. Cover and reduce heat. Simmer 15 minutes. Preheat oven to 350F (175C). Spoon half the vegetable mixture into buttered baking dish. Arrange halibut or sea bass over vegetables. Top with remaining vegetables. Cover. Bake 45 minutes or until fish flakes with a fork. Serve with lemon wedges. Serve immediately. Makes 6 servings.

Asparagus & Shrimp Nordic-Style

The Scandinavian way of combining crayfish with asparagus works beautifully with shrimp also.

1 lb. asparagus spears
3 tablespoons butter
4 hot poached eggs
1/2 lb. cooked small shrimp
2 tablespoons brandy or Cognac
1/2 cup whipping cream
1 teaspoon Dijon-style mustard

1/2 cup shredded samso or
   Gruyère cheese (2 oz.)
1/4 teaspoon dried leaf tarragon
1/8 teaspoon white pepper
2 tablespoons caviar or
   chopped fresh parsley, if desired

Butter 4 individual ramekins. In a large saucepan, cook asparagus in boiling salted water 5 to 7 minutes or cook in a steamer 12 to 15 minutes. Asparagus should be crisp-tender. Drain well. Melt 1 tablespoon butter in a large skillet over medium heat. Add cooked asparagus. Cook 1 minute, shaking skillet occasionally. Place 1 poached egg in each ramekin. Divide asparagus spears between 4 ramekins. Melt 2 tablespoons butter in a small saucepan over medium heat. Add shrimp and brandy or Cognac. Heat until warm, about 150F (65C). Using a long match, carefully ignite brandy or Cognac and shrimp. When flame goes out, spoon liquor and shrimp over eggs and asparagus. Stir cream and mustard into small saucepan used for liquor. Bring cream mixture to a boil. Cook over medium-high heat to reduce liquid by 1/3. Add cheese, tarragon and white pepper. Heat until cheese melts. Spoon cream sauce over eggs and asparagus. Top each serving with a dollop of caviar or parsley, if desired. Serve immediately. Makes 4 servings.

Chinese Pea Pods & Shrimp

A fast and delectable stir-fry to serve with hot steamed rice.

2 tablespoons safflower oil or
  peanut oil
3/4 lb. medium-size raw shrimp,
  peeled, slit lengthwise, deveined
1/2 teaspoon salt
1/3 cup clam juice
1/2 lb. Chinese pea pods, trimmed or
  1 (6-oz.) pkg. frozen pea pods

3 green onions, cut in 1-inch pieces
1 cup water chestnuts, thinly sliced
2 teaspoons cornstarch
2 teaspoons cold water
1 teaspoon soy sauce
4 to 5 sprigs cilantro

Heat oil in a wok or large skillet. Add shrimp and salt. Stir-fry 1 minute or until shrimp become pink. Add clam juice, pea pods, green onions and water chestnuts. Cover. Cook 2 minutes, stirring once or twice. Stir together cornstarch, cold water and soy sauce. Add to shrimp mixture. Cook, stirring until thickened. Garnish with cilantro sprigs. Serve immediately. Makes 4 servings.

Chicken & Artichokes Jubilee

A delectable wine sauce blends chicken and artichokes.

4 medium artichokes
4 split chicken breasts
  (about 1-1/3 lbs.)
3/4 cup chicken broth
1 teaspoon chopped fresh tarragon or
  1/4 teaspoon dried leaf tarragon
2 tablespoons butter

2 tablespoons all-purpose flour
1 teaspoon Dijon-style mustard
1/2 cup half and half
1/4 cup white wine
1 cup shredded Jarlsberg or
  Gruyère cheese (4 oz.)

Butter 4 individual casseroles. Remove all leaves and stems from artichokes. Cut each artichoke in half. Using a spoon or melon-baller, scrape or scoop out the fuzzy choke center. Cut each artichoke piece in half again. In a covered medium saucepan, cook artichoke hearts over medium heat in boiling salted water until tender, 10 to 15 minutes. Drain well. Place chicken breasts in a large skillet. Add broth and tarragon. Poach chicken over medium heat 15 minutes or until flesh has lost its pink color and is tender. Drain broth and reserve. Measure broth. Reduce broth to 3/4 cup by cooking over medium-high heat or add water to make 3/4 cup broth. Remove and discard skin and bones from chicken. Melt butter in a small saucepan over medium heat. Stir in flour and mustard. Cook 2 minutes, stirring constantly. Blend in reserved broth and half and half. Cook until thickened, 4 to 5 minutes. Stir in wine and 3/4 cup cheese. Divide chicken and artichokes between buttered casseroles. Spoon sauce over chicken. Sprinkle remaining cheese over sauce. Place under broiler and broil until cheese is bubbly. Serve immediately. Makes 4 servings.

How To Make Cashew Chicken & Vegetables

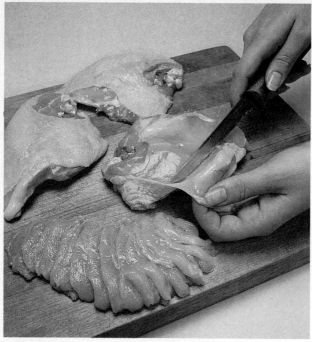

1/Remove skin and bone from chicken. Slice chicken wafer thin.

2/Stir-fry chicken mixture in a wok or large skillet.

Cashew Chicken & Vegetables

Once ingredients are assembled, this dish goes together with split-second timing.

1/2 cup cashews, roasted
4 split chicken breasts (about 1-1/3 lbs.)
1 teaspoon cornstarch
2 tablespoons peanut oil or safflower oil
1/4 lb. mushrooms, sliced
6 oz. Chinese pea pods, trimmed, or
   1 (6-oz.) pkg. frozen pea pods
1 (4-oz.) can water chestnuts,
   thinly sliced

1/2 cup chicken broth
1 tablespoon soy sauce
1/4 teaspoon white pepper
4 drops sesame oil
1-1/2 teaspoons cornstarch
1 tablespoon cold water

Preheat oven to 300F (150C). Scatter cashews in a 9-inch pie dish. Bake 10 minutes or until lightly toasted; set aside. Skin and bone chicken. Slice chicken wafer thin. Place 1 teaspoon cornstarch in a plastic bag. Add chicken and shake until coated. Heat a wok or large skillet over high heat. Add peanut oil or safflower oil and heat. Add chicken pieces. Stir-fry over high heat 1 minute or until chicken is completely white. Add mushrooms and pea pods. Stir-fry 30 seconds. Add water chestnuts and broth. Cover. Cook over medium heat 1-1/2 minutes. Add soy sauce, white pepper and sesame oil. In a small bowl, combine 1-1/2 teaspoons cornstarch and cold water. Stir cornstarch paste into chicken mixture. Stir over medium heat until thickened, 2 to 3 minutes. Spoon chicken mixture onto a warm platter. Sprinkle with toasted cashews. Serve immediately. Makes 4 servings.

Cassoulet

This French bean stew tastes even better when reheated.

2 cups dried Great Northern beans or
   cranberry beans
4 slices bacon, diced
2 medium onions, chopped
1 lb. boneless lamb, cut in 1-inch cubes
1 lb. boneless pork, cut in 1-inch cubes
2-1/2 cups red wine
1-1/2 cups beef broth
3 tablespoons brandy or Cognac
4 garlic cloves, minced

3 tablespoons tomato paste
1 teaspoon salt
1/2 teaspoon freshly ground pepper
1/2 teaspoon dried leaf thyme
1 lb. smoked bratwurst, mettwurst or
   mild Italian sausage
1/2 cup breadcrumbs,
   made from sourdough bread
2 tablespoons butter, melted
3 tablespoons chopped fresh parsley

Wash beans. Place in a large saucepan. Cover with cold water. Cover. Bring to boil. Boil 2 minutes. Remove from heat. Let stand 1 hour. Drain well. Preheat oven to 350F (175C). Oil a 4-quart casserole dish. In a large skillet, sauté bacon and onion over medium heat until glazed. Pour off drippings. Add lamb and pork cubes. Cook meat until browned. In a large bowl, combine beans, bacon, onions and browned meat. Add wine, broth, brandy or Cognac, garlic, tomato paste, salt, pepper and thyme. Mix lightly. Place in oiled casserole dish. Cover. Bake 2 hours or until beans are tender. Place sausages in a medium saucepan. Cover with water. Bring to a boil. Remove from heat. Let stand 15 minutes. Drain sausages. Slice diagonally. Arrange sausages on bean mixture. In a small bowl, toss breadcrumbs with butter. Sprinkle crumbs over sausages. Bake uncovered 20 to 30 minutes. Sprinkle parsley over top. Serve immediately. Makes 8 servings.

Oven-Baked Lima Beans & Sausages

Savory baked limas and sausages make a hearty dish.

2 cups dried lima beans
1-1/2 qts. (6 cups) water
1 meaty ham bone (about 1 lb.)
1 tablespoon butter
1 large onion, chopped
2 garlic cloves, minced
2 teaspoons Dijon-style mustard

2 teaspoons Worcestershire sauce
1-1/2 cups tomato sauce
1/3 cup cider vinegar
2 tablespoons dark molasses
1/4 teaspoon freshly ground pepper
2 lbs. garlic sausage or Polish sausage

Butter a 3-quart casserole dish. Wash lima beans. Place beans in a large saucepan. Cover with water. Cover and bring to a boil over high heat. Boil 2 minutes. Remove from heat. Let stand 1 hour. Add ham bone. Simmer, covered, over low heat 1 hour. Drain excess liquid. Remove ham bone. Dice meat. Discard fat and bone. Spoon beans into buttered casserole dish. Add diced ham. Preheat oven to 350F (175C). Melt butter in a large skillet over medium heat. Add onion. Sauté until glazed. Add garlic, mustard, Worcestershire sauce, tomato sauce, vinegar, molasses and pepper. Stir tomato mixture into beans. Bake, uncovered, 30 minutes. Arrange sausages on top. Bake 15 minutes or until beans are tender. Serve immediately. Makes 8 servings.

Linguine with Vegetables & Provolone

Smoky-flavored provolone and garden vegetables adorn hot pasta.

1/2 lb. linguine or flat spaghetti
2 tablespoons butter
1 garlic clove, minced
2 green onions, chopped
2 small zucchini, ends trimmed,
   thinly sliced
1/4 lb. mushrooms, sliced
1 medium tomato, peeled, chopped

2 teaspoons chopped fresh basil or
   1/2 teaspoon dried leaf basil
1/2 teaspoon salt
1/4 teaspoon freshly ground pepper
1 cup shredded provolone cheese (4 oz.)
3 tablespoons freshly grated Parmesan cheese
2 tablespoons chopped fresh parsley

In a 3-quart saucepan, bring salted water to a boil. Add linguine or spaghetti to boiling water and cook over medium heat until al dente, about 11 minutes. Drain well. Return pasta to saucepan. Melt butter in a large skillet over medium-high heat. Add garlic, green onions, zucchini and mushrooms. Sauté 2 minutes. Add tomato, basil, salt and pepper. Cover and reduce heat. Simmer 3 to 4 minutes, or until zucchini is crisp-tender. Add vegetable mixture and cheeses to pasta. Mix gently until cheese is melted. Sprinkle with parsley. Serve immediately. Makes 3 to 4 servings.

Sausage-Stuffed Cabbage Rolls

The rice-meat filling plumps inside tender cabbage leaves during cooking.

1 (3-lb.) head green cabbage
1 tablespoon olive oil
1 small onion, chopped
1/2 lb. bulk Italian sausage
1/2 lb. lean ground pork
2 tablespoons uncooked long- or
   short-grain white rice
2 tablespoons chopped fresh parsley
1/2 teaspoon salt
1/4 teaspoon freshly ground pepper

1/2 teaspoon ground allspice
1/2 teaspoon dried leaf oregano
2 tablespoons butter
2 medium carrots, shredded
1 large onion, chopped
1-1/2 cups tomato sauce
1/2 cup beef broth
1 lemon, cut in wedges
2 to 3 tablespoons chopped fresh parsley
Dairy sour cream

Remove core from cabbage. Carefully remove outer cabbage leaves and discard. Separate inner leaves. In a 3-quart saucepan, bring salted water to a boil. Drop inner cabbage leaves into boiling water. Cook 3 to 4 minutes. Drain well and cool. Select 24 leaves; set aside. Heat oil in a medium skillet. Add small onion. Sauté until golden brown. Place onion in a medium bowl. Add Italian sausage, ground pork, rice, parsley, salt, pepper, allspice and oregano. Mix to blend. Spread a cabbage leaf flat. Place 2 tablespoons meat filling on cabbage leaf near leaf base. Fold bottom of leaf over filling. Fold sides toward center. Roll up tightly. Repeat with remaining filling and leaves. Melt butter in a large saucepan over medium heat. Add carrots and large onion. Sauté until glazed. Place cabbage rolls in layers on top of carrots and onion. In a small bowl, combine tomato sauce and beef broth. Pour liquid over cabbage rolls. Cover. Cook over low heat 1 hour or until fork tender. Place on a large platter. Garnish with lemon wedges and parsley. Serve hot with sour cream. Makes 4 to 6 servings.

1/Use a spoon to scoop out tomato pulp, leaving a 3/4-inch shell.

2/Spoon meat mixture into hollowed-out tomatoes.

Stuffed Tomatoes Avgolemono

A tangy lemon sauce covers these tomatoes stuffed with meat and pine nuts.

12 medium tomatoes
2 tablespoons olive oil
1 bunch green onions,
    finely chopped (white part only)
1/3 cup chopped fresh parsley
3 tablespoons uncooked
    short-grain white rice
1 lb. lean ground beef or
    1/2 lb. ground turkey and
    1/2 lb. ground pork

1/2 teaspoon salt
1/4 teaspoon freshly ground pepper
1/2 teaspoon ground allspice
1/3 cup pine nuts
1-1/2 cups beef broth
2 eggs
2 tablespoons lemon juice

Slice tops off tomatoes. Use a spoon to scoop out pulp, leaving a 3/4-inch shell. Finely chop tomato pulp; set aside along with any tomato juice. Heat oil in a large skillet over medium heat. Add green onions. Sauté until limp. Add parsley, rice, reserved tomato pulp and juice, ground meat, salt, pepper and allspice. Cover and reduce heat. Simmer 20 minutes, stirring occasionally. Mix in pine nuts. Cook, uncovered, until juices evaporate, 3 to 4 minutes. Spoon meat mixture into hollowed-out tomatoes. Arrange stuffed tomatoes in a large skillet. Add broth. Cover and simmer 3 to 4 minutes or until tomatoes are just tender. Transfer tomatoes to a serving platter. Keep warm. Measure broth. Reduce broth to 1-1/2 cups by cooking over medium-high heat or add water to make 1-1/2 cups broth. Bring broth to a boil. In a medium bowl, beat eggs until light. Mix in lemon juice. Pour in half the hot broth, stirring constantly. Return broth mixture to skillet. Cook over very low heat, stirring occasionally, until thickened. Pour lemon sauce around stuffed tomatoes. Serve immediately. Makes 6 servings.

 Cook the lemon sauce over low heat. High heat or boiling may cause curdling.

Ham & Cheese Stuffed Artichokes

Minced ham and melted cheese fill these whole artichokes for a luncheon or dinner entree.

Bechamel Sauce, see below
4 large artichokes
1 tablespoon olive oil
1 tablespoon lemon juice
1 cup finely chopped cooked ham
3/4 cup shredded Gruyère or
   feta cheese (3 ozs.)

1/2 cup freshly shredded Parmesan or
   Romano cheese (2 ozs.)
2 tablespoons fine dry bread crumbs
1 tablespoon butter, melted

Bechamel Sauce:
2 tablespoons butter
2 tablespoons all-purpose flour
1 cup milk

1/4 teaspoon salt
Dash white pepper

Prepare Bechamel Sauce. Lightly butter an 8'' x 8'' baking dish. Cut off artichoke stems. Remove and discard hard outer leaves of artichokes. Using scissors cut sharp tips off remaining leaves. Place 2 quarts of salted water in a 3-quart saucepan. Bring to a boil. Add artichokes, olive oil and lemon juice. Cook over medium heat until tender, but not soft, 35 to 40 minutes. Drain well. Cool slightly. Preheat oven to 350F (175C). Using a spoon or melon-baller, scrape or scoop out fuzzy choke center. Place artichokes upright in buttered baking dish. In a medium bowl, combine Bechamel Sauce, ham, Gruyère or feta cheese and 1/4 cup Parmesan or Romano cheese. Mix well. Arrange ham mixture between artichoke leaves and in centers. Sprinkle with crumbs and remaining Parmesan or Romano cheese. Drizzle butter over artichokes. Bake 20 minutes or until cheese topping browns lightly. Makes 4 servings.

Bechamel Sauce:
In a small saucepan melt butter over medium heat. Stir in flour and cook 2 minutes, stirring until smooth. Slowly pour in half the milk, stirring constantly until smooth and thick. Add remaining milk and stir constantly until sauce is smooth and thick. Season with salt and pepper. Set aside until ready to use.

Insight on Artichokes

Artichokes, generally considered a vegetable, are actually an edible thistle blossom. Cool rainy mornings and warm sunny afternoons of the Pacific coastline are ideal conditions for growing artichokes. As the thistle stalk develops, artichokes form on the stalk. The largest develops at the top with smaller artichokes developing farther down the stalk and the smallest or artichoke hearts forming at the base. Size will vary from tiny hearts, 1 to 1-1/2 inches in diameter, to the largest up to 6 inches in diameter. Size is no indication of quality or flavor. The order in which the artichoke is borne on the plant determines its potential size. Growers wait for buds to reach their full size, then harvest just before ready to open. Artichokes are great when counting calories. A medium-size artichoke averages 50 to 60 calories. They are also a good source of vitamins and minerals.

Spaghetti Squash with Greek Meat Sauce

The interior of this intriguing squash separates into spaghetti-like strands when cooked.

Greek Meat Sauce, see below
1 (3-lb.) spaghetti squash
1/4 teaspoon salt
1/4 teaspoon freshly ground pepper
1/4 cup butter

1 avocado, peeled, sliced
8 cherry tomatoes
1/2 cup freshly grated Parmesan or
    Romano cheese (1-1/2 oz.)
2 tablespoons chopped fresh parsley

Greek Meat Sauce:
1 tablespoon mixed pickling spice
1 lb. ground turkey
1 lb. lean ground pork
2 medium onions, chopped
1 (6-oz.) can tomato paste

2/3 cup dry red wine
2 garlic cloves, minced
1-1/2 teaspoons salt
1 teaspoon freshly ground pepper
1 cinnamon stick

Prepare Greek Meat Sauce. With a Chinese cleaver, split spaghetti squash in half lengthwise. Scoop out seeds. Place cut-side down in a large saucepan. Add water to a depth of 2 inches. Cover. Simmer over medium-low heat 30 to 40 minutes or until center of squash is crisp-tender. Remove from pan. Cool slightly. Using a fork, fluff squash and scoop out spaghetti-like strands. Place on a large warm platter. Add salt and pepper. Melt butter in a small saucepan over medium heat until it turns light brown. Pour melted butter over squash strands. Toss with a fork to blend. Top squash with hot Greek Meat Sauce. Arrange avocado in a pinwheel on top of meat sauce. Garnish with cherry tomatoes. Sprinkle with cheese and parsley. Serve immediately. Makes 8 servings.

Greek Meat Sauce:
Tie pickling spice in a cheesecloth bag or place in a tea ball. In a large saucepan, combine spice bag or tea ball, ground meats, onions, tomato paste, wine, garlic, salt, pepper and cinnamon stick. Cover and simmer over medium-low heat 2 to 2-1/2 hours. Stir occasionally to keep meat crumbly. Sauce can be made in advance and refrigerated. Remove fat from top of chilled sauce. Set aside until ready to use.

Variation

Substitute spaghetti-squash cooking method found in recipe for Spaghetti Squash with Tomato Sauce, page 129. The 2 methods are interchangeable.

The cooking time is not precise for this hard-shelled squash. It is best to test for doneness by piercing the squash with a fork. It will seem tender to the touch when it is cooked.

How To Make Spaghetti Squash with Greek Meat Sauce

1/Using a fork, fluff squash and scoop out spaghetti-like strands.

2/Garnish with cherry tomatoes and parsley. Sprinkle with grated cheese.

Spaghetti Squash with Tomato Sauce

This pasta-like squash makes a great base for robust sausages and tomato sauce.

1 (2-1/2- to 3-lb.) spaghetti squash	1/2 teaspoon freshly ground pepper
3 tablespoons butter	1/2 teaspoon dried leaf oregano
2 tablespoons olive oil	1/4 cup half and half
2 tablespoons water	2 tablespoons chopped fresh parsley
1 medium onion, finely chopped	6 mild Italian sausages
5 medium tomatoes, peeled, chopped	12 whole black oil-cured Italian olives
2 garlic cloves, chopped	1/2 cup freshly grated Parmesan cheese
1/2 teaspoon salt	(1-1/2 oz.)

Preheat oven to 375F (190C). Place squash in a 13" x 9" baking dish. Add water to a depth of 1 inch. Bake 45 to 55 minutes or until squash is tender when pierced with a fork. Cool 5 minutes. Cut in half lengthwise. With a spoon, scoop out seeds. Discard. Using a fork, fluff squash and scoop out spaghetti-like strands. Place on a large warm platter. Toss squash with 2 tablespoons plus 2 teaspoons butter. Heat oil in a large skillet over medium heat. Add water and onion. Cook until onion is soft and water evaporates. Add tomatoes. Cover and reduce heat. Simmer 10 minutes. Add garlic, salt, pepper and oregano. Simmer, uncovered, 10 minutes. Stir in half and half and parsley. Place sausages in a medium saucepan. Cover with water and bring to a boil. Remove sausages from heat. Let stand 15 minutes. Drain well. Melt 1 teaspoon butter in a large skillet over medium heat. Add sausages. Turn sausages frequently to brown completely. Spoon tomato sauce over squash. Place sausages and olives around squash. Serve hot with Parmesan cheese. Makes 6 servings.

Variation

Add 3 medium zucchini, sliced, to tomato sauce during last 10 minutes of cooking.

Pilgrim Stew in Butternut Shells

Golden squash shells form a succulent container for a zesty stew.

1 cup dry white wine
3 tablespoons white-wine vinegar
2 garlic cloves, minced
1 teaspoon dried leaf thyme
1/2 teaspoon salt
1/2 teaspoon freshly ground pepper
2 lbs. boneless pork,
   cut in 1-inch cubes

1 tablespoon butter
3 tablespoons tomato paste
1/2 cup chicken broth
3 small butternut squash
Salt and freshly ground pepper to taste
1 tablespoon butter, melted
3 tablespoons roasted sunflower seeds or
   chopped pistachio nuts

In a medium bowl, combine wine, vinegar, garlic, thyme, salt and pepper. Stir in pork. Cover. Refrigerate 6 to 8 hours or overnight. Drain meat well. Pat dry with paper towel. Reserve marinade. Melt 1 tablespoon butter in a 3-quart saucepan over medium-high heat. Add marinated pork cubes. Brown on all sides. Add reserved marinade, tomato paste and broth. Cover and reduce heat. Simmer 1-1/2 hours or until pork is tender when pierced with a fork. Preheat oven to 400F (205C). While cooking pork, cut squash in half lengthwise. Remove seeds. Place cut-side down in a large shallow baking dish. Add water to a depth of 1 inch. Bake 40 minutes or until squash is tender when pierced with a fork. Remove from pan. Place squash cut-side up on a platter. Season with salt and pepper. Drizzle 1 tablespoon melted butter over squash. Spoon stew inside each squash half. Sprinkle each serving with sunflower seeds or pistachio nuts. Serve immediately. Makes 6 servings.

Stuffed Eggplant Boats

Tiny slender eggplants make neat individual servings for this Turkish-style entree.

8 (6-inch) slender eggplants or
   2 medium eggplants
Salt
1 tablespoon olive oil
1 large onion, chopped
1 lb. lean ground lamb or ground turkey
3 large tomatoes
2 tablespoons chopped fresh parsley

3/4 teaspoon salt
1/2 teaspoon freshly ground pepper
2 garlic cloves, minced
1/2 teaspoon ground allspice
1/2 cup freshly shredded Parmesan cheese
   (2 oz.)
1 (8-oz.) can tomato sauce

Slit eggplants lengthwise to within 1 inch of each end. Sprinkle salt lightly into slits. Let stand 15 minutes. Salt draws out bitter juices from eggplant. Preheat oven to 400F (205C). Rinse eggplants under cold water. Pat dry with paper towel. Place in a 13" x 9" baking dish. Cover with foil. Bake 30 minutes. Heat oil in a large skillet over medium heat. Add onion. Sauté until golden. Add ground meat. Cook until browned and crumbly. Peel and chop 2 tomatoes. Add chopped tomatoes, parsley, 3/4 teaspoon salt, pepper, garlic and allspice to meat mixture. Cover and reduce heat. Simmer 15 minutes. Fill slits in baked eggplants with stuffing. Return to 13" x 9" baking dish. Cut remaining tomato into wedges. Place on top of eggplants. Sprinkle with cheese. Pour tomato sauce over eggplants. Cover with foil. Reduce oven temperature to 375F (190C). Bake 50 minutes. Remove foil. Broil 1 minute or until top is lightly browned. Serve hot or warm. Makes 4 servings.

Spinach Gnocchi Balls

Make spinach balls in advance and chill to retain shape during cooking.

3 (12-oz.) bunches spinach or
  3 (10-oz.) pkgs. frozen chopped spinach,
  thawed, drained
2 eggs
2 cups ricotta cheese (1 lb.)
1-1/4 cups freshly grated Parmesan or
  Romano cheese, or
  mixture of both (3-3/4 oz.)
1/2 cup dry breadcrumbs,
  made from French bread

3 tablespoons chopped fresh parsley
2 garlic cloves, minced
All-purpose flour
2 qts. chicken broth
1/3 cup butter
1/4 cup freshly grated Parmesan cheese
  (3/4 oz.)

Wash fresh spinach thoroughly in several changes of cold water. Discard stems and bruised or tough leaves. Chop spinach. Blanch spinach in boiling water 3 minutes. Drain well. In a large bowl, beat eggs until blended. Mix in ricotta cheese and 1-1/4 cups cheese, breadcrumbs, spinach, parsley and garlic. Shape spinach mixture into 1-1/2-inch balls. Roll spinach balls in flour. Cover and refrigerate until firm. In a large saucepan, bring broth to a boil over medium heat. Add a few spinach balls. Reduce heat. Simmer until spinach balls float, 8 to 10 minutes. With a slotted spoon, lift out spinach balls to a heatproof serving platter. Repeat with remaining spinach balls. Melt butter in a small saucepan over medium heat. Heat butter until it begins to brown. Pour hot butter over spinach balls. Sprinkle 1/4 cup cheese over top. Serve immediately. Makes 8 servings.

Sauerkraut & Sausage

This Alsatian dish known as Choucroute Garni makes a congenial party dish with a variety of sausages.

4 lbs. sauerkraut
3 slices thick-sliced bacon, diced
1 medium onion, chopped
2 cooking apples, peeled, cored, diced
1 meaty ham bone (about 1 lb.)
1 bay leaf
3 garlic cloves

4 whole cloves
2 cups white wine
3 to 4 lbs. assorted sausages:
  mild Italian sausage, bockwurst,
  smoked bratwurst, cocktail links,
  mettwurst or Polish sausage
1 tablespoon butter

Preheat oven to 300F (150C). Oil a 4-quart casserole dish. Wash sauerkraut under running cold water. Drain well. Sauté bacon in a large skillet over medium heat until crisp. Remove bacon from skillet. Add onion. Sauté onion in bacon drippings until golden brown. In oiled casserole, combine sauerkraut, bacon, onion, apples, ham bone, bay leaf, garlic, cloves and wine. Cover. Bake 2-1/2 to 3 hours or until flavors have blended. Flavor continues to improve with longer baking. Place sausages in a large saucepan. Cover with water. Bring to a boil. Remove from heat. Let stand 15 minutes. Drain sausages. Melt butter in a large skillet over medium heat. Add sausages. Brown sausages in melted butter. Arrange sausages on top of sauerkraut. Serve immediately. Makes 10 to 12 servings.

SIDE DISHES

As seasons change, produce markets bring forth an ever-changing array of colorful and tasty vegetables. This offers creative cooks opportunities to develop a range of side dishes. Spring's supply of early shoots, summer's abundance of fresh green leaves, fall's bounty of colorful squash and winter's storehouse of roots and tubers each offers new opportunities.

Whatever your source, the key to good eating lies in young, tender fresh vegetables. Selection, storage and preparation are all-important in making the most from fresh vegetables. Wash vegetables thoroughly just before cooking. Cook to perfection. Overcooking destroys flavor, nutrients, color and texture.

Young, fresh vegetables have a natural sweet tenderness. Just-picked Blue Lake green beans, fresh ears of golden-yellow corn harvested just before grilling, or a salad made from scarlet tomatoes still warm from the sun's rays are incomparable treats.

Served lightly buttered, seasoned with herbs or in combination with other foods, vegetables are the perfect accompaniment. Zucchini gains a new flavor with a coating of cheese in Parmesan-Coated Zucchini. Beets pick up a tangy zest in Orange-Glazed Beets. Brussels sprouts gain a tangy sweetness with the flavor of grapes in Brussels Sprouts Véronique.

Serve all-time favorites such as carrots, potatoes and cabbage in new, mouth-watering recipes. Try Brandied Orange Carrots, Red Cabbage & Apples, and Ranch-House Stuffed Potatoes.

With such boundless variety this chapter offers, family and friends many delightful dishes.

Family Holiday Reunion
Grandma's Favorite Beef Roast
Creamy Scalloped Potatoes, page 138
Herb-Tossed Blue-Lake Beans, page 140
Limas and Onions in Sour Cream, page 144
Pickled Beets, page 78
Sweet & Sour Hot Slaw, page 73
Garlic-Potato Bread, page 176
Carrot Pudding with
Brandied Hard Sauce, page 185

Stir-Fried Pea Pods & Cucumbers

Serve this quick, crunchy side dish with barbecued meat or poultry.

2 tablespoons safflower oil or
  peanut oil
2 green onions, chopped (white part only)
1 medium cucumber, peeled,
  halved lengthwise, sliced thinly
1/2 lb. Chinese pea pods, trimmed, or
  1 (6-oz.) pkg. frozen pea pods, thawed

1 tablespoon cider vinegar
1 teaspoon soy sauce
1/4 teaspoon grated gingerroot or
  1/8 teaspoon ground ginger
2 drops sesame oil
1/4 teaspoon brown sugar
Dash red (cayenne) pepper

Heat safflower oil or peanut oil in a wok or large skillet over medium-high heat. Add green onions. Stir-fry 1 minute. Add cucumber. Stir-fry 1 minute. Add pea pods. Stir-fry 2 minutes. Remove from heat. Stir in vinegar, soy sauce, ginger, sesame oil, brown sugar and red pepper. Mix well. Serve immediately. Makes 4 servings.

Variation
Refrigerate cooked mixture and serve as a salad over watercress.

Stir-Fried Chinese Vegetables

A fast vegetable combination great to serve with steak teriyaki or fish kabobs.

3 tablespoons safflower oil or
  peanut oil
2 celery stalks,
  sliced diagonally 1/2-inch thick
1 red bell pepper, seeded, diced
1 bunch green onions,
  cut in 1-inch pieces

1/2 lb. mushrooms, sliced
1/2 lb. bean sprouts
6 oz. Chinese pea pods, trimmed, or
  1 (6-oz.) pkg. frozen pea pods,
  thawed
2 tablespoons soy sauce
1/2 teaspoon sesame oil

Heat safflower oil or peanut oil in a wok or large skillet over medium-high heat. Add celery, bell pepper and green onions. Stir-fry until vegetables are slightly softened, 2 minutes. Add mushrooms, bean sprouts and pea pods. Stir-fry until vegetables are crisp-tender, 1 minute. Add soy sauce and sesame oil. Serve immediately. Makes 6 to 8 servings

To store gingerroot, place it in a small jar. Add sherry to cover gingerroot. Cover with a tight sealing lid. Refrigerate until ready to use. Gingerroot can also be frozen. When ready to use, just shave or grate off the amount called for in the recipe.

1/With a sharp knife, cut tofu into 1-inch squares.

2/Fry squares of tofu in hot oil until evenly browned.

Chinese Cabbage & Tofu Stir-Fry

Chinese cabbage, also known as Napa cabbage, makes a fast side dish to accompany an Oriental meal.

**2 dried shiitake mushrooms or
  6 sliced fresh mushrooms
1 tablespoon soy sauce
1-1/2 teaspoons mirin or sherry
1/2 teaspoon grated gingerroot or
  1/4 teaspoon ground ginger**

**1/4 lb. tofu, cut in 1-inch squares
2 tablespoons safflower oil or peanut oil
1/2 head (1-lb.) Chinese cabbage,
  cut in 1/4-inch strips
1 garlic clove, minced
4 to 5 sprigs cilantro**

In a small bowl, place shiitake mushrooms and 1/4 cup water. Let stand 5 minutes. In a small bowl, combine soy sauce, mirin or sherry and ginger. Add tofu cubes. Turn cubes in sauce to coat well. Let stand 5 minutes. Drain off sauce and reserve. Heat oil in a wok or large skillet over medium-high heat. Add tofu squares. Stir-fry until browned on all sides, about 2 minutes. Remove tofu from wok or skillet; set aside. Add cabbage and garlic to wok or skillet. Stir-fry 3 minutes. Thinly slice soaked mushrooms. Add shiitake or fresh mushrooms to cabbage. Stir-fry 1 minute. Spoon onto a hot serving plate. Top with fried tofu cubes. Sprinkle with cilantro sprigs. Serve immediately. Makes 2 to 3 servings.

Potatoes Anna

These beautifully crusted potato slices are buttery tender inside.

1/2 cup butter, melted
6 large baking potatoes, peeled,
   sliced wafer thin

1/2 teaspoon salt
1/4 teaspoon freshly ground pepper

Preheat oven to 450F (230C). Pour 2 to 3 tablespoons melted butter into a round 12-inch baking dish. Swirl to coat dish. In buttered baking dish, arrange potato slices in slightly overlapping circles. Pour remaining butter over potatoes. Sprinkle with salt and pepper. Bake 25 minutes. Reduce heat to 400F (205C). Continue baking until potatoes are tender when pierced with a fork, 15 minutes. Run a knife under potatoes around edge of pan. Invert potatoes onto a serving plate. Cut into wedges. Makes 6 servings.

Garlic-Buttered Potato Dollars

These crispy potatoes are a cross between a potato chip and a baked potato.

2 tablespoons butter
2 garlic cloves, minced
3 to 4 large baking potatoes, scrubbed,
   unpeeled, sliced 1/8-inch thick

1/4 teaspoon salt
1/4 teaspoon freshly ground pepper

Preheat oven to 450F (230C). Place 1 tablespoon butter and half the garlic in each of two 9-inch pie dishes. Place in oven until butter melts. Pour off most of the melted butter into a small saucepan; set aside. Place potato slices, slightly overlapping, in circles in pie dishes. Sprinkle with salt and pepper. Pour reserved butter and garlic over potatoes. Bake until crisp underneath and potatoes are tender when pierced with a fork, about 30 minutes. Serve immediately. Makes 4 servings.

Swedish Whipped Rutabagas & Potatoes

An unusual accompaniment to pork, duck or game.

4 medium rutabagas, peeled, cut in cubes
2 medium potatoes, peeled, quartered
1 small onion, chopped
2 tablespoons butter
1/4 cup half and half

1 teaspoon brown sugar
1/2 teaspoon ground allspice
1/4 teaspoon freshly ground pepper
2 tablespoons chopped fresh parsley

Place rutabagas in a medium saucepan with salted water to a 1-inch depth. Cover and bring to a boil over medium heat. Reduce heat and simmer 20 minutes. Add potatoes and onions. Cook until vegetables are tender when pierced with a fork, about 15 minutes. Drain well. Mash vegetables with potato masher or puree in a food processor fitted with a steel blade. Add butter, half and half, brown sugar, allspice and pepper. Process well. Sprinkle with parsley. Serve immediately. Makes 6 servings.

Ranch-House Stuffed Potatoes

Bacon, cheese and onions flavor a stuffed baked potato.

6 medium baking potatoes,
   unpeeled, scrubbed
3 tablespoons butter
1/3 cup dairy sour cream
1/4 cup milk
1/2 teaspoon salt

1/2 teaspoon freshly ground pepper
1/2 lb. bacon, cooked crisp, crumbled
1 bunch green onions, chopped
1 cup shredded Gruyère or
   Jarlsberg cheese (4 oz.)
1 cup dairy sour cream

Preheat oven to 425F (220C). Prick potatoes with a fork in several places for steam to escape. Place potatoes on oven rack. Bake 1 hour or until tender to the touch when lightly squeezed. Remove from oven and cool slightly. Cut a thin slice from top of each potato. With a spoon, scoop out potato flesh and place in a medium bowl. Reserve potato shells. Mash potato flesh with a potato masher or wire whip. Beat in butter, 1/3 cup sour cream, milk, salt and pepper. Spoon mashed-potato mixture into reserved potato shells. Place stuffed potatoes in a 13'' x 9'' baking dish. Bake until heated through and lightly browned, about 15 minutes. Serve potatoes with toppings of bacon, green onions, cheese and sour cream. Makes 4 servings.

Baked Potatoes with Toppings

An array of toppings will dress up baked potatoes for a party.

6 large baking potatoes, scrubbed

Nordic Toppings:
1 (2-oz.) jar lumpfish caviar
1 cup dairy sour cream

1/4 cup chopped chives or green-onion tops
6 lemon wedges

American Toppings:
8 slices bacon, cooked crisp, crumbled
1 cup dairy sour cream

1 cup shredded sharp Cheddar cheese (4 oz.)
3 green onions, chopped

Mexican Toppings:
1 cup shredded Monterey Jack cheese (4 oz.)
1 red bell pepper, seeded, chopped
2 canned green chili peppers,
   seeded, chopped

1 cup dairy sour cream or plain yogurt

Preheat oven to 425F (220C). Prick potatoes with a fork in several places for steam to escape. Place potatoes on oven rack. Bake 1 hour or until tender to the touch when lightly squeezed. Remove from oven. Split potatoes. Serve immediately with choice of suggested toppings. Makes 6 servings.

1/Slide uncooked side of potato cake back into skillet with melted butter. Cook until golden brown.

2/ Garnish potato cake with chopped green onion.

Swiss Potato Cake

Known as Roesti, this hearty potato cake is a favorite to serve with grilled bratwurst.

6 large baking potatoes, whole, unpeeled
1 cup shredded Gruyère or
   Jarlsberg cheese (4 oz.)
3 green onions, chopped

1/4 teaspoon salt
1/4 teaspoon freshly ground pepper
1/2 cup butter

Place potatoes in a medium saucepan with salted water to a 1-inch depth. Cook over medium heat until tender, about 20 minutes. Place cooked potatoes in a colander and cool under cold running water. Peel potatoes. Shred potatoes coarsely using a hand shredder or a food processor fitted with a shredding blade; should have approximately 6 cups shredded potato. In medium bowl, combine shredded potatoes, cheese, 2 chopped green onions, salt and pepper. Melt 1/4 cup butter in a large skillet over medium heat. Add potato mixture, patting it smooth on top to make a flat cake. Cook over medium heat until browned on the bottom, about 10 minutes. Loosen potato cake with a spatula. Invert potato cake onto a plate. Add remaining 1/4 cup butter to skillet and melt. Slide uncooked side of potato cake back into skillet. Cook until golden brown on the bottom, about 10 minutes. Garnish with 1 chopped green onion. Serve in skillet or turn out onto a platter. Cut in wedges. Serve immediately. Makes 6 servings.

Creamy Scalloped Potatoes

In France, scalloped potatoes with milk and cheese are known as Gratin Dauphinois.

1/4 cup butter
6 large boiling potatoes (about 2 lbs.),
  peeled, sliced 1/8-inch thick
1/4 teaspoon salt
1/4 teaspoon freshly ground pepper

1 garlic clove, minced
1 cup shredded Gruyère, Jarlsberg or
  samso cheese (4 oz.)
1 cup half and half

Preheat oven to 425F (220C). Generously butter a round 10-inch baking dish with 2 tablespoons butter. Spread half the potatoes in baking dish. Sprinkle half the salt, pepper and garlic over potatoes. Dot with 1 tablespoon butter. Sprinkle with 1/2 cup cheese. Cover with remaining potatoes. Sprinkle with remaining salt, pepper, garlic and cheese. Dot potatoes with 1 tablespoon butter. Scald half and half by heating in a small saucepan over medium heat until bubbles appear around the edge. Pour over potatoes. Bake until potatoes are tender when pierced with a fork and top is golden brown, 25 to 30 minutes. Serve immediately. Makes 6 servings.

Variation

Substitute 1 cup chicken broth or beef broth for the half and half. This is a version from the Savoy region of France.

New Potatoes with Caviar

Makes an elegant accompaniment to barbecued salmon or a great appetizer.

16 small new potatoes (uniform size)
2 tablespoons butter
1/2 cup dairy sour cream

1/3 cup caviar
2 to 3 tablespoons chopped chives or
  fresh parsley

In a 2-quart saucepan, bring salted water to a boil. Add potatoes to boiling water and cook over medium heat until tender, 10 minutes. Drain well. Using a small melon-baller, hollow out a scoop on top of each potato. Melt butter in a large skillet over medium heat. Add potatoes. Sauté until coated with butter. Place on a serving platter. Spoon sour cream into each potato. Top with caviar and chives or parsley. Serve immediately. Makes 4 servings.

Orange-Glazed Yams

A zesty orange sauce, seasoned with smoky bacon and crunchy nuts, enhances golden yams.

6 yam-type sweet potatoes, cooked,
  peeled, sliced 1-inch thick
1 (6-oz.) can frozen orange-juice
  concentrate, thawed

2 tablespoons brown sugar
6 slices bacon, cooked crisp, crumbled
1/2 cup chopped filberts or pecans or
  slivered almonds

Preheat oven to 375F (190C). Butter a 2-quart baking dish. Arrange potato slices in buttered baking dish. In a small bowl, combine orange-juice concentrate, sugar and bacon. Pour juice mixture over potatoes. Sprinkle with nuts. Bake until heated through, about 20 minutes. Serve immediately. Makes 6 servings.

Pecan-Coated Sweet-Potato Casserole

The perfect side dish to a Thanksgiving turkey.

6 large sweet potatoes, cooked, peeled
1/4 cup butter, room temperature
1/2 cup orange juice or half and half
1/2 teaspoon salt

1/2 teaspoon ground cinnamon
2/3 cup packed brown sugar
3/4 cup pecan halves or walnut halves

Preheat oven to 375F (190C). Butter a 2-quart baking dish. Mash sweet potatoes in a large bowl. Beat in butter, orange juice or half and half, salt, cinnamon and 1/3 cup sugar. Spoon sweet-potato mixture into buttered baking dish. Sprinkle pecans or walnuts and remaining sugar over top. Bake, uncovered, until heated through and nuts are lightly toasted, about 20 minutes. Serve immediately. Makes 8 servings.

Marmalade-Glazed Parsnips

Use your favorite marmalade and create your own variation of glazed parsnips.

4 medium parsnips (about 1-1/4 lbs.)
   peeled, thickly sliced diagonally
1 tablespoon butter

1 tablespoon orange marmalade
1/8 teaspoon white pepper

In a large skillet, bring a small amount of salted water to a boil. Add parsnips to boiling water and cook over medium-high heat until tender, 10 to 15 minutes. Drain well. Add butter, marmalade and white pepper. Sauté until parsnips are glazed, 2 to 3 minutes. Serve immediately. Makes 4 servings.

Kohlrabi with Sour Cream & Chives

Kohlrabi is the German name for cabbage-turnip.

4 medium kohlrabi, thickly sliced
1 tablespoon butter
1/4 cup dairy sour cream

1 tablespoon finely chopped chives
1/8 teaspoon freshly ground pepper

In a 2-quart saucepan, bring salted water to a boil. Add kohlrabi to boiling water and cook over medium heat until tender, about 20 minutes. Drain well. Add butter, stirring constantly to coat kohlrabi. Stir in sour cream and chives. Heat through. Sprinkle with freshly ground pepper. Serve immediately. Makes 4 servings.

Herb-Tossed Blue-Lake Beans

A quick and effective styling for slender green beans.

**1-1/2 lbs. green beans, trimmed, or
  2 (10-oz.) pkgs. frozen French-cut
  green beans, thawed
2 tablespoons butter
1 shallot or green onion, finely chopped**

**1 garlic clove, minced
2 teaspoons chopped fresh tarragon or
  1/2 teaspoon dried leaf tarragon
2 tablespoons chopped fresh parsley**

Leave slender green beans whole. If green beans are large, slice lengthwise. In a 3-quart saucepan, bring salted water to a boil. Drop green beans into boiling water. Cook until crisp-tender, 5 to 7 minutes. Drain well. Melt butter in a large skillet over medium heat. Add shallot or green onion. Sauté until glazed, 2 to 3 minutes. Add garlic, tarragon and green beans. Sauté until green beans are glazed, 2 to 3 minutes. Sprinkle with parsley. Serve immediately. Makes 6 servings.

Indian Green Beans

Coconut and almonds give an elegant finish to these seasoned green beans.

**1/4 cup unsalted butter
1/2 cup blanched almonds,
  slivered or chopped
1 teaspoon black mustard seeds, if desired
1 large onion, chopped
1 teaspoon grated gingerroot or
  1/2 teaspoon ground ginger
1/4 teaspoon salt
1/4 teaspoon freshly ground pepper
1-1/2 lbs. green beans, trimmed,
  cut in 2-inch pieces or
  2 (10-oz.) pkgs. frozen cut
  green beans, thawed**

**Dash of red (cayenne) pepper
1/4 cup grated fresh coconut or
  unsweetened shredded coconut
2 tablespoons chopped fresh cilantro
2 tablespoons lemon juice
4 to 5 sprigs cilantro**

Melt 1 tablespoon butter in a large skillet over medium heat. Add almonds and mustard seeds, if desired. Sauté until nuts are lightly browned; set aside. Melt 3 tablespoons butter in large skillet over medium heat. Add onion, ginger, salt and pepper. Sauté until onions become soft, but not browned, 2 to 3 minutes. Add beans, red pepper, coconut and chopped cilantro. Mix lightly. Cover and reduce heat. Cook until beans are crisp-tender, 5 to 7 minutes, stirring occasionally. Stir in reserved almond mixture. Sprinkle with lemon juice. Garnish with cilantro sprigs. Serve immediately. Makes 6 servings.

How To Make Endive with Lemon Sauce

1/Using a paring knife, remove core from endive.

2/Spoon Lemon Sauce over cooked endive.

Endive with Lemon Sauce

Slightly bitter Belgian endive takes well to a rich lemon sauce.

8 Belgian endive (about 12 oz.)
3 tablespoons butter
1 cup chicken broth

2 eggs, slightly beaten
2 tablespoons lemon juice

Remove core from endive. In a large skillet, bring salted water to a boil. Add endive to boiling water and cook over medium heat 5 minutes. Drain well. Reduce heat and add butter. Sauté endive 5 minutes. Add broth and cover. Simmer until endive are tender, about 15 minutes. Arrange endive on a serving platter. Keep warm. Measure broth. If necessary, add water to make 1 cup or reduce liquid by cooking over high heat to make 1 cup. In a medium bowl, combine eggs and lemon juice. Slowly whisk in broth from cooked endive. Return lemon sauce to skillet. Stir constantly over medium heat until sauce thickens. Do not boil sauce. Pour lemon sauce over endive. Serve immediately. Makes 4 servings.

Sugar Snaps Voilà   Photo on pages 148 and 149.

Quickly stir-fry this new vegetable for a crisp, tasty treat.

**2 tablespoons safflower oil or
  peanut oil**
1/2 lb. Sugar Snap peas, trimmed
1/2 cup sliced water chestnuts
1 garlic clove, minced

**1/2 teaspoon grated gingerroot or
  1/4 teaspoon ground ginger**
1 teaspoon soy sauce
Dash hot-pepper sauce
4 to 5 sprigs cilantro

Heat oil in a wok or large skillet over medium-high heat. Add peas. Stir-fry 2 minutes. Add water chestnuts, garlic, ginger, soy sauce and hot-pepper sauce. Cook 2 minutes, or until peas are crisp-tender. Garnish with cilantro sprigs. Serve immediately. Makes 3 to 4 servings.

Peas with Prosciutto

An easy Italian way to dress up peas.

2 tablespoons butter
1/4 cup finely chopped onion
**2-1/2 cups fresh shelled peas or
  2 (10-oz.) pkgs. frozen baby peas**
1/3 cup chicken broth
1/4 teaspoon salt

1/4 teaspoon freshly ground pepper
**2 oz. prosciutto or cooked ham,
  cut in strips**
**2 tablespoons toasted pine nuts,
  if desired**

Melt butter in a medium saucepan over medium heat. Add onion. Sauté until soft but not browned, 2 to 3 minutes. Add peas, broth, salt and pepper. Cover and reduce heat. Simmer until tender, about 3 to 5 minutes. Remove cover. Stir in prosciutto or cooked ham and pine nuts, if desired. Cook over medium-low heat until juices evaporate, stirring occasionally. Serve immediately. Makes 4 to 6 servings.

Saffron Rice with Peas

Golden rice studded with green peas enhances a seafood menu.

1/4 cup butter
1 small onion, finely chopped
2 cups uncooked long-grain white rice
1 cup dry white wine
3 cups chicken broth

1/4 teaspoon saffron threads
**1/2 cup freshly grated Parmesan cheese
  (1-1/2 oz.)**
1 (10-oz.) pkg. frozen baby peas, thawed

Melt butter in a large saucepan over medium heat. Add onion. Sauté until glazed but not browned, 2 to 3 minutes. Add rice. Toss with a fork 2 to 3 minutes until rice is glazed. Pour in wine and 2-1/2 cups broth. Cover and reduce heat. Simmer until rice is tender and broth is absorbed, about 20 minutes. In a small bowl or cup, blend saffron with remaining broth. Stir broth, cheese and peas into rice mixture. Cover and remove from heat. Let stand 5 to 10 minutes. Serve immediately. Makes 8 servings.

Sausage-Stuffed Onions

With a meaty stuffing, onions become a delicious entree or festive buffet side dish.

6 medium onions, peeled
1 tablespoon butter
1/4 lb. mushrooms, chopped
1 lb. well-seasoned bulk pork sausage
1/2 cup soft white breadcrumbs or
   breadcrumbs made from French bread

1 tablespoon chopped fresh parsley
1/4 teaspoon salt
1/4 teaspoon freshly ground pepper
1/2 cup chicken broth
1/2 cup white wine

Preheat oven to 375F (190C). Cut a thin slice from bottom of each onion. Onions should stand upright. Using a sharp knife, scoop out inside of each onion from top, leaving a 1/4-inch-thick shell. Chop scooped-out onion flesh. Cook onion shells in a medium saucepan of boiling water over medium heat 5 minutes. Drain well. Melt butter in a large skillet over medium heat. Add chopped onion. Sauté until lightly browned, 4 to 5 minutes. Add mushrooms. Sauté until glazed. Spoon onion mixture into a medium bowl. Place sausage in large skillet. Sauté until lightly browned. Add sausage to onion mixture. Stir in breadcrumbs, parsley, salt and pepper. Spoon stuffing into onion shells. Place stuffed onions in a 9-inch square baking dish. Pour broth and wine over onions. Bake until onions are tender, 25 to 30 minutes. Baste several times while baking. Serve immediately. Makes 6 servings.

Golden Puree with Caramelized Onion

Rutabagas and carrots blend in this bright-orange puree topped with caramelized chopped onions.

5 large carrots, cut in 1-inch pieces
2 large rutabagas, peeled,
   cut in 1-inch pieces
2 tablespoons butter
2 tablespoons whipping cream

1/4 teaspoon mace
1/4 teaspoon salt
1/4 teaspoon white pepper
2 tablespoons butter
1 large sweet Spanish onion, chopped

Place carrots and rutagabas in a large saucepan with a small amount of salted water. Bring to a boil. Cook over medium heat until tender, 25 minutes. Drain well. Place vegetables in a blender or food processor fitted with a steel blade. Add 2 tablespoons butter, cream, mace, salt and white pepper. Process until pureed. Melt 2 tablespoons butter in a large skillet over medium-low heat. Add onion. Sauté 20 minutes or until caramelized. Spoon vegetable puree into a serving bowl. Top with caramelized onion. Serve immediately. Makes 4 to 6 servings.

Sautéing onions slowly until golden brown gives a caramelized sweetness.

Okra & Tomato Medley

Very small okra are best for this medley.

3 tablespoons olive oil
2 medium onions, coarsely chopped
2 garlic cloves, minced
3/4 lb. small okra, trimmed
1 (29-oz.) can whole plum tomatoes
1/4 teaspoon salt

1/4 teaspoon freshly ground pepper
1/2 teaspoon ground allspice
2 tablespoons chopped fresh cilantro or
   1/2 teaspoon ground coriander
1 lemon, cut in wedges
4 to 5 sprigs cilantro

Heat oil in a large skillet over medium heat. Add onions. Sauté until soft but not browned, 2 to 3 minutes. Add garlic and okra. Cook, stirring gently, until onion is lightly browned. Add tomatoes and liquid, salt, pepper, allspice and chopped cilantro or coriander. Cover and reduce heat. Simmer until an okra pod tests tender when pierced with a fork, 12 to 15 minutes. Refrigerate. Serve chilled with lemon wedges and cilantro sprigs. Makes 4 to 6 servings.

Red Cabbage & Apples

Here's an Austrian accompaniment to roast duck or pork loin.

1 large red cabbage, shredded
2 tablespoons butter
1 medium onion, chopped
2 tart cooking apples, cored, diced
1 tablespoon vinegar

1 tablespoon brown sugar
1/4 teaspoon freshly ground pepper
1/4 teaspoon ground nutmeg
3/4 cup red wine
3/4 cup water

In a 3-quart saucepan, bring salted water to a boil. Add cabbage to boiling water and cook over medium heat until crisp-tender, about 10 minutes. Drain well. Melt butter in a large skillet over medium heat. Add onion. Sauté until glazed, 2 to 3 minutes. Add cooked cabbage, apples, vinegar, sugar, pepper, nutmeg, wine and water. Cover and reduce heat. Simmer 30 minutes or until tender. Serve immediately. Makes 6 to 8 servings.

Limas & Onions in Sour Cream   Photo on page 148.

A fast side dish that accents pork roast or chops.

1 (10-oz.) pkg. frozen lima beans or
   2 cups fresh lima beans
1 tablespoon butter
3 green onions, chopped
1/8 teaspoon salt

1/8 teaspoon white pepper
1/2 teaspoon dried leaf tarragon
1 cup cherry tomatoes, halved
1/3 cup dairy sour cream
1 tablespoon chopped chives

In a 2-quart saucepan, bring salted water to a boil. Add lima beans to boiling water and cook over medium-high heat until tender, 7 to 10 minutes. Drain well. Melt butter in a large skillet over medium heat. Add onions. Sauté until glazed, 2 minutes. Add salt, white pepper, tarragon, cooked lima beans and tomatoes. Heat through. Stir in sour cream. Sprinkle with chopped chives. Serve immediately. Makes 3 to 4 servings.

How To Clean Asparagus

1/Snap asparagus spears near the white ends. Discard tough woody ends.

2/Use a peeler to remove outer layer of asparagus spears.

Dutch Asparagus

The Dutch use this spring vegetable as finger food.

1 lb. asparagus spears
1/8 teaspoon ground nutmeg
3 tablespoons butter

1 hard-cooked egg
2 tablespoons chopped fresh parsley

In a large saucepan, cook asparagus in boiling salted water 5 to 7 minutes or cook in a steamer 12 to 15 minutes. Asparagus should be crisp-tender. Drain well. Place asparagus spears on a platter. Sprinkle with nutmeg. In a small saucepan, melt butter until it bubbles and starts to brown. Pour butter over asparagus. Separate yolk from egg white. Chop or shred yolk and white separately. Sprinkle egg yolk and egg white in rows on top of asparagus. Sprinkle with parsley. Serve immediately. Makes 2 to 3 servings.

Broccoli Duo

Broccoli gets a double billing when handled in this fashion.

1 large bunch broccoli
3 tablespoons butter
5 tablespoons dairy sour cream
1/4 teaspoon salt

1/4 teaspoon freshly ground pepper
1/4 teaspoon ground nutmeg
1/4 cup toasted chopped walnuts or pecans
3 garlic cloves, minced

Cut off broccoli flowerets. Place flowerets in a steamer. Steam until crisp-tender, about 8 minutes. Place flowerets in a medium bowl. Keep warm. Peel broccoli stems. Shred stems using a hand shredder or a food processor fitted with a shredding blade. Steam shredded broccoli stems until crisp-tender, about 8 minutes. Place cooked broccoli stems in a small bowl. Add 1 tablespoon butter, 3 tablespoons sour cream, 1/8 teaspoon salt, 1/8 teaspoon pepper and nutmeg. Mix lightly. Transfer to a small serving dish. Dollop with remaining 2 tablespoons sour cream. Sprinkle with nuts. Melt 2 tablespoons butter in a small saucepan over medium heat. Add garlic. Sauté until butter browns lightly. Pour garlic butter over broccoli flowerets. Add 1/8 teaspoon each salt and pepper. Serve immediately. Flowerets and stems can be served in 2 separate dishes or combined as 1 dish. Makes 3 to 4 servings.

Cauliflower Curry

The Indian name for this delicious vegetable dish is Aloo Gobi.

1/4 cup oil or vegetable shortening
1 teaspoon cumin seeds
1 small onion, chopped
2 potatoes, peeled, thinly sliced
1 small cauliflower, cut in flowerets
1 teaspoon ground coriander
2 teaspoons ground turmeric

1/4 teaspoon salt
1/2 teaspoon chili powder
1 tomato, chopped
1/2-inch piece gingerroot, peeled, cut in julienne strips
1/4 cup water
3 to 4 sprigs cilantro

Heat oil or shortening in a large wok or skillet over medium-high heat. Add cumin seeds. Stir-fry 10 to 15 seconds. Add onion. Sauté until lightly browned, 4 to 5 minutes. Add potatoes and stir-fry 2 minutes. Add cauliflower, coriander, turmeric, salt and chili powder. Stir-fry 2 minutes. Add tomato, gingerroot and water. Cover wok or skillet and cook 5 minutes or until potatoes are tender when pierced with a fork. Place in a serving dish. Garnish with cilantro. Serve hot. Makes 4 servings.

Herb-Coated Radishes

For a change, cook radishes instead of using them raw as a relish or salad.

1 large bunch radishes, trimmed
1 tablespoon butter
1/8 teaspoon dried leaf thyme

1/8 teaspoon dried leaf basil
1/8 teaspoon fennel seed
Dash white pepper

Place radishes in a small saucepan. Cover with salted water. Simmer over low heat, covered, until tender, 10 to 12 minutes. Drain well. Add butter, thyme, basil, fennel seed and white pepper. Stir over medium heat until radishes are well coated. Serve immediately. Makes 3 servings.

Carrots Grand Marnier

Tangy orange marmalade flavors this quick and easy carrot dish.

1 lb. carrots, sliced diagonally,
  1 (1-lb.) pkg. frozen carrot slices,
   thawed, or 1 (1-lb.) can sliced carrots
2 tablespoons butter

1-1/2 tablespoons orange marmalade
Pinch of ground nutmeg
1 tablespoon Grand Marnier or
  other orange-flavored liqueur

In a large skillet, bring salted water to a boil. Add carrots to boiling water and cook over medium heat until tender, about 10 minutes. Drain well. Add butter, marmalade and nutmeg to carrots. Sauté over medium-high heat, stirring, until carrots are glazed. Pour liqueur over carrots. Heat until liqueur is warm, 150F (65C). Using a long match, carefully ignite liqueur. When flame diminishes, serve. Makes 4 servings.

Brandied Orange Carrots   Photo on pages 148 and 149.

Honey and orange juice give a sweet shiny glaze to whole baby carrots.

1 bunch baby carrots, trimmed,
  1 (12-oz.) pkg. frozen baby carrots,
   thawed, or 3 medium carrots,
   sliced diagonally

2 tablespoons thawed frozen orange-juice
  concentrate
1-1/2 teaspoons honey
1 tablespoon brandy or Cognac

Cook carrots in a medium saucepan of boiling salted water over medium-high heat. Cook until tender when pierced with a fork, 7 to 10 minutes. Drain well. Add orange-juice concentrate, honey and brandy or Cognac. Sauté over medium-high heat until carrots are glazed and lightly browned, 2 to 3 minutes. Garnish as desired. Serve immediately. Makes 2 to 3 servings.

Orange-Glazed Beets   Photo on pages 148 and 149.

Fresh gingerroot sparks this tangy sauce for beets.

1 bunch beets (about 1-1/4 lbs.)
3/4 cup orange juice
2 teaspoons grated orange peel
2 teaspoons sugar
1 teaspoon grated gingerroot or
  1/2 teaspoon ground ginger

1-1/2 teaspoons cornstarch
1/8 teaspoon salt
1/8 teaspoon freshly ground pepper
1 tablespoon butter

Cut beet greens 1/4 inch from beet. Do not remove beet tap root. Place beets in a medium saucepan. Cover with water. Bring to a boil. Reduce heat and cover. Simmer 30 to 40 minutes or until tender. Place beets in a colander and cool under cold running water. Remove beet tops and slip off beet skins. Slice beets thinly or julienne. In a small bowl, combine orange juice, 1 teaspoon orange peel, sugar, ginger, cornstarch, salt and pepper. Melt butter in a medium skillet over medium heat. Add beets and orange-juice mixture. Stir over medium heat until sauce boils and thickens. Pour into serving dish. Garnish with remaining orange peel. Serve immediately. Makes 4 servings.

Crookneck Squash Mediterranean-Style

A choice way to serve crookneck squash or cauliflower is with Italian sausage and vegetable sauce.

2 mild Italian sausages,
   casings removed, crumbled
1 tablespoon olive oil
1 large onion, finely chopped
2 medium carrots, shredded
1 small celery stalk, finely chopped
1 garlic clove, minced

1 tablespoon tomato paste
2 tablespoons white wine
1 teaspoon chopped fresh basil or
   1/4 teaspoon dried leaf basil
6 crookneck or straightneck yellow squash,
   ends trimmed

In a large skillet, brown crumbled sausages over medium heat. Add oil, onion, carrots, celery and garlic. Cook until soft and glazed, 5 to 10 minutes, stirring occasionally. Add tomato paste, wine and basil; set aside. Cut squash lengthwise. In a 2-quart saucepan, bring a small amount of salted water to a boil. Add squash halves to boiling water and cook over medium heat until crisp-tender, 8 to 10 minutes. Drain well. Add squash to sausage mixture. Bring to a boil and heat through. Serve immediately. Makes 6 servings.

Variation

Substitute 1 large head cauliflower for crookneck or straightneck squash. Break cauliflower into flowerets.

Mexican Corn & Squash   Photo on pages 148 and 149.

A flamboyant Mexican dish to enliven a barbecued chicken or roast pork dinner.

3 tablespoons butter
1 medium onion, finely chopped
2 medium zucchini, ends trimmed,
   sliced 3/8-inch thick
2 crookneck squash, ends trimmed,
   sliced 3/8-inch thick
1 small red or green bell pepper,
   seeded, diced
1/3 cup water

3 ears yellow sweet corn, husked,
   1 (10-oz.) pkg. frozen whole-kernel corn,
   or 1 (15-oz.) can whole-kernel corn,
   drained
1 large tomato, peeled, diced
1/4 teaspoon salt
1/4 teaspoon freshly ground pepper
2 tablespoons minced fresh parsley

Melt butter in a large skillet over medium heat. Add onion, zucchini, crookneck squash and bell pepper. Sauté until glazed, 4 to 5 minutes. Add water. Cover and reduce heat. Simmer 5 minutes. If using fresh sweet corn, cut kernels from corn cob using a sharp knife. Stir corn into squash mixture. Add tomato, salt and pepper. Cook until vegetables are tender, about 3 minutes. Sprinkle with parsley. Serve immediately. Makes 6 servings.

Shown on the preceding pages: Limas & Onions in Sour Cream, page 144; Brandied Orange Carrots, page 147; Sugar Snaps Voilà, page 142; Mexican Corn & Squash, page 150; Orange-Glazed Beets, page 147; Green-Onion & Parmesan Loaf, page 174.

Zucchini with Quick Pesto Sauce

This quick-to-make basil sauce is an ideal topping for zucchini or crookneck squash.

Quick Pesto Sauce, see below
4 small zucchini, ends trimmed,
   thinly sliced diagonally
1 tablespoon butter

1/4 teaspoon salt
1/4 teaspoon freshly ground pepper
8 cherry tomatoes, halved

Quick Pesto Sauce:
1/4 cup chopped fresh basil
2 tablespoons chopped fresh parsley
1 tablespoon olive oil
2 tablespoons freshly grated Parmesan or
   Romano cheese

1 garlic clove, minced
1 tablespoon pine nuts or
   toasted chopped walnuts

Prepare Quick Pesto Sauce. In a 2-quart saucepan, bring salted water to a boil. Add zucchini to boiling water and cook until crisp-tender, about 5 minutes. Drain well. Add butter. Sauté to coat zucchini lightly. Add salt and pepper. Spoon zucchini onto a serving platter. Place cherry tomatoes in saucepan. Heat through, about 30 seconds. Place tomatoes in a circle around zucchini. Spoon Quick Pesto Sauce over zucchini. Serve immediately. Makes 4 servings.

Quick Pesto Sauce:
Place all ingredients in a blender or food processor fitted with a steel blade. Process until minced.

Parmesan-Coated Zucchini

Italians finish zucchini with a crusty cheese topping.

3 tablespoons olive oil
6 small zucchini, ends trimmed,
   thinly sliced
1/4 teaspoon salt
1/4 teaspoon freshly ground pepper
2 teaspoons finely chopped fresh basil or
   1/2 teaspoon dried leaf basil

1 garlic clove, finely minced
2 tablespoons chopped fresh parsley
1/3 cup freshly grated Parmesan or
   Romano cheese (1-1/2 oz.)

Heat 2 tablespoons oil in a large skillet over low heat. Add zucchini, salt, pepper, basil, garlic and parsley. Cover. Simmer 3 to 5 minutes or until zucchini are crisp-tender. Place zucchini mixture on an ovenproof serving platter. Sprinkle with cheese. Drizzle remaining oil over zucchini. Place under broiler. Broil until cheese is melted and slightly browned, about 2 minutes. Serve immediately. Makes 6 servings.

Pattypan with Cheese & Chilies

This Mexican dish goes well with barbecued chicken or grilled sausages.

4 pattypan or scalloped squash,
 peeled, sliced 1/2-inch thick
1 small onion, chopped
2 garlic cloves, minced
2 medium tomatoes, peeled, chopped
2 green chili peppers, seeded, diced

1/4 teaspoon ground coriander
1/4 teaspoon salt
1 tablespoon butter
1/4 lb. teleme or Monterey Jack cheese,
 cut in strips
4 to 5 sprigs cilantro

Butter a 1-1/2-quart baking dish. In a medium saucepan, combine squash, onion, garlic, tomatoes, peppers, coriander and salt. Cook over low heat, covered, until tender, 10 minutes. Add butter. Stir to coat vegetables. Place vegetables in buttered baking dish. Top with cheese strips. Place under broiler. Broil until cheese is slightly melted, about 2 minutes. Garnish with cilantro sprigs. Serve immediately. Makes 6 servings.

Chayote Mexicana

Pronounced chy-OH-tay, this pear-shaped gourd goes by several names.

2 chayote (about 1 lb.), peeled
1 tablespoon butter
1/4 teaspoon ground cumin

1/4 teaspoon chili powder
1/4 teaspoon dried leaf oregano
Dash seasoned pepper

Slice or dice chayote, cutting through the flat inner seed. The seed is edible and has a nut-like flavor after cooking. In a 2-quart saucepan, bring salted water to a boil. Add chayote to boiling water and cook over low heat until tender, about 15 minutes. Drain well. Add butter, cumin, chili powder, oregano and pepper. Stir over medium heat until chayote is glazed with seasonings, 2 minutes. Serve immediately. Makes 4 servings.

Jerusalem Artichokes & Celery au Gratin

These artichokes may be called sunchokes in your local markets.

1/2 lb. Jerusalem artichokes,
 whole, scrubbed, unpeeled
4 inner celery stalks,
 thinly sliced diagonally
1 tablespoon butter

1/8 teaspoon white pepper
1/4 cup toasted chopped pecans or walnuts
1/4 cup crumbled Danish blue castello
 cheese or other blue cheese (1 oz.)

Butter a 1-quart baking dish. In a 2-quart saucepan, bring salted water to a boil. Add Jerusalem artichokes to boiling water and cook over medium heat until tender, about 15 minutes. Remove Jerusalem artichokes with a slotted spoon. Cool slightly. Peel Jerusalem artichokes and slice thinly. Add celery to saucepan of boiling water. Simmer, covered, until crisp-tender, about 5 minutes. Drain well. Combine Jerusalem artichokes, celery and butter in saucepan. Sauté until butter melts and vegetables are lightly glazed. Add white pepper. Place in buttered baking dish. Sprinkle with nuts and blue cheese. Place under broiler. Broil until cheese is slightly melted, about 2 minutes. Serve immediately. Makes 4 servings.

1/Scoop out eggplant pulp, leaving a 3/4-inch shell.

2/Spoon vegetable mixture into eggplant. Top with eggplant lid.

Yaya's Stuffed Eggplant

The Greek way of stuffing eggplant shows off its natural beauty.

3 tablespoons olive oil
1 large onion, finely chopped
1 carrot, finely chopped
1 celery stalk, chopped
1/2 cup chopped fresh parsley
3 tomatoes, peeled, chopped
6 fresh mint leaves
2 garlic cloves, minced

1 teaspoon salt
Freshly ground pepper to taste
2 teaspoons chopped fresh basil or
   1/2 teaspoon dried leaf basil
1 large eggplant
Salt
2 tablespoons uncooked
   long-grain white rice

Heat oil in a large skillet over medium heat. Add onion. Sauté until lightly browned, 4 to 5 minutes. Add carrot, celery, parsley, tomatoes, mint, garlic, 1 teaspoon salt, pepper and basil. Cover and reduce heat. Simmer until carrot and celery are tender, about 25 minutes. While vegetables cook, slice off stem-end of eggplant to make a lid. With a spoon, scoop out eggplant pulp, leaving a 3/4-inch-thick shell. Sprinkle inside of eggplant shell lightly with salt. Let stand 15 minutes. Salt draws out bitter juices from eggplant. Chop eggplant pulp into cubes. Add to vegetables. Simmer vegetable mixture 15 minutes. Stir in rice. Preheat oven to 350F (175C). Rinse salted eggplant. Drain well. Spoon vegetable mixture into eggplant. Replace eggplant lid and secure with wooden picks. Place eggplant on its side in a large baking dish or roasting pan. Pour in 1/2 cup water. Cover and bake until eggplant is tender, about 1 hour. Slice. Serve immediately. Makes 6 to 8 servings.

Variation
Brown 1 pound ground lamb, pork or turkey with the onion.

Layered Eggplant Slices

For a choice vegetarian entree, stack 4 vegetables atop eggplant.

1 medium eggplant,
    cut in 1/2-inch slices crosswise
Salt
1 tablespoon olive oil or butter
2 medium onions, thinly sliced
1 tablespoon olive oil
1/2 cup plain yogurt or
    dairy sour cream

2 medium tomatoes, thinly sliced
1/4 teaspoon ground allspice
1/4 teaspoon ground coriander
1/2 red or green bell pepper, seeded,
    cut in thin strips
8 mushrooms, sliced
1-1/2 cups shredded Jarlsberg or
    Monterey Jack cheese (6 oz.)

Sprinkle eggplant lightly with salt. Let stand 15 minutes. Salt draws out bitter juices from eggplant. Rinse under cold water. Pat dry with paper towel. Heat 1 tablespoon oil or butter in a large skillet over medium-high heat. Add onions. Sauté until soft but not browned, 2 to 3 minutes. Arrange eggplant slices in a 15" x 10" baking pan. Brush eggplant slices with 1 tablespoon oil. Place under broiler. Broil 5 minutes. Preheat oven to 350F (175C). Spoon onions over eggplant slices. Top each slice with a dollop of yogurt or sour cream. Arrange tomato slices over eggplant. Sprinkle with allspice and coriander. Bake 30 minutes. Sprinkle with bell pepper, mushrooms and cheese. Bake 10 minutes or until cheese melts. Serve immediately. Makes 6 servings.

Southern Okra & Corn Stew

Here is an old Southern dish, especially good with fried chicken or pork chops.

2 tablespoons butter
1 large onion, finely chopped
1 garlic clove, chopped
1 green bell pepper, seeded, chopped
2 cups canned tomatoes, drained, or
    5 fresh tomatoes, peeled
8 small okra, trimmed, thinly sliced

2 cups fresh kernel corn,
    1 (10-oz.) pkg. frozen whole-kernel
    corn, thawed, or 1 (15-oz.) can
    whole-kernel corn, drained
1/4 teaspoon salt
1/4 teaspoon freshly ground pepper

Melt butter in a large skillet over medium heat. Add onion and garlic. Sauté until glazed and slightly soft, 2 to 3 minutes. Add bell pepper and tomatoes. Reduce heat and simmer 15 minutes. Add okra and simmer 5 minutes. Add corn, salt and pepper. Simmer until heated through, about 2 minutes. Serve immediately. Makes 6 servings.

Indian Eggplant

A tantalizing blend of colors, flavors and temperatures.

Gingered Tomato Sauce, see below
1 large eggplant,
   cut in 1-inch slices crosswise
Salt

1 to 2 tablespoons olive oil
1 cup plain yogurt
1 tablespoon minced chives or
   fresh parsley

Gingered Tomato Sauce:
2 tablespoons butter
1 medium onion, finely chopped
1/3 cup tomato paste
1/2 lb. pear-shaped tomatoes, peeled,
   chopped, or 1 (12-oz.) can
   Italian tomatoes

1 teaspoon grated gingerroot or
   1/4 teaspoon ground ginger
Salt and freshly ground pepper to taste

Prepare Gingered Tomato Sauce. Sprinkle eggplant lightly with salt. Let stand 15 minutes. Salt draws out bitter juices from eggplant. Rinse under cold water. Pat dry with paper towel. Preheat oven to 425F (220C). Pour a thin film of oil in a 15"x 10" baking pan. Turn eggplant slices in oil, coating both sides. Arrange slices in a single layer. Bake 30 minutes or until tender. Arrange eggplant on a serving platter. Top with Gingered Tomato Sauce. In a small bowl, combine yogurt and chives or parsley. Top each serving with a dollop of yogurt mixture. Serve immediately. Makes 4 to 6 servings.

Gingered Tomato Sauce:
Melt butter in a large skillet over medium heat. Add onion. Sauté until lightly browned, 4 to 5 minutes. Add tomato paste, tomatoes and ginger. Cover and reduce heat. Simmer 20 minutes. Process tomato mixture in a blender or food processor fitted with a steel blade until smooth. Season with salt and pepper. Set aside until ready to use.

Brussels Sprouts Véronique

Nutmeg gives an added flavor to this member of the cabbage family.

1 lb. Brussels sprouts
1 tablespoon butter
2 tablespoons whipping cream
1/4 teaspoon salt

1/4 teaspoon ground nutmeg
1 cup seedless red or green grapes,
   whole or halved

In a 2-quart saucepan, bring salted water to a boil. Add Brussels sprouts and cook over medium heat until tender, 5 to 7 minutes. Drain well. Melt butter in a large skillet over medium heat. Add Brussels sprouts. Sauté to coat Brussels sprouts lightly. Add cream, salt, nutmeg and grapes. Boil pan juices, shaking pan slightly, until juices are reduced to 1 tablespoon and grapes are heated through. Serve immediately. Makes 4 servings.

When preparing Brussels sprouts, make a shallow cut in the bottom of the stem so that they will cook evenly and quickly.

Butter-Glazed Vegetables   Photo on cover.

A quick way to prepare a colorful array of vegetables that will delight anyone.

1/4 cup dairy sour cream or plain yogurt
2 teaspoons minced chives
2 medium zucchini, ends trimmed,
   cut in 3-inch strips
2 medium crookneck squash, ends trimmed,
   cut in 1/4-inch slices
2 medium ears of corn, cut in 2-inch pieces
1 cup broccoli flowerets

1/4 cup water
3 tablespoons butter
12 tomato wedges
1/4 teaspoon salt
1/4 teaspoon freshly ground pepper
1/4 cup freshly grated Parmesan cheese
   (3/4 oz.)

In a small bowl, combine sour cream or yogurt and chives; set aside. Place zucchini, crookneck squash, corn and broccoli in a large skillet. Add water and 2 tablespoons butter. Cover and bring to a boil over medium heat. Reduce heat and simmer 4 to 5 minutes. Add 1 tablespoon butter, cherry tomatoes, salt and pepper. Cook, covered, 1 minute or until vegetables are crisp-tender, shaking pan occasionally. Serve with sour cream or yogurt mixture and cheese. Makes 4 servings.

Variation

Substitute 1 cup cauliflowerets for crookneck squash and 2 small carrots, thinly sliced diagonally, for corn. Replace tomatoes with 12 trimmed Chinese pea pods and 1/4 lb. mushrooms.

Summer Vegetable Platter

Chilled carrots and broccoli make a flavorful summer combination.

1 medium bunch broccoli
1 tablespoon olive oil
3 garlic cloves, minced
1/2 teaspoon freshly ground pepper
6 large carrots, sliced diagonally

2 teaspoons olive oil
1-1/2 teaspoons red-wine vinegar or
   raspberry vinegar
1 teaspoon brown sugar
1 lemon, cut in wedges

Peel broccoli stalks. Separate broccoli into long flowerets. In a 3-quart saucepan bring salted water to a boil. Add broccoli flowerets to boiling water and cook over medium-high heat until crisp-tender, about 7 minutes. Drain flowerets in a colander. Refresh under cold water. Place flowerets in a medium bowl. In a small skillet, heat 1 tablespoon olive oil over medium heat. Add garlic and sauté until lightly browned, 4 to 5 minutes. Spoon oil and garlic over flowerets. Sprinkle with 1/4 teaspoon pepper. Cover broccoli and refrigerate. In a 2-quart saucepan, bring salted water to a boil. Add carrots to boiling water and cook covered over medium heat until crisp-tender, about 7 minutes. Drain well. Add 2 teaspoons olive oil, vinegar and sugar to carrots. Cook over medium heat, stirring occasionally, until sugar dissolves and carrots are glazed. Place carrots in a medium bowl. Sprinkle with 1/4 teaspoon pepper. Cover and refrigerate. To serve, arrange chilled broccoli spears on a large platter in a fan-shape. Place carrots at the base of the fan. Garnish with lemon wedges. Makes 6 servings.

Peperonata

Sautéed bell peppers make a colorful accompaniment to barbecued meats or Mexican dishes.

3 tablespoons olive oil
1 medium onion, chopped
2 red bell peppers, seeded,
   cut in strips
2 green bell peppers, seeded,
   cut in strips
2 garlic cloves, minced

2 tomatoes, peeled, cut in thin wedges
1/4 teaspoon salt
1/4 teaspoon freshly ground pepper
2 teaspoons chopped fresh basil or
   cilantro
1 tablespoon chopped fresh parsley

Heat oil in a large skillet over medium heat. Add onion. Sauté until lightly browned, 4 to 5 minutes. Add bell peppers. Sauté until peppers are limp. Add garlic, tomatoes, salt, pepper and basil or cilantro. Heat through. Sprinkle with parsley. Serve immediately. Makes 4 servings.

Vegetables à la Grecque

Aromatic herbs season a pretty array of cooked vegetables.

2-1/2 cups water
1/4 cup dry vermouth
3 tablespoons lemon juice
3 tablespoons olive oil
1 shallot or green onion, chopped
3/4 teaspoon salt
6 black peppercorns

1/4 teaspoon dried leaf thyme
3 sprigs parsley
2 lbs. assorted vegetables: mushrooms,
   green beans, carrots, zucchini,
   crookneck squash, leeks
1/4 cup minced fresh parsley

In a large saucepan, combine water, vermouth, lemon juice, oil, shallot or green onion, salt, peppercorns, thyme and parsley sprigs. Cover. Simmer over medium-low heat 10 minutes to blend seasonings. Prepare vegetables. If small, leave mushrooms whole. If large, cut mushrooms in half. Trim green beans. If small, leave beans whole. If large, split beans lengthwise. Cut carrots lengthwise. Trim ends from zucchini and crookneck squash. Cut zucchini and crookneck in quarters. Trim ends and tough outer leaves from leeks. Cut leeks lengthwise. Wash under cold running water, pulling layers apart so grit is removed. Simmer prepared vegetables separately in vermouth mixture. Simmer mushrooms 5 minutes, green beans 5 to 7 minutes, carrots 8 to 10 minutes, zucchini and crookneck 5 to 7 minutes and leeks 10 minutes. Vegetables should each be cooked until crisp-tender. Using a slotted spoon, place vegetables in a serving dish. Rapidly boil pan juices until reduced to 2/3 cup. Ladle juices over vegetables. Sprinkle with parsley. Serve hot, cold or at room temperature. Makes 8 servings.

 Cook the light-colored vegetables first. This prevents the cooking broth from becoming discolored and coloring those light vegetables.

Ratatouille

Accompany this Provençal vegetable stew with grilled Italian sausage, French bread and fruit.

1 large eggplant
Salt
6 tablespoons olive oil
2 large onions, coarsely chopped
4 garlic cloves, minced
4 medium zucchini, ends trimmed,
   thinly sliced
1 red or green bell pepper, seeded,
   cut in 1-inch squares

3 large tomatoes, peeled, diced
3/4 teaspoon salt
1/2 teaspoon freshly ground pepper
1 tablespoon chopped fresh basil or
   3/4 teaspoon dried leaf basil
1/4 cup minced fresh parsley

Cut eggplant lengthwise. Cut in 1-1/2-inch cubes. Place eggplant pieces in a colander. Sprinkle lightly with salt. Let stand 15 minutes. Salt draws out bitter juices from eggplant. Rinse under cold water. Pat dry with paper towel. Preheat oven to 350F (175C). Heat 3 tablespoons oil in a large skillet. Add onions. Sauté until soft, 2 to 3 minutes. Add garlic, zucchini and red or green pepper. Sauté until glazed, 2 to 3 minutes. Place sautéed vegetables and eggplant in a 2-1/2-quart baking dish. Add tomatoes, 3/4 teaspoon salt, pepper and basil. Pour remaining oil over vegetables. Cover. Bake 1-1/2 to 2 hours or until vegetables are tender when pierced with a fork. While baking, baste vegetables 1 or 2 times with pan juices. Serve hot or cold sprinkled with parsley. Makes 8 servings.

Shredded Vegetable Trio

Serve 3 colorful vegetables as an eye-catching accompaniment for any meal.

3 medium carrots, shredded
3/4 teaspoon salt
3/8 teaspoon freshly ground pepper
1/4 teaspoon ground nutmeg
4-1/2 teaspoons butter
3 medium, yellow crookneck squash,
   ends trimmed, shredded

1/4 teaspoon dried leaf tarragon
3 medium zucchini, ends trimmed, shredded
1 teaspoon chopped fresh basil or
   1/4 teaspoon dried leaf basil

In a 1-quart saucepan, bring salted water to a boil. Add carrots, 1/4 teaspoon salt, 1/8 teaspoon pepper and nutmeg to boiling water. Cook over medium heat until crisp-tender, 3 to 4 minutes. Drain well. Stir in 1-1/2 teaspoons butter. In a 1-quart saucepan, bring salted water to a boil. Add crookneck squash, 1/4 teaspoon salt, 1/8 teaspoon pepper and tarragon to boiling water. Cook over medium heat until crisp-tender, 2 to 3 minutes. Drain well. Stir in 1-1/2 teaspoons butter. In a 1-quart saucepan, bring salted water to a boil. Add zucchini, 1/4 teaspoon salt, 1/8 teaspoon pepper and basil to boiling water. Cook over medium heat until crisp-tender, 2 to 3 minutes. Drain well. Stir in 1-1/2 teaspoons butter. Spoon a trio of vegetables on each plate. Serve immediately. Makes 6 servings.

Vegetable Garden Stew

The Greeks turn summer's garden bounty into a savory stew.

2 tablespoons olive oil
1 large red or yellow onion, chopped
2 garlic cloves, minced
3 tablespoons tomato paste
1-1/4 cups chicken broth
2 carrots, cut in 1-inch pieces
2 potatoes, peeled,
   cut in 1/2-inch strips
3/4 lb. green beans,
   cut in 1-1/2-inch pieces

2 zucchini, ends trimmed,
   cut in 3/4-inch slices
2 yellow crookneck squash, ends trimmed,
   cut in 3/4-inch slices
1/2 teaspoon freshly ground pepper
2 tablespoons chopped fresh parsley
2 to 3 tablespoons freshly grated Parmesan
   or Romano cheese

Heat oil in a large pot over medium-high heat. Add onion. Sauté until lightly browned, 4 to 5 minutes. Add garlic, tomato paste, broth, carrots and potatoes. Cover and reduce heat. Simmer 10 minutes. Add green beans, zucchini and crookneck squash. Simmer until squash is crisp-tender, about 5 minutes. Sprinkle with pepper and parsley. Ladle stew into bowls. Sprinkle with cheese. Serve immediately. Makes 4 to 5 servings.

Artichokes Constantinople

A dill-flavored vinaigrette flavors this vegetable medley as it simmers.

2 (9-oz.) pkgs. frozen artichoke hearts,
   thawed, or 1-1/2 lbs.
   fresh baby artichokes or
   artichoke hearts, page 40
6 medium carrots, cut in 1-1/2-inch pieces
2 large potatoes, scrubbed, unpeeled,
   cut in 1-inch cubes
2 bunches green onions,
   cut in 1-1/2-inch pieces

1/2 cup olive oil
1/3 cup lemon juice
1 cup water
1/2 teaspoon salt
1/4 teaspoon freshly ground pepper
2 teaspoons chopped fresh dill or
   1/2 teaspoon dried dill weed

If using fresh artichokes, pull off lower outer leaves. Trim stem ends. Cut each artichoke in half. Using the tip of a peeler or paring knife, scrape or scoop out the fuzzy choke center. In a large saucepan, combine artichokes, carrots, potatoes, green onions, oil, 1/3 cup lemon juice, water, salt, pepper and dill. Cover. Simmer over medium-low heat until vegetables are tender, about 25 minutes. Place vegetables in a serving dish. Cook pan juices over medium-high heat until reduced to a sauce. Spoon sauce over vegetables. Serve immediately. Makes 8 servings.

 To prevent prepared artichokes from discoloring, soak in a lemon-juice bath. In a medium bowl, combine 3 tablespoons lemon juice, 2 tablespoons all-purpose flour and 2 to 3 cups water. Add prepared artichokes and let stand until ready to use. Drain well before using.

Turkish Skewered Vegetables

Crisp broiled vegetables in the Turkish manner make an ideal side dish to barbecued meats.

1/4 cup olive oil
2 tablespoons lemon juice
1/4 teaspoon salt
1/4 teaspoon freshly ground pepper
1 small eggplant,
   cut in 12 (1-inch) pieces

1 large green bell pepper, seeded,
   cut in 1-1/4-inch pieces
12 large cherry tomatoes
12 small boiling onions, cooked, or
   1 (15-oz.) can whole onions
12 large mushrooms, stems removed

In a large bowl, combine oil, lemon juice, salt and pepper. Add eggplant, bell pepper, tomatoes, onions and mushrooms. Mix well. Let stand at least 1 hour, turning vegetables occasionally. Drain vegetables. Thread vegetables alternately on 8-inch skewers. Broil or grill 3 to 4 minutes, turning to brown evenly. Brush vegetables with marinade 2 to 3 times during cooking. Serve immediately. Makes 6 servings.

Grilled Sweet Corn with Garlic Butter

When the barbecue is going, tuck ears of sweet corn on the grill.

Garlic Butter, see below

6 ears yellow or white sweet corn

Garlic Butter:
6 tablespoons butter, room temperature
1 to 2 garlic cloves, minced
1/8 teaspoon salt

1 tablespoon chopped fresh parsley or
   chives

Prepare Garlic Butter. Pull husks away from corn but do not tear off. Remove silk and replace husks. If necessary, tie husks in place. Soak corn in a pan or pail of cold water 20 minutes. Drain well. Place on preheated barbecue grill. Cook, turning occasionally until husks are charred and corn is cooked through, 15 to 20 minutes. Serve with Garlic Butter. Makes 6 servings.

Garlic Butter:
In a small bowl, combine butter, garlic, salt and parsley or chives. Mix well. Refrigerate until ready to use.

Turkish Skewered Vegetables and Grilled Sweet Corn with Garlic Butte

Steamed Artichokes with Dipping Sauces

Whole artichokes are a beautiful vegetable to serve hot or cold with your favorite sauce.

4 large artichokes
1 tablespoon olive oil
2 garlic cloves, minced
Dipping Sauces:
   Pistachio Mayonnaise, see below
   Mustard Mayonnaise, see below
   Tarragon-Vinaigrette, page 66
   Provençal Mayonnaise, page 35

Pistachio Mayonnaise:

1 egg
1-1/2 tablespoons lemon juice
1-1/2 tablespoons white-wine vinegar
1/2 teaspoon salt
1/2 teaspoon dry mustard

7/8 cup safflower oil
1 garlic clove, minced
1/2 teaspoon dried leaf tarragon
1 tablespoon chopped fresh parsley
1/4 cup chopped pistachio nuts

Mustard Mayonnaise:

1/4 cup mayonnaise
3 tablespoons sour cream
1 tablespoon lemon juice

1/4 teaspoon dried leaf tarragon
1/2 teaspoon Dijon-style mustard

Prepare choice of dipping sauces. Cut off artichoke stems. Remove and discard hard outer leaves of artichokes. Cut sharp tips off remaining leaves with scissors. Place artichokes upright in a steamer. Drizzle olive oil over artichokes. Sprinkle garlic over artichokes. Steam over medium-low heat 45 to 50 minutes or until tender. Serve hot or cover and refrigerate until ready to serve.

Pistachio Mayonnaise:

In a blender or food processor fitted with a steel blade, place egg, lemon juice, vinegar, salt and dry mustard. Process until smooth. With motor running, gradually pour in oil in a slow, steady stream, blending to a smooth sauce. Add garlic, tarragon, parsley and nuts. Process until minced. Turn into a small bowl and cover. Refrigerate until ready to serve. Makes about 1-1/2 cups.

Mustard Mayonnaise:

In a small bowl, combine mayonnaise, sour cream, lemon juice, tarragon and mustard. Mix well. Cover and refrigerate until ready to serve. Makes 1/2 cup.

Green Rice

Spinach and leeks give a distinct flavor and color to this rice side dish for seafood.

1 bunch leeks, 2 large or 3 small
2 (1-lb.) bunches spinach
1/4 cup olive oil
1 medium onion, finely chopped
3/4 cup uncooked long-grain white rice

1 garlic clove, minced
1-1/2 cups chicken broth
1/4 teaspoon salt
1/4 teaspoon freshly ground pepper
1 lemon, cut in wedges

Trim ends and tough outer leaves from leeks. Quarter lengthwise, cutting almost to the root. Wash under cold running water, pulling layers apart so grit is removed. Finely chop leeks. Wash spinach thoroughly in several changes of cold water. Discard stems and bruised or tough leaves. Drain well. Chop washed spinach. Heat oil in a large saucepan over medium heat. Add leeks and onion. Sauté until soft but not browned, 2 to 3 minutes. Add spinach, rice, garlic, broth, salt and pepper. Cover and reduce heat. Simmer until rice is tender and broth is absorbed, about 20 minutes. Serve hot with lemon wedges. Makes 6 servings.

Mushroom Risotto

Fresh shiitake mushrooms give a wonderful meaty flavor to this Italian risotto or braised rice.

3 tablespoons butter
1/4 cup chopped onion
1 cup uncooked long-grain white rice
1/2 teaspoon salt
1/3 cup dry white wine
2 cups hot chicken broth

1/2 cup sliced or
  chopped shiitake mushrooms or
  fresh mushrooms
1/3 cup freshly grated Parmesan cheese
  (1 oz.)

Melt 2 tablespoons butter in a large saucepan over medium-high heat. Add onion. Sauté until glazed, 2 to 3 minutes. Add rice and salt. Toss with a fork 2 to 3 minutes until rice is glazed. Add wine. Cook, stirring constantly, until wine has evaporated. Add in 3/4 cup broth or enough to cover rice. Stir until broth has been absorbed. Continue stirring in broth a little at a time, until rice is tender but firm to the bite, 15 to 20 minutes. Melt 1 tablespoon butter in a small skillet over medium heat. Add mushrooms. Sauté until glazed. Stir mushrooms and cheese into rice. Fluff rice with a fork. Serve immediately. Makes 4 servings.

Freshly grated Parmesan or Romano cheese melts more smoothly into a hot dish than packaged grated cheese.

SAUCES & RELISHES

The trademark of an inspired cook is a creative sauce or a zestful relish or pickle which adds that special touch to a dish. Sauces may be simple combinations of textures and colors such as Mexican Salsa, a blending of chopped tomatoes and onions seasoned with peppers to serve with your favorite Mexican dish. They can also be rich and elegant like the subtly flavored Swiss Buttered Herb Sauce or pungent Greek Garlic Mayonnaise.

For those with limited time, try the quick Pesto Sauce, easily made in a blender or food processor. Flavored with fresh basil, it lends a delicious touch to countless dishes.

During peak tomato season, plan to make and freeze several batches of Cooked Tomato Sauce, perfect to serve with zucchini or your favorite pasta. An old favorite to serve with hamburgers hot off the barbecue is Chili Sauce seasoned with a variety of herbs and spices. Pints of relishes and sauces make perfect offerings for the holiday season or thoughtful hostess gifts through the year.

Zucchini is a favorite for cooking and preserving. Try it in Zucchini Bread & Butter Pickles. For a relish with flair, try Gingered Cherry Preserves. Little cherry tomatoes are preserved in a spicy sauce, perfect to serve with meats.

For a novel touch, try Fried Parsley. Fresh parsley is easily fried in hot oil until crisp; then use as a garnish to any dish.

This year, capture both beauty and bounty of vegetables in a variety of sauces and preserves to enjoy all year long.

Dinner for 6

Baked Salmon with
Greek Garlic Mayonnaise, page 166
Potatoes Anna, page 135
Steamed Asparagus Spears with
Hollandaise, page 165
Continental Salad, page 64
Fresh Berries & Ice Cream

Swiss Buttered Herb Sauce

A Swiss cafe uses this sauce on baked potatoes, grilled steak, salmon or lamb.

1/2 cup butter
1 tablespoon Dijon-style mustard
1 tablespoon lemon juice
2 tablespoons chopped capers
2 anchovy fillets, chopped

3/4 cup minced fresh parsley
3 shallots or green onions, chopped
2 garlic cloves, minced
1 tablespoon chopped chives

In a small saucepan, combine butter, mustard, lemon juice and capers. Stir over medium heat until butter is melted. Add anchovies, parsley, shallots or green onions, garlic and chives. Heat through. Serve hot over vegetables or meats. Makes 1 cup.

Béarnaise Sauce

A choice companion to Italian green beans, asparagus or artichokes.

1/4 cup white-wine vinegar
2 tablespoons dry vermouth
1 green onion, chopped
1/2 teaspoon dried leaf tarragon

1 to 2 sprigs parsley
1 to 1-1/4 cups butter
4 egg yolks
1 teaspoon Dijon-style mustard

In a small saucepan, combine vinegar, vermouth, green onion, tarragon and parsley. Bring to a boil over medium heat. Boil until reduced to 2 tablespoons. Strain, discarding herbs. In a small saucepan, melt butter over low heat until bubbly. Rinse a blender container with hot water. Drain well. In blender, combine egg yolks, strained vinegar mixture and mustard. Process 30 seconds. With blender running, slowly pour in melted butter in a thin steady stream. Keep back any watery residue at bottom of saucepan. Process until thickened, 30 seconds. Pour into a sauce bowl. Keep sauce warm by setting sauce bowl in a pan of warm water until ready to serve. Makes 1-3/4 cups.

Hollandaise Sauce

A rich golden sauce to serve with cooked asparagus, artichokes, broccoli or cauliflower.

1/2 cup butter
3 egg yolks
2 tablespoons lemon juice

1/2 teaspoon grated lemon peel
1/2 teaspoon Dijon-style mustard

In a small saucepan, melt butter over low heat until bubbly. Rinse a blender container with hot water. Drain well. In blender, combine egg yolks, lemon juice, lemon peel and mustard. Process 4 to 5 seconds. With blender running, slowly pour in melted butter in a thin steady stream. Keep back any watery residue at bottom of saucepan. Process until smooth, 30 seconds. Pour into a sauce bowl. Keep sauce warm by setting sauce bowl in a pan of warm water until ready to serve. Makes 1 cup.

To make sauce thicker, blend in an additional 2 or 3 tablespoons melted butter.

Greek Garlic Mayonnaise

This robust mayonnaise called Skordalia is great for dipping or as a sauce for cooked vegetables.

1 egg
3/4 teaspoon salt
1/4 teaspoon white pepper
3/4 teaspoon Dijon-style mustard
1-1/2 tablespoons lemon juice
1-1/2 tablespoons white-wine vinegar

3 garlic cloves, chopped
1/3 cup olive oil
About 2/3 cup safflower oil
1/3 cup lightly toasted pine nuts or
toasted blanched almonds

In a blender or food processor fitted with a steel blade, combine egg, salt, white pepper, mustard, lemon juice, vinegar and garlic. Process 30 seconds or until smooth. With blender running, slowly pour in olive oil in a thin steady stream. Then slowly pour in safflower oil. Add enough safflower oil to make a thick consistency. If sauce is too thin, add more safflower oil. Add pine nuts or almonds. Process 1 to 2 seconds or until coarsely chopped. Pour into a small sauce bowl. Cover and refrigerate. Makes 1-1/4 cups.

Aioli Sauce

A flavorful garlic sauce—great with artichokes, tomatoes, asparagus, broccoli and seafood.

1 egg
3 tablespoons white-wine vinegar
3/4 teaspoon salt
1-1/2 teaspoons Dijon-style mustard

4 or 5 garlic cloves, chopped
1/3 cup olive oil
About 2/3 cup safflower oil

In a blender or food processor fitted with a steel blade, combine egg, vinegar, salt, mustard and garlic. Process until smooth, 30 seconds. With blender running, slowly pour in olive oil in a thin steady stream. Then slowly pour in safflower oil. Add enough safflower oil to make a thick consistency. If sauce is too thin, add more safflower oil. Pour into a small sauce bowl. Cover and refrigerate. Makes 1-1/4 cups.

Crème Fraîche

Serve as a garnish to hot or cold cream soup.

1 cup pasteurized whipping cream

1/2 cup dairy sour cream

In a small stainless-steel saucepan, combine whipping cream and sour cream. Stir to blend. Over low heat, bring cream mixture to 85F (30C). Remove from heat. Cover. Let stand at room temperature 12 hours or overnight. Cream mixture will become very thick. Refrigerate. Will keep up to 10 days. Makes 1-1/2 cups.

 Ultra-pasteurized cream will not ferment and become thick. Be sure to select regular whipping cream.

How To Make Green-Tomato Relish

1/Sprinkle green-tomato mixture with 1/3 cup salt. Let stand 3 hours.

2/When filling jars, be sure to leave 1/2-inch headspace.

Green-Tomato Relish

A different way to use the last of the tomato harvest.

4 qts. chopped, cored green tomatoes
1 large head cabbage, shredded
4 medium, red bell peppers,
   seeded, chopped
1 large onion, chopped
1/3 cup salt

1-1/2 cups packed brown sugar
4-1/2 cups distilled white vinegar
2 tablespoons mustard seed
1 tablespoon celery seed
1 tablespoon prepared horseradish

In a large bowl, combine tomatoes, cabbage, peppers and onion. Sprinkle with salt. Mix well. Let stand 3 hours. Drain well. Place in a colander and rinse. Drain well, squeezing to remove excess moisture. In a large saucepan, combine sugar, vinegar, mustard seed, celery seed and horseradish. Bring to a boil. Remove from heat and let stand 15 minutes. Add vegetables. Return to heat and heat to boiling. Ladle boiling hot relish into hot sterilized jars, leaving 1/2-inch headspace. Use self-sealing lids. Adjust lids. Place jars on a rack in a large pot of boiling water. Water should cover jars 1 to 2 inches and have additional 2 inches for boiling space. Cover pot. Bring water to a boil. At sea level, boil 10 minutes. For every 1000 feet altitude, add 1 minute to boiling time. Makes 7 pints.

Cooked Tomato Sauce

A handy sauce for pasta or serving with zucchini or green beans.

2 tablespoons olive oil
1 small onion, finely chopped
2 cups chopped, peeled tomatoes
   (preferably Italian plum-style) or
   2 cups drained canned tomatoes
3 tablespoons tomato paste

2 garlic cloves, minced
1 tablespoon chopped fresh basil or
   3/4 teaspoon dried leaf basil
1/2 teaspoon brown sugar
1/2 teaspoon salt
1/4 teaspoon freshly ground pepper

Heat oil in a medium saucepan over medium heat. Add onion. Sauté until soft, but not browned, 2 to 3 minutes. Reduce heat. Add tomatoes, tomato paste, garlic, basil, sugar, salt and pepper. Simmer, uncovered, 40 minutes, stirring occasionally. For a thicker sauce, continue to cook over low heat until desired consistency is reached. Makes 1-1/2 cups.

Gingered Cherry Preserves

Serve this colorful preserve with roast lamb or pork.

1 qt. cherry tomatoes
1-1/2 cups sugar
1 lemon, thinly sliced
1 cinnamon stick, broken into pieces

1/2 cup distilled white vinegar
3 whole cloves
1/3 cup (3 oz.) minced candied ginger

In a large saucepan, combine all ingredients. Bring to a boil over medium heat. Cover and reduce heat. Simmer 10 minutes. Remove cover and simmer, stirring until thickened, 40 to 45 minutes. Ladle hot preserves into hot sterilized jars, leaving 1/2-inch head space. Use self-sealing lids. Adjust lids. Place jars on a rack in a large pot of boiling water. Water should cover jars 1 to 2 inches and have additional 2 inches for boiling space. Cover pot. Bring water to a boil. At sea level, boil 10 minutes. For every 1000 feet altitude, add 1 minute to boiling time. Makes 3 to 4 half-pints.

Pesto Sauce

A classic Italian herb sauce to serve in countless ways.

2 cups loosely packed fresh basil leaves,
   well rinsed
3 or 4 garlic cloves
1/2 teaspoon salt
1/2 teaspoon freshly ground pepper

1/2 cup olive oil
3 tablespoons pine nuts or
   toasted chopped walnuts
1/2 cup freshly grated Parmesan or
   Romano cheese (1-1/2 oz.)

In a blender or food processor fitted with a steel blade, combine basil, garlic, salt, pepper and oil. Process until finely minced. Add nuts and cheese. Process to mix in. Makes 2 cups.

Front to back: Gingered Cherry Preserves, page 168; Mexican Salsa, page 171; Dilly Beans, page 170; Zucchini Bread & Butter Pickles, page 170.

Dilly Beans   Photo on page 169.

Young slender beans are ideal for pickling.

1-1/2 cups water	3 garlic cloves, peeled
1 pint (2 cups) distilled white vinegar	1 small onion, sliced
1 teaspoon salt	2 lbs. small green beans, trimmed
3 tablespoons sugar	3 sprigs fresh dill or
1 hot red pepper	1/2 teaspoon dried dill weed
1 bay leaf	

In a medium saucepan, combine water, vinegar, salt, sugar, red pepper, bay leaf, garlic and onion. Bring to a boil over medium-high heat. Cover and reduce heat. Simmer 10 minutes. Pack beans upright in 3 hot sterilized jars. Insert a sprig of dill in each jar. If using dill weed, add to vinegar mixture. Add hot vinegar mixture to cover beans, leaving 1/2-inch headspace. Use self-sealing lids. Adjust lids. Place jars on a rack in a large pot of boiling water. Water should cover jars 1 to 2 inches and have additional 2 inches for boiling space. Cover pot. Bring water to a boil. At sea level, boil 10 minutes. For every 1000 feet altitude, add 1 minute to boiling time. Makes 3 pints.

Zucchini Bread & Butter Pickles   Photo on page 169.

An abundant crop of zucchini makes crunchy pickles.

1 pint (2 cups) distilled white vinegar	1 teaspoon dill seed
1 cup sugar	1/2 teaspoon dry mustard
1-1/2 tablespoons salt	2 qts. sliced zucchini
1 teaspoon celery seed	2 cups thinly sliced onions

In a 4-1/2-quart saucepan, combine vinegar, sugar, salt, celery seed, dill seed and mustard. Bring to a boil over medium-high heat. In a large heatproof bowl, combine zucchini and onions. Pour hot vinegar mixture over zucchini and onions. Let stand 1 hour. Return zucchini mixture to saucepan. Bring to a boil. Cook 3 minutes. Pack hot zucchini mixture into hot sterilized jars, leaving 1/2-inch headspace. Use self-sealing lids. Adjust lids. Place jars on a rack in a large pot of boiling water. Water should cover jars 1 to 2 inches and have additional 2 inches for boiling space. Cover pot. Bring water to a boil. At sea level, boil 10 minutes. For every 1000 feet altitude, add 1 minute to boiling time. Makes 3 pints.

Salsa Verde

A perfect accompaniment to an Italian boiled dinner of chicken, sausage and vegetables.

3/4 cup minced fresh parsley	1/4 cup olive oil
2 green onions, chopped	2 tablespoons white-wine vinegar
2 tablespoons chopped capers	1/4 teaspoon salt
3 garlic cloves, minced	1/4 teaspoon freshly ground pepper

In a small bowl or blender container, combine all ingredients. Mix well. Cover and refrigerate. Makes 1 cup.

California Vegetable Sauce

A colorful sauce, great for filling an omelet.

2 tablespoons butter
1 small red onion, chopped
1/2 lb. mushrooms, sliced
1 garlic clove, minced
1 cup cherry tomatoes, halved

2 tablespoons chopped fresh parsley
1 tablespoon chopped fresh basil or
   3/4 teaspoon dried leaf basil
1 small avocado

Melt 1 tablespoon butter in a large skillet over medium heat. Add onion. Sauté onion 5 minutes. Add remaining butter and mushrooms. Sauté mushrooms 1 minute. Add garlic and tomatoes. Heat through, shaking pan occasionally. Remove from heat. Sprinkle with parsley and basil. Peel and dice avocado. Scatter over vegetables. Serve as an omelet filling or an accompaniment to hamburgers or tacos. Makes 4 servings.

Mexican Salsa   Photo on page 169.

The perfect fresh sauce to spoon over burritos, tacos and barbecued meats.

4 large ripe tomatoes, peeled, chopped
1 small red onion, chopped
1 or 2 canned green chilies,
   seeded, chopped
2 garlic cloves, minced

1/2 teaspoon salt
1/2 teaspoon brown sugar
1 teaspoon cider vinegar
2 tablespoons chopped fresh cilantro
Dash hot-pepper sauce

Combine all ingredients in a medium bowl. Mix well. Refrigerate 1 to 2 hours for flavors to blend. Makes 2 cups.

Guacamole

Serve this creamy Mexican sauce as an accompaniment to pizza or a dip for vegetables and chips.

2 avocados
1/3 cup lemon or lime juice
1/2 teaspoon salt

1/4 cup minced fresh cilantro
1 green onion, finely chopped
Dash hot-pepper sauce

Cut avocados in half, removing seed. Scoop avocado pulp from shell and place pulp in a small bowl. Mash pulp with a fork. Stir in lemon or lime juice, salt, cilantro, green onion and hot-pepper sauce. Spoon into a serving bowl. Cover and refrigerate until ready to serve. Makes about 1-1/2 cups.

Place an avocado seed in the center of the sauce to prevent it from darkening during chilling. Remove seed at serving time.

Red-Tomato Relish

A crimson-colored relish to accompany hot dogs, hamburgers and shredded pot roast.

1 lb. onions, coarsely chopped
1 red bell pepper, seeded, chopped
1 green bell pepper, seeded, chopped
6 cups (3 lbs.) coarsely chopped,
    peeled, ripe tomatoes
1 pint (2 cups) distilled white vinegar
1 cup light corn syrup

1 cup sugar
4 teaspoons salt
1 tablespoon dry mustard
2 teaspoons celery seed
1/2 teaspoon ground allspice
1/4 teaspoon crushed dried red pepper
1 bay leaf

In a 5-quart saucepan, combine all ingredients. Bring to a boil over medium heat, stirring constantly. Reduce heat. Simmer 1 hour, stirring occasionally. Ladle boiling hot relish into hot sterilized jars, leaving 1/2-inch headspace. Use self-sealing lids. Adjust lids. Place jars on a rack in a large pot of boiling water. Water should cover jars 1 to 2 inches and have additional 2 inches for boiling space. Cover pot. Bring water to a boil. At sea level, boil 10 minutes. For every 1000 feet altitude, add 1 minute to boiling time. Makes 5 half-pints.

Chili Sauce

An old-fashioned condiment great with a pot roast, barbecued beef or grilled hamburger.

12 large ripe tomatoes, peeled, chopped
4 green bell peppers, chopped
4 medium onions, chopped
1 bunch celery, chopped
3 bay leaves
1-1/2 cups sugar
2-1/2 cups cider vinegar

2 tablespoons salt
1 teaspoon freshly ground pepper
1 teaspoon ground cloves
1 teaspoon ground cinnamon
1 teaspoon ground ginger
1 teaspoon dry mustard

Combine all ingredients in a large pot. Bring to a boil over medium-high heat. Cover and reduce heat. Simmer 3 to 4 hours. Continue cooking to desired thickness. Ladle hot sauce into hot sterilized jars, leaving 1/2-inch headspace. Use self-sealing lids. Adjust lids. Place jars on a rack in a large pot of boiling water. Water should cover jars 1 to 2 inches and have additional 2 inches for boiling space. Cover pot. Bring water to a boil. At sea level, boil 10 minutes. For every 1000 feet altitude, add 1 minute to boiling time. Makes 6 pints.

Fried Parsley

Try this novel garnish to give variety to your dishes.

2 large bunches parsley

Oil for deep-frying

Wash parsley; **dry completely to prevent spattering.** Trim off extra-long stems, but leave parsley in sprigs. Heat 1-1/2 inches oil in a deep-fat fryer or heavy saucepan to 375F (190C). At this temperature, a 1-inch cube of bread will turn golden brown in 40 seconds. Drop parsley sprigs into hot oil. Cook until crisp, less than 1 minute. Remove parsley with a slotted spoon. Drain on paper towel. Serve as a garnish to roast meats, poultry or fish.

BREADS & DESSERTS

The wonderful aroma of fresh home-baked breads or the mouth-watering appearance of delicious sweets lends a special touch to any meal. Including vegetables in these special treats provides added flavor, valuable nutrients and extra moistness.

Vegetable-enriched breads suit a variety of occasions. A few bites of a Super Healthy Carrot-Bran Muffin will convert even a dedicated non-breakfast eater. Green-Onion & Parmesan Loaf is splendid fare for dinner guests, a picnic or for any salad luncheon. Chili peppers and cheese add flavor and color to Mexican Corn Bread.

Garlic-Potato Bread is a nutritious whole-wheat bread with moistness added from potato. Serve it with kabobs or your next back-yard cookout. Quick breads are always a joy to make because of the ease with which they go together.

Pumpkin-Walnut Bread is no exception.

Winter squash brings body and flavor to Praline-Topped Squash Pie and the elegant Squash Flambé. Perfect for lunch bags or a picnic basket are moist Orange-Carrot Cookies. Carrots also jewel everyone's all-time favorite—Frosted Carrot Bundt Cake.

Chocolate lovers will delight in Chocolate-Potato Cake, Speckled Chocolate-Carrot Cake and Sprouted Zucchini Brownies. Who said eating chocolate desserts couldn't be healthy!

For a cool treat, try Pumpkin-Eggnog Bombe flavored lightly with spices. Use your favorite mold for added interest.

Desserts and breads made with vegetables are fun, creative and nutritious.

Back-yard Barbecue for Dad

Ruby-Glazed Pork Loin
Grilled Sweet Corn with
Garlic Butter, page 160
Vegetable Platter Salad, page 69
Green-Onion & Parmesan Loaf, page 174
Carrot Picnic Cake, page 181

Green-Onion & Parmesan Loaf   Photo on page 148.

A green-onion-and-cheese filling keeps this bread moist.

3/4 cup warm water (105F, 40C)
1 (1/4-oz.) pkg. (1 tablespoon)
   active dry yeast
1/2 cup butter, room temperature
2 tablespoons sugar
1 teaspoon salt

3 eggs
3 to 4 cups all-purpose flour
Cheese Filling, see below
1 egg yolk
2 teaspoons water

Cheese Filling:
2 tablespoons butter
1 bunch green onions, chopped
1 egg
1 cup shredded Monterey Jack or
   Jarlsberg cheese (4 oz.)

1/2 cup freshly grated Parmesan cheese
   (1-1/2 oz.)
1/2 teaspoon dried leaf oregano

Place warm water in a small bowl. Sprinkle yeast into water. Let stand until yeast has dissolved, about 5 minutes. In a large bowl, beat butter until creamy. Beat in sugar, salt and eggs. Add 1 cup flour. Beat well. Add yeast mixture and 1 cup flour. Beat 5 minutes. Gradually add enough remaining flour to make a soft dough. Turn out dough on a lightly floured board. Knead until smooth and satiny, about 5 minutes. Place dough in a greased bowl. Cover. Let rise in a warm place until doubled in size, about 2 hours. Prepare Cheese Filling. Butter a 2-quart baking dish or soufflé dish. Punch down dough by pushing your fist into center. Pull edges of dough over center. Turn out dough on a lightly floured board. Knead lightly. Roll out dough into a 16'' x 10'' rectangle. Spread dough with Cheese Filling. Roll up dough firmly from longest side. Shape dough into a round coil. Place coiled dough, seam-side down, in buttered baking dish. Cover. Let rise until doubled in size, 45 to 60 minutes. In a small bowl, combine egg yolk and water. Brush egg yolk mixture over top surface of dough. Preheat oven to 350F (175C). Bake 40 minutes or until loaf sounds hollow when tapped with your fingers. Cool 5 to 10 minutes in baking dish. Remove from baking dish and place on a rack. Serve warm or at room temperature. Makes 1 loaf.

Cheese Filling:

Melt butter in a small skillet over medium heat. Add onions and sauté until glazed, about 2 minutes. Beat egg in a medium bowl. Add cheeses, oregano and sautéed onion. Mix well. Set aside until ready to use.

Variation

Substitute 1-1/2 cups sharp Cheddar cheese for Monterey Jack or Jarlsberg and Parmesan cheese; 1 chopped red bell pepper for green onions; and 1/2 teaspoon chili powder for oregano.

Pumpkin-Walnut Bread

For a tea sandwich, spread this bread with a mixture of cream cheese and candied ginger.

2 eggs
1-1/2 cups packed brown sugar
1/2 cup oil
2 cups pureed cooked pumpkin,
    banana squash or Hubbard squash, or
    canned pumpkin
1 cup whole-wheat flour

1-2/3 cups all-purpose flour
2 teaspoons baking soda
3/4 teaspoon salt
3/4 teaspoon ground cinnamon
1/4 teaspoon ground nutmeg
1/4 teaspoon ground cloves
1 cup chopped walnuts

Preheat oven to 350F (175C). Lightly butter three 7" x 3" loaf pans. In a large bowl, beat eggs and brown sugar until light and fluffy. Stir in oil and pumpkin or squash. In a medium bowl, stir together whole-wheat and all-purpose flours, baking soda, salt, cinnamon, nutmeg and cloves. Add flour mixture to egg mixture. Mix just until blended. Stir in walnuts. Pour mixture into buttered pans. Bake 40 to 45 minutes or until a wooden pick inserted in the center comes out clean. Cool in pans 5 minutes. Remove from pans and cool completely on a rack. Makes 3 loaves.

Zucchini Tea Loaf

Shredded zucchini keeps this quick bread moist. Slice thinly for open-face tea sandwiches.

1/2 cup safflower oil
1/2 cup granulated sugar
1/2 cup packed brown sugar
2 eggs
3/4 cup whole-wheat flour
3/4 cup all-purpose flour
1 teaspoon baking powder

1/2 teaspoon baking soda
1/2 teaspoon salt
1 teaspoon ground cinnamon
1 teaspoon vanilla extract
1 cup finely shredded zucchini
3/4 cup chopped walnuts or pecans

Preheat oven to 350F (175C). Butter and flour an 8" x 4" loaf pan. In a large bowl, combine oil, granulated sugar and brown sugar. Add eggs, one at a time, beating well after each addition. In a medium bowl, stir together whole-wheat and all-purpose flours, baking powder, baking soda, salt and cinnamon. Add flour mixture to egg mixture. Mix well. Stir in vanilla, zucchini and nuts. Spoon into buttered loaf pan. Bake 50 minutes or until a wooden pick inserted in the center comes out clean. Cool in pan 10 minutes. Remove from pan and cool completely on a rack. Makes l loaf.

1/Braid the 3 dough ropes evenly into 1 loaf.

2/Slice braid and spread evenly with Herb Glaze.

Garlic-Potato Bread

Fresh garlic adds flavor to this chewy whole-wheat potato bread. It's perfect with a barbecue.

1 large potato, unpeeled, scrubbed	2 teaspoons honey
1/4 cup warm water (105F, 40C)	1 teaspoon salt
1 (1/4-oz.) pkg. (1 tablespoon)	1-1/2 to 2-1/2 cups all-purpose flour
active dry yeast	1-1/4 to 2 cups whole-wheat flour
2 garlic cloves, minced	1 egg yolk
1 tablespoon olive oil	2 teaspoons water

Butter a 9-inch springform pan or soufflé dish. Place potato in a small saucepan. Add water to cover. Cover and bring to a boil over high heat. Reduce heat and simmer 15 minutes or until potato is tender. Drain off potato water, reserving 1 cup. Cool potato slightly. Peel and shred potato. Place 1/4 cup warm water in a large bowl. Sprinkle yeast in warm water. Let stand until yeast has dissolved, about 5 minutes. Add shredded potato, reserved potato water, garlic, oil, honey and salt. Add 1/2 cup each all-purpose and whole-wheat flours. Beat until smooth. Gradually add remaining flour to make a soft dough. Turn out dough on a lightly floured board. Knead until smooth and satiny, about 5 minutes. Place dough in a greased bowl. Cover and let rise in a warm place until doubled in size, about 1-1/2 hours. Punch down dough by pushing your fist into center. Pull edges of dough over center. Turn out dough on a lightly floured board. Knead lightly and shape into a 9-inch round. Place in buttered baking dish. Let rise until doubled in size, about 50 minutes. In a small bowl, combine egg yolk and water. Brush egg yolk mixture over top surface of dough. Preheat oven to 375F (190C). Bake 30 to 35 minutes or until loaf sounds hollow when tapped with your fingers. Cool in pan 10 minutes. Remove from pan and cool completely on a rack. Makes 1 large loaf.

Vintners' Herb Braided Bread

A colorful braided bread to add to a salad luncheon or buffet.

1/2 cup warm water (105F, 40C)
1 (1/4-oz.) pkg. (1 tablespooon)
   active dry yeast
6 tablespoons butter, room temperature
1/4 cup packed brown sugar
2 eggs

1/4 teaspoon ground turmeric
1 teaspoon salt
1/2 cup white wine, room temperature
3-1/2 to 4 cups all-purpose flour
Herb Glaze, see below

Herb Glaze:
1/2 cup olive oil
1/4 cup white wine
3 tablespoons lemon juice
2 garlic cloves, minced
2 green onions, minced
2 tablespoons minced fresh parsley

1 tablespoon chopped fresh basil or
   3/4 teaspoon dried leaf basil
1/4 teaspoon ground turmeric
1 teaspoon dried dill weed
1/8 teaspoon white pepper

Place warm water in a small bowl. Sprinkle yeast into water. Let stand until yeast has dissolved, about 5 minutes. In a large bowl, beat butter, sugar, eggs, turmeric and salt. Add yeast mixture, wine and 1 cup flour. Beat well. Gradually add enough remaining flour to make a soft dough. Turn out dough on a lightly floured board. Knead until smooth and satiny, about 5 minutes. Place dough in a greased bowl. Cover. Let rise in a warm place until doubled in size, about 1-1/2 hours. Grease a baking sheet. Punch down dough by pushing your fist into center. Pull edges of dough over center. Turn out dough on a lightly floured board. Knead lightly. Divide dough into 3 pieces. Roll each piece into an 18-inch rope. Pinch 3 ropes together at 1 end. Braid evenly. Place on greased baking sheet. Cover. Let rise until doubled in size, about 50 minutes. Preheat oven to 350F (175C). Bake 30 to 35 minutes or until loaf sounds hollow when tapped with your fingers. Cool 5 to 10 minutes. Remove from baking sheet and place on a rack. Prepare Herb Glaze. At serving time, brush braid with Herb Glaze. Slice braid and spread each slice with Herb Glaze. Place loaf back together on a platter. Makes 1 large braid.

Herb Glaze:
Combine all ingredients in a small bowl. Stir to blend. Set aside until ready to use.

Variation

Substitute 2 cups whole-wheat flour for 2 cups all-purpose flour. Also substitute 2 teaspoons Herbs of Provence, page 111, for basil, turmeric and dill weed.

Wrap sliced, glazed bread in foil. Place in a 300F (150C) oven 10 to 15 minutes to warm through.

Mexican Corn Bread

Accompany baked ham or pork loin with this spicy cheese-laced bread.

2 eggs
1 (15-oz.) can cream-style corn
3/4 cup milk
1/3 cup butter, melted
1/2 teaspoon baking soda
1/2 teaspoon salt

1/2 teaspoon freshly ground pepper
1 cup yellow cornmeal
1 (4-oz.) can green chilies,
   seeded, chopped
1-1/2 cups shredded Monterey Jack or
   Cheddar cheese (6 oz.)

Preheat oven to 400F (205C). Lightly butter a 9-inch square baking dish. In a medium bowl, beat eggs until blended. Stir in corn, milk, butter, baking soda, salt, pepper and cornmeal. Mix just until blended. Spread half the batter in buttered baking dish. Sprinkle batter with half of chilies and cheese. Spread remaining batter over cheese and chilies. Sprinkle with remaining chilies and cheese. Bake 45 minutes or until topping is golden brown and center springs back when lightly touched. Cut in squares. Serve warm. Makes 8 to 10 servings.

Squash Soufflé Custard

As it bakes, this pudding becomes a custard base topped with a soufflé.

3 eggs, separated
1/8 teaspoon cream of tartar
1/2 cup packed brown sugar
1-1/2 teaspoons ground cinnamon
1 teaspoon ground ginger
1/4 teaspoon ground cloves
1/4 teaspoon salt

1 cup pureed cooked squash or
   pumpkin, or canned pumpkin
1 cup milk
2 tablespoons butter, melted
Whipped cream flavored with
   chopped candied ginger or rum

Preheat oven to 375F (190C). Lightly butter a 1-1/2-quart baking dish or soufflé dish. In a medium bowl, beat egg whites until foamy. Add cream of tartar. Beat until soft peaks form. Gradually beat in 1/4 cup brown sugar. Beat until mixture is stiff but not dry; set aside. In a large bowl, beat egg yolks until light. Beat in remaining 1/4 cup brown sugar, cinnamon, ginger, cloves and salt. Stir in squash or pumpkin and milk. Fold 1/3 of egg-white mixture into egg-yolk mixture. Blend until smooth. Gently fold in remaining egg-white mixture and melted butter. Pour into buttered baking dish. Place baking dish in a large baking pan. Pour in water to a depth of 1 inch. Bake 35 to 40 minutes or until a knife inserted in the center comes out clean. Cool slightly. Serve with flavored whipped cream. Makes 6 to 8 servings.

 Hard-shelled winter squash, such as butternut, acorn and banana, are good in desserts in place of pumpkin.

Squash Flambé

Flame this caramelized custard ring for a dramatic show.

1/2 cup granulated sugar
6 eggs
3/4 cup packed brown sugar
3/4 teaspoon ground cinnamon
1/2 teaspoon ground ginger
1/4 teaspoon ground nutmeg
1/4 teaspoon ground allspice
1/2 teaspoon salt

1-1/2 cups milk or half and half
1-1/2 cups pureed cooked squash or
　pumpkin, or canned pumpkin
1/4 cup pecan halves
3 tablespoons rum
Vanilla or eggnog ice-cream balls,
　if desired

Preheat oven to 350F (175C). Place granulated sugar in a small saucepan. Heat over medium-high heat, shaking pan, until sugar melts and caramelizes. Immediately pour melted sugar into bottom of a 1-1/2-quart ring mold. Tilt mold to coat bottom. Cool mold slightly. Lightly butter mold sides where caramelized sugar does not cover. In a large bowl, beat eggs until blended. Mix in brown sugar, cinnamon, ginger, nutmeg, allspice and salt. Scald milk or half and half by heating in a small saucepan over medium heat until bubbles appear around the edge. Stir into egg mixture. Add squash or pumpkin. Beat until smooth. Pour mixture into caramel-lined mold. Set mold in a large baking pan. Add hot water to a depth of 1 inch. Bake 30 minutes or until a knife inserted in center comes out clean. Cool on a rack 15 minutes. Insert a knife around mold edges to loosen custard. Place a serving plate or platter on top of mold. Invert mold and plate, releasing custard from pan. Refrigerate, if desired. At serving time, garnish top of custard with pecan halves. In a small saucepan, heat rum until warm, about 150F (65C). Using a long match, carefully ignite rum. Spoon flaming rum over custard. Serve custard with vanilla or eggnog ice-cream balls, if desired. Makes 8 servings.

Sprouted Zucchini Brownies

Chocolate chips make a self-frosted topping on these wonderfully moist and healthy bar cookies.

Chocolate-Chip Topping, page 181
1/2 cup butter, room temperature
1 cup granulated sugar
1/2 cup packed brown sugar
2 eggs
1 cup alfalfa sprouts

1-1/2 cups shredded zucchini
1 cup whole-wheat flour
1 cup all-purpose flour
3 tablespoons unsweetened cocoa
1/2 teaspoon salt
1 teaspoon baking soda

Prepare Chocolate-Chip Topping. Preheat oven to 350F (165C). Butter a 13″ x 9″ baking dish. In a large bowl, beat butter until creamy. Gradually add granulated sugar and brown sugar. Beat until fluffy. Beat in eggs, one at a time, until smooth. Stir in sprouts and zucchini. In a medium bowl, stir together whole-wheat and all-purpose flours, cocoa, salt and baking soda. Add flour mixture to batter. Mix until blended. Pour into buttered baking dish. Smooth batter with a spatula. Sprinkle Chocolate-Chip Topping over the batter. Bake 25 minutes or until a wooden pick inserted in the center comes out clean. Place on a rack to cool. Cut in squares. Makes 48 servings.

Desserts

Super Healthy Carrot-Bran Muffins

Freeze a supply of these whole-grain muffins for a fresh-tasting breakfast treat.

1-1/2 cups whole-bran cereal
1 cup boiling water
1/2 cup safflower oil
1-1/2 cups packed brown sugar
1/4 cup honey or molasses
3 eggs
1 pint (2 cups) buttermilk

2-1/2 cups whole-wheat flour
3-1/2 teaspoons baking soda
1 teaspoon salt
1-1/2 cups flaked bran cereal or granola
1-1/3 cups shredded carrots
3/4 cups raisins
1/2 cup chopped walnuts

Place whole-bran cereal in a small heatproof bowl. Pour boiling water over cereal. Let stand 10 minutes. In a large bowl, beat oil, sugar and honey or molasses until blended. Add eggs, one at a time, beating well after each addition. Stir in buttermilk and soaked bran cereal. In a medium bowl, stir together whole-wheat flour, baking soda and salt. Add flour mixture to egg mixture. Mix well. Stir in bran cereal or granola, carrots, raisins and walnuts. Let stand 1 hour or refrigerate batter for baking at a later time. Preheat oven to 400F (205C). Grease 36 muffin cups or line with paper liners. Fill prepared muffin cups 2/3 to 3/4 full with batter. Bake 25 to 35 minutes or until a wooden pick inserted in the center of a muffin comes out clean. Chilled batter will take 4 to 5 minutes longer to bake than room-temperature batter. Cool muffins on a rack. Makes 36 muffins.

Orange-Carrot Cookies

These moist cookies burst with healthy ingredients—a good choice for a lunch bag or snack.

3/4 cup butter, room temperature
1-1/4 cups packed brown sugar
2 eggs
3 tablespoons thawed frozen
   orange-juice concentrate
1-1/4 cups whole-wheat flour
1/4 cup instant or non-instant milk powder
1/2 teaspoon salt

1 teaspoon baking powder
1/4 cup toasted wheat germ
1-3/4 cups rolled oats
1 teaspoon grated orange peel
1 cup shredded carrots
1 cup chopped walnuts
1/2 cup raisins or shredded coconut

Preheat oven to 350F (175C). Lightly grease baking sheets. In a large bowl, beat together butter and sugar until creamy. Mix in eggs. Add orange-juice concentrate, beating until blended. In a medium bowl, stir together flour, milk powder, salt, baking powder, wheat germ and rolled oats. Add to butter mixture. Mix well. Stir in orange peel, carrots, walnuts and raisins or coconut. Drop by heaping teaspoons onto greased baking sheets. Bake 10 to 12 minutes or until lightly browned. Cool on racks. Makes about 50 cookies.

Carrot Picnic Cake

This moist healthy cake frosts itself while it bakes.

Chocolate-Chip Topping, see below
3/4 cup safflower oil
1 cup packed brown sugar
3/4 cup granulated sugar
2 eggs
1 cup all-purpose flour
1 cup whole-wheat flour
1-1/2 teaspoons baking soda

1/2 teaspoon baking powder
1/2 teaspoon salt
1 teaspoon ground cinnamon
1-1/4 cups shredded carrots
2 cups diced tart apples
1/2 cup raisins
1/2 cup chopped walnuts

Chocolate-Chip Topping:
1 cup (6 oz.) semisweet chocolate pieces
1 tablespoon granulated sugar

1 teaspoon ground cinnamon

Prepare Chocolate-Chip Topping. Preheat oven to 350F (175C). Butter and flour a 10-inch tube pan or Bundt pan. In a large bowl, combine oil, brown sugar and granulated sugar. Add eggs, one at a time, beating well after each addition. In a medium bowl, combine all-purpose and whole-wheat flours, baking soda, baking powder, salt and cinnamon. Add flour mixture to egg mixture. Mix well. Stir in carrots, apples, raisins and nuts. Pour batter into buttered pan. Sprinkle Chocolate-Chip Topping over batter. Bake 45 to 50 minutes or until a wooden pick inserted in the center comes out clean. Cool in pan 15 minutes. Invert onto a rack. Remove pan. Turn cake right-side up. Cool completely. Makes 12 servings.

Chocolate-Chip Topping
In a small bowl, combine chocolate pieces, sugar and cinnamon. Set aside until ready to use.

Speckled Chocolate-Carrot Cake

This nut sponge cake retains moistness during aging thanks to the carrots.

1/2 cup (3 oz.) semisweet chocolate pieces
1 cup almonds
6 eggs, separated
1/4 teaspoon salt
1/4 teaspoon cream of tartar
1 cup sugar
1/2 teaspoon almond extract

1 tablespoon grated orange peel
1 teaspoon baking powder
1-1/4 cups shredded carrots
3/4 cup fine brioche crumbs or
  freshly crumbled white bread
Whipped cream or ice cream

Preheat oven to 350F (175C). Place chocolate pieces in a blender or food processor fitted with a steel blade. Process chocolate until coarsely ground. Place ground chocolate in a small bowl. Place almonds in blender or food processor. Process until finely ground. Add ground almonds to chocolate. Stir until well blended; set aside. In a large bowl, beat egg whites until foamy. Add salt and cream of tartar to egg whites. Beat until soft peaks form. Beat in 2 tablespoons sugar. In a medium bowl, beat egg yolks until pale yellow. Gradually beat in remaining sugar, almond extract, orange peel and baking powder. Fold in carrots and half the chocolate mixture. Mix until well blended. Fold in crumbs. Gently fold in egg-white mixture and remaining chocolate mixture. Turn into a 9-inch ungreased springform pan. Bake 35 to 40 minutes or until a wooden pick inserted in the center comes out clean. Cool in pan 10 minutes. Invert onto a rack and remove pan. Cool completely. Serve with whipped cream or ice cream. Makes 12 servings.

Praline-Topped Squash Pie

A crunchy nut glaze seals the top of this spicy custard pie.

Sweet Butter Crust, see below
Nut Topping, see below
3 eggs
3/4 cup packed brown sugar
1/2 teaspoon ground cinnamon
1/2 teaspoon ground ginger

1/4 teaspoon ground cloves
1/4 teaspoon ground nutmeg
1/2 teaspoon salt
1-2/3 cups pureed cooked butternut,
   acorn or banana squash
1-1/2 cups half and half or milk

Sweet Butter Crust:
1-1/4 cups all-purpose flour
1 tablespoon sugar
1/2 cup butter,
   cut in 1/2-inch pieces

1 egg yolk
1-1/2 tablespoons ice water

Nut Topping:
1-2/3 cups walnut halves or
   pecan halves

1/3 cup packed brown sugar

Preheat oven to 375F (190C). Prepare Sweet Butter Crust. Prepare Nut Topping. In a large bowl, beat eggs until blended. Mix in sugar, cinnamon, ginger, cloves, nutmeg and salt. Stir in squash and half and half or milk. Pour into pastry shell. Bake 35 minutes. Sprinkle Nut Topping over pie. Bake 5 minutes longer or until pie is set and a knife inserted in the center comes out clean. Change oven temperature to broil. Broil pie 30 seconds to caramelize sugar. Watch pie carefully to avoid scorching. Cut in wedges. Serve warm or at room temperature. Makes 6 to 8 servings.

Sweet Butter Crust:
In a medium bowl, combine flour, sugar and butter. Mix with pastry blender or fork until mixture resembles fine crumbs. Add egg yolk and toss with fork until blended. Add ice water and mix until dough clings together in a ball. Roll dough on a lightly floured board to fit a 9-inch pie dish. Place in pie dish and flute edges. Refrigerate until dough is firm. Preheat oven to 425F (220C). Bake 8 minutes; set aside until ready to use.

Nut Topping:
In a medium bowl, combine nuts and brown sugar. Mix well; set aside until ready to use.

Variation
Substitute 1/2 cup whipping cream, 1/4 cup chopped walnuts or pecans and 2 tablespoons praline or caramel sauce for nut topping. In a small bowl, beat whipping cream until soft peaks form. Place whipped cream in dollops over center of baked pie. Sprinkle chopped nuts in a 2-inch border around edge of pie. Drizzle praline or caramel sauce over whipped cream.

Praline-Topped Squash Pie

How To Make Pumpkin-Eggnog Bombe

1/Pack ice cream into selected mold in 3/4-inch layer. Freeze until firm.

2/Spoon pumpkin mixture into lined mold.

3/Garnish bombe as desired.

4/Slice bombe and serve immediately.

Pumpkin-Eggnog Bombe

The surprise inside this festive eggnog ice-cream bombe is a spicy pumpkin center.

1 qt. vanilla or eggnog ice cream
2 cups pureed cooked pumpkin,
  banana squash or Hubbard squash, or
  canned pumpkin
2/3 cup packed brown sugar
1 teaspoon ground cinnamon

1/4 teaspoon ground ginger
1/4 teaspoon ground cloves
1/4 teaspoon ground nutmeg
1/4 teaspoon salt
1 cup whipping cream
3 tablespoons Grand Marnier or rum

Using a 1-1/2-quart ice-cream mold or salad mold, pack ice cream in 3/4-inch-thick layer on bottom and sides of mold. Place mold in freezer. Freeze until ice cream is firm. In a large bowl, combine pumpkin or squash, sugar, cinnamon, ginger, cloves, nutmeg and salt. In a medium bowl, whip cream until stiff. Stir in Grand Marnier or rum. Fold whipped-cream mixture into pumpkin or squash mixture. Spoon mixture into center of ice-cream-lined mold. Cover. Freeze until firm, at least 8 hours. To unmold, dip mold in a pan of hot water 5 seconds. Invert on a serving platter. Garnish as desired. Cut in wedges. Serve immediately. Makes 8 to 10 servings.

Carrot Pudding

A steamed pudding makes a hearty holiday dessert accompanied by a fluffy hard sauce.

Brandied Hard Sauce, see below
1 cup shredded carrots
1 cup grated, peeled apples
1 cup chopped raisins
1 cup packed brown sugar
1 cup all-purpose flour

1 teaspoon baking soda
1 teaspoon ground cinnamon
1 teaspoon ground allspice
1/2 teaspoon ground cloves
1/3 cup butter, melted
1 egg, lightly beaten

Brandied Hard Sauce:
6 tablespoons butter, room temperature
1-1/2 cups powdered sugar

1 egg yolk
2 tablespoons brandy or rum

Prepare Brandied Hard Sauce. Butter a 1-1/2-quart pudding mold or charlotte mold. In a large bowl, combine carrots, apples, raisins, brown sugar, flour, baking soda, cinnamon, allspice, cloves, melted butter and egg. Mix until ingredients are moistened. Spoon into buttered mold. Cover. Place in a large saucepan. Add enough hot water to fill pan half-way up the side of the mold. Cover. Steam 3 hours or until a wooden pick inserted in the center comes out clean. Periodically check water supply. Add additional water if saucepan is becoming low on water. Cool in mold 10 minutes. Invert to remove pudding from mold. Serve warm with Brandied Hard Sauce. Makes 8 servings.

Brandied Hard Sauce:
In a medium bowl, beat butter, sugar, egg yolk and brandy or rum until fluffy. Refrigerate until ready to use.

Frosted Carrot Bundt Cake

Pineapple, coconut and walnuts enhance this favorite cake.

2 cups all-purpose flour
1 cup whole-wheat flour
1-1/2 teaspoons baking soda
1 teaspoon ground cinnamon
1/2 teaspoon salt
2 cups sugar
1-1/3 cups corn oil
3 eggs

1 teaspoon vanilla extract
2-1/4 cups shredded carrots
1 (8-oz.) can crushed pineapple
 with juice
1-1/2 cups chopped walnuts or pecans
3/4 cup shredded coconut
Cream-Cheese Frosting, see below

Cream-Cheese Frosting:
1 (3-oz.) pkg. cream cheese,
 room temperature
1/4 cup butter, room temperature

2-1/2 cups powdered sugar
1 teaspoon vanilla extract

Preheat oven to 350F (175C). Butter and lightly flour a 10-inch Bundt pan or tube pan. In a medium bowl, stir together all-purpose and whole-wheat flours, baking soda, cinnamon and salt. In a large bowl, beat together sugar and oil until blended. Add eggs, one at a time, beating well after each addition. Add half the flour mixture. Mix well. Add remaining flour mixture, vanilla, carrots, pineapple and juice, nuts and coconut. Mix until well blended. Pour batter into buttered pan. Bake 1 hour 10 minutes or until a wooden pick inserted in the center comes out clean. Cool in pan 10 minutes. Invert onto a rack and remove pan. Cool completely. Prepare Cream-Cheese Frosting. Spread frosting over top and sides of cake. Makes 16 servings.

Cream-Cheese Frosting:
In a medium bowl, combine cream cheese, butter, sugar and vanilla. Beat until smooth and creamy.

Chocolate-Potato Cake

Potatoes give moistness to this lightly spiced chocolate cake.

1 cup cold cooked potatoes
1 cup butter, room temperature
2 cups sugar
4 eggs, separated
2 cups all-purpose flour
1 teaspoon ground cinnamon

1/2 teaspoon salt
1/2 teaspoon ground cloves
1 cup ground chocolate or
 sweetened cocoa mix (not cocoa)
1/2 cup milk
1 cup chopped walnuts or pecans

Preheat oven to 325F (165C). Lightly butter and flour a 10-inch Bundt pan or tube pan. Mash potatoes thoroughly or put through a ricer. In a large bowl, beat butter until creamy. Add sugar gradually, creaming until light and fluffy. Beat in egg yolks. Mix in potatoes. Sift together flour, cinnamon, salt, cloves and chocolate. Alternately add flour mixture and milk to potato mixture. Mix until blended. In a medium bowl, beat egg whites until stiff but not dry. Gently fold 1/3 of beaten egg whites into the chocolate batter. Fold in remaining beaten egg whites and nuts. Turn batter into buttered pan. Bake 1 hour 10 minutes or until a wooden pick inserted in the center comes out clean. Cool 10 minutes in pan. Invert onto a rack and remove pan. Cool completely. Sprinkle with powdered sugar or serve with a coffee or orange liqueur-flavored whipped cream. Makes 16 servings.

INDEX

A

a la Grecque, Vegetables 157
Acidulated water 7
Al dente 7
Abalone Mushrooms 21
Acorn Squash 29
Aioli Sauce 166
Almond Pâté, Mushroom & 34
Anchovy Sauce, Hot Garlic & 32
Anise 17
Anna, Potatoes 135
Antipasto, Italian 40
Appetizers 31-43
Apples, Red Cabbage & 144
Artichoke:
    Artichoke & Filbert Soup 49
    Artichoke & Sausage Frittata 89
    Artichoke Dip & Rye Wafers, Hot 34
    Artichokes Constantinople 159
    Chicken & Artichokes Jubilee 121
    Globe Artichoke 9
    Ham & Cheese Stuffed Artichokes 127
    Insight on Artichokes 127
    Steamed Artichokes with Dipping
      Sauces 162
Artichoke, Jerusalem:
    Jerusalem Artichoke 9, 26
    Jerusalem Artichoke & Leek Bisque 52
    Jerusalem Artichoke & Seafood Salad 77
    Jerusalem Artichokes & Celery
      au Gratin 152
Asparagus:
    Asparagus 10, 15
    Asparagus & Eggs Milanese 88
    Asparagus & Shrimp Nordic-Style 120
    Dutch Asparagus 145
Avgolemono, Stuffed Tomatoes 126

B

Babie with Mushroom Center, Dutch 87
Bacon & Potato Squares 86
Bacon Filling, Onion & 99
Bacon Pie, Bavarian Onion & 99
Bacon Salad Flambé, Hot Spinach & 70
Baked Fish & Vegetables Piraeus 120
Baked Lima Beans & Sausages, Oven- 123
Baked Potatoes with Toppings 136
Baking 8
Banana Squash 29
Barley Soup, Beef & 56
Basic Pizza Crust 98
Basic Vegetable Preparation 6-7
Basics, Vegetable 5-8
Basil Dressing, Lemon- 72
Basil Vinaigrette 67
Basil, Pasta with Fresh Tomato & 101
Batavian Endive 17, 20
Batter, Tempura 37
Bavarian Onion & Bacon Pie 99
Beans:
    Bean Sprouts 11
    Cassoulet 123
    Dilly Beans 169-170
    Dried Beans 10-11

    Green Bean & Mushroom Salad 67, 90
    Green, Lima, Wax Beans 10-11
    Herb-Tossed Blue-Lake Beans 140
    Indian Green Beans 140
    Lentil Soup 54
    Marinated Four-Bean Salad 81
    Minestrone 53
    Oven-Baked Lima Beans & Sausages 123
    Yellow Split-Pea Soup 54
Béarnaise Sauce 165
Bechamel Sauce 127
Beef & Barley Soup 56
Beef & Celery-Root Soup, German 58
Beet Greens 11, 18-19
Beets:
    Beets 11
    Borscht 57
    Orange-Glazed Beets 147-149
    Pickled Beets 78
Belgian Endive 17, 20
Bell Peppers 24
Bibb Lettuce 20
Bisque, Jerusalem Artichoke & Leek 52
Blanching 8
Blue-Cheese Dip with Vegetables 32
Blue-Lake Beans, Herb-Tossed 140
Boiling 7
Bok Choy 12, 15
Bolognese, Pasta 99
Bombe, Pumpkin-Eggnog 184-185
Böreks, California-Style 108-109
Borscht 57
Boston Lettuce 20
Braising/Stewing 8
Bran Muffins, Super Healthy Carrot- 180
Brandied Hard Sauce 185
Brandied Orange Carrots 147, 148-149
Breads & Desserts 173-182
Bread & Butter Pickles, Zucchini 169-170
Broccoli:
    Broccoli 12
    Broccoli Duo 146
    Cream of Broccoli Soup 48
    Spinach & Chèvre Quiche 102
    Summer Vegetable Platter 156
Broiling/Grilling 8
Brownies, Sprouted Zucchini 179
Brussels Sprouts 12
Brussels Sprouts Véronique 155
Buckwheat Crepes 106
Bunching Lettuce 20
Bundt Cake, Frosted Carrot 186
Butter Pastry 102
Butter Pastry, Sweet 183
Butter Pickles, Zucchini Bread & 169-170
Butter, Grilled Sweet Corn
    with Garlic 160-161
Butter-Glazed Vegetables 156
Buttercrunch Lettuce 20
Buttercup Squash 29
Buttered Herb Sauce, Swiss 165
Buttered Potato Dollars, Garlic- 135
Butterhead Lettuce 20

Butternut Shells, Pilgrim Stew in 130
Butternut Squash 29
Buying Vegetables 6

C

Cabbage:
    Cabbage 12-13
    Chinese Cabbage 13
    Chinese Cabbage & Tofu Stir-Fry 134
    Green Cabbage 12-13
    Napa Cabbage 12-13
    Red Cabbage 12-13
    Red Cabbage & Apples 144
    Sausage-Stuffed Cabbage Rolls 124
    Savoy Cabbage 12-13
    Sweet & Sour Hot Slaw 73
Cakes:
    Carrot Picnic Cake 181
    Chocolate-Potato Cake 186
    Frosted Carrot Bundt Cake 186
    Speckled Chocolate-Carrot Cake 181
Cake, Swiss Potato 137
California Soup in a Pumpkin Tureen,
    Early 60-61
California Vegetable Sauce 171
California-Style Böreks 108-109
Carrots:
    Brandied Orange Carrots 147, 148-149
    Carrot-Fontina Squares 87
    Carrot Picnic Cake 181
    Carrot Pudding 185
    Carrots 13
    Carrots Grand Marnier 147
    Carrot Soup 48
    Carrot Timbales 93
    Frosted Carrot Bundt Cake 186
    Golden Puree with Caramelized
      Onions 143
    Orange-Carrot Cookies 180
    Speckled Chocolate-Carrot Cake 181
    Summer Vegetable Platter 156
    Super Healthy Carrot-Bran Muffins 180
Cashew Chicken & Vegetables 122
Casserole, Pecan-Coated Sweet-Potato 139
Cassoulet 123
Cauliflower:
    Cauliflower 14
    Cauliflower Curry 146
    Cauliflower Soufflé 83
Caviar, Eggplant 33
Caviar, New Potatoes with 138
Caviar Tart, Decorative 108
Celeriac 14
Celery-Root Soup, German Beef & 58
Celery 14-15
Celery au Gratin, Jerusalem
    Artichokes & 152
Celery Root 14
Celery-Root Soup, German Beef & 58
Champignon de Paris Mushrooms 21
Chard Stuffing, Italian Swiss 110
Chard, Swiss 14-15, 30
Chayote 15, 28
Chayote Mexicana 152

Index

Cheese:
Blue-Cheese Dip with Vegetables 32
Cheese Crust 111
Cheese Filling 174
Cheese Soup with Pumpkin 61
Cheese-Tipped Fennel 38-39
Cream-Cheese Frosting 186
Cream-Cheese Pastry 42
Grilled Shiitake Mushrooms
  with Cheese 41
Ham & Cheese Stuffed Artichokes 127
Herb Cream Cheese 35, 74-75
Pattypan with Cheese & Chilies 152
Scandinavian Vegetable &
  Cheese Salad 77
Cherry Preserves, Gingered 168-169
Chestnut:
Chestnut & Vegetable Stuffing 107
Chestnut Soufflé 84
Chestnut Soup 62
Chèvre Quiche, Spinach & 102
Chicken:
Cashew Chicken & Vegetables 122
Chicken & Artichokes Jubilee 121
Chinese Chicken Salad 73-75
Chicons 17, 20
Chicory 15
Chicory, Witloof 17, 20
Chile con Queso 37, 97
Chili Sauce 172
Chilies, Pattypan with Cheese & 152
Chinese Cabbage 13
Chinese Cabbage & Tofu Stir-Fry 134
Chinese Chicken Salad 73-75
Chinese Pea Pods 11, 24
Chinese Pea Pods & Shrimp 121
Chinese Vegetables, Stir-Fried 133
Chives:
Chive-Stuffed Pea Pods 38-39
Kohlrabi with Sour Cream & Chives 139
Spinach Soufflé with Chive Sauce 84
Chocolate-Carrot Cake, Speckled 181
Chocolate-Potato Cake 186
Cilantro 20
Citrus Dressing 64
Clams Hiely, Spinach & 119
Cobb Salad, Western 65
Cocozelle Squash 28
Collards 15, 18-19
Con Queso, Chile 37, 97
Constantinople, Artichokes 159
Continental Salad 64
Cooked Tomato Sauce 168
Cookies, Orange-Carrot 180
Cooking Techniques 7-8
Corn:
Cornmeal Crust 96-97
Grilled Sweet Corn with
  Garlic Butter 160-161
Mexican Corn & Squash 148-150
Mexican Corn Bread 178
Southern Corn Pudding 92
Southern Okra & Corn Stew 154
Sweet Corn 16, 29
Cos Lettuce 20
Country Salad, Greek 77
Cream Cheese, Herb 35, 74-75
Cream Vegetable Pancakes, Sour- 104-105
Cream of Broccoli Soup 48
Cream-Cheese Frosting 186

Cream-Cheese Pastry 42
Creamy Scalloped Potatoes 138
Crème Fraîche 166
Crepes, Buckwheat 106
Crisphead Lettuce 20
Crisp-tender 7
Crookneck Squash
  Mediterranean-Style 150
Crookneck Squash, Yellow 28
Crust:
Basic Pizza Crust 98
Cheese Crust 111
Cornmeal Crust 96-97
Lemon-Butter Crust 108
Whole-Wheat Pizza Crust 95
Cucumber:
Cucumber 16
Dilled Cucumber Soup 46-47
Gingered Cucumber Salad 68
Stir-Fried Pea Pods & Cucumbers 133
Swedish-Style Cucumbers in Dill 78
Curried Pea Vichyssoise 56
Curried Shrimp, Endive with 38-39
Curry Dressing 70
Curry, Cauliflower 146
Custard Sauce 113
Custard, Squash Soufflé 178

D
Daikon, Radish 26
Dandelion 16, 19
Danish Hash 117
Decorative Caviar Tart 108
Deep-Frying 8
Deli Salad, Washington Square 67
Dill Dressing 77
Dill, Swedish-Style Cucumbers in 78
Dilled Cucumber Soup 46-47
Dilly Beans 169-170
Dips & Spreads 32-35
Dipping Sauces, Steamed
  Artichokes with 162
Dolmas 36
Dressings:
Basil Vinaigrette 67
Citrus Dressing 64
Curry Dressing 70
Dill Dressing 77
Garlic-Wine Dressing 64
Gingered Soy Dressing 68
Herb Vinaigrette 67
Italian Dressing 69
Lemon Dressing 68
Lemon-Basil Dressing 72
Mexican Dressing 76
Mustard-Tarragon Dressing 71
Oil & Lime Dressing 71
Oil & Vinegar Dressing 77
Parsley-Vinaigrette Dressing 65
Red-Wine Vinaigrette Dressing 81
Sesame-Soy Dressing 73
Shallot Dressing 79
Shallot-Mustard Vinaigrette Dressing 78
Spicy Dressing 80
Tarragon-Vinaigrette Dressing 66
Dried Beans:
Cassoulet 123
Dried Beans 10-11
Lentil Soup 54
Minestrone 53
Oven-Baked Lima Beans & Sausages 123

Yellow Split-Pea Soup 54
Dumpling Squash 29
Dutch Asparagus 145
Dutch Babie with Mushroom Center 87

E
Early California Soup in a Pumpkin
  Tureen 60-61
Edible Pea Pods 11, 24
Egg & Radish Salad, Shredded 80
Eggnog Bombe, Pumpkin- 184-185
Eggplant:
Eggplant 16
Eggplant Caviar 33
Indian Eggplant 155
Layered Eggplant Slices 154
Stuffed Eggplant Boats 130
Yaya's Stuffed Eggplant 153
Eggs & Soufflés 82-93
Leek & Italian Sausage Quiche 103
Spinach & Chèvre Quiche 102
Zucchini & Walnut Quiche 103
Endive:
Batavian Endive 17, 20
Belgian Endive 17, 20
Endive 17, 20
Endive with Curried Shrimp 38-39
Endive with Lemon Sauce 141
French Endive 17, 20
Watercress & Endive Salad 66
Enoki Mushrooms 21
Escarole 17, 20
Escarole & Sausage Bistro Salad 81

F
Fennel 17
Fennel, Cheese-Tipped 38-39
Filbert Soup, Artichoke & 49
Fillings:
Cheese Filling 174
Mushroom Filling 88
Onion & Bacon Filling 99
Finocchio 17
Fish & Vegetables Piraeus, Baked 120
Flambé, Hot Spinach & Bacon Salad 70
Flambé, Squash 179
Flats, Tortilla 100
Florentine Meatballs 41
Fontina Squares, Carrot- 87
Four-Bean Salad, Marinated 81
Fraîche, Crème 166
French Endive 17, 20
French Potato Salad 71
French Vegetable Soup 50
French-Fried Potato Skins 43
Fried Parsley 172
Fried Potato Skins, French- 43
Frittata, Artichoke & Sausage 89
Frosted Carrot Bundt Cake 186
Frosting, Cream-Cheese 186
Fruited Vegetable Soup 62

G
Galettes Sarasin 106
Garbanzo-Sesame Spread 33
Garden Greens with Nasturtium
  Blossoms 71
Garden Stew, Vegetable 159
Garlic:
Garlic 18, 23
Garlic-Buttered Potato Dollars 135
Garlic-Potato Bread 176

Garlic-Wine Dressing 64
Greek Garlic Mayonnaise 166
Grilled Sweet Corn with
    Garlic Butter 160-161
    Hot Garlic & Anchovy Sauce 32
Gazpacho Monterey 45
Gazpacho Salad, Multi-Layered 64, 74-75
German Beef & Celery-Root Soup 58
Gingered Cherry Preserves 168-169
Gingered Cucumber Salad 68
Gingered Soy Dressing 68
Gingerroot 18
Glazed Beets, Orange- 147-149
Glazed Parsnips, Marmalade- 139
Glazed Vegetables, Butter- 156
Glazed Yams, Orange- 138
Globe Artichoke 9
Gnocchi Balls, Spinach 131
Goddess Dip, Green 32
Golden Puree with Caramelized
    Onions 143
Grand Marnier, Carrots 147
Grape Leaves, Stuffed (Dolmas) 36
Greek Country Salad 77
Greek Garlic Mayonnaise 166
Greek Meat Sauce, Spaghetti
    Squash with 128-129
Green Beans:
    Green Beans 10-11
    Green Bean & Mushroom Salad 67, 90
    Indian Green Beans 140
Green Cabbage 12-13
Green Goddess Dip 32
Green Onions 22-23
Green Peppers 24
Green Rice 163
Green-Onion & Parmesan
    Loaf 148-149, 174
Green-Tomato Relish 167
Greens:
    Beet Greens 11, 18-19
    Collard Greens 15, 18-19
    Dandelion Greens 16, 19
    Garden Greens with Nasturtium
        Blossoms 71
    Greens 18-19
    Mustard Greens 18-19, 22
    Sorrel 19, 27
    Turnip Greens 18-19, 30
Grilled Shiitake Mushrooms
    with Cheese 41
Grilled Sweet Corn with
    Garlic Butter 160-161
Grilling/Broiling 8
Gruyère Salad, Mushroom- 68, 74-75
Guacamole 171

H
Ham & Cheese Stuffed Artichokes 127
Ham-Filled Spinach Soufflé Roll 90-91
Hard Sauce, Brandied 185
Hash, Danish 117
Healthy Carrot-Bran Muffins, Super 180
Herb Braided Bread, Vintners' 176-177
Herb Cream Cheese 35, 74-75
Herb Sauce, Swiss Buttered 165
Herb Vinaigrette 67
Herb-Coated Radishes 146
Herb-Tossed Blue-Lake Beans 140
Herbs of Provence 111
Hiely, Spinach & Clams 119

Hollandaise Sauce 165
Hot Artichoke Dip & Rye Wafers 34
Hot Garlic & Anchovy Sauce 32
Hot Mushroom & Sausage Triangles 42
Hot Peppers 24
Hot Spinach & Bacon Salad Flambé 70
Hubbard Squash 29

I
Iceberg Lettuce 20
Index of Vegetables 9-30
Indian Eggplant 155
Indian Green Beans 140
Insight on Artichokes 127
Italian Antipasto 40
Italian Dressing 69
Italian Marrow Squash 28
Italian Salad 72
Italian Sausage & Mushroom Pizza 98
Italian-Sausage Quiche, Leek & 103
Italian Swiss-Chard Stuffing 110

J
Jícama 19, 26
Jícama & Orange Salad, Mexican 76
Jerusalem Artichoke:
    Jerusalem Artichoke 9, 26
    Jerusalem Artichoke & Leek Bisque 52
    Jerusalem Artichoke & Seafood Salad 77
    Jerusalem Artichokes & Celery
        au Gratin 152

K
Kale 18-19
Kohlrabi 19
Kohlrabi with Sour Cream & Chives 139

L
Layered Eggplant Slices 154
Leeks:
    Jerusalem Artichoke & Leek Bisque 52
    Leek & Italian Sausage Quiche 103
    Leeks 20, 23
Lemon Dressing 68
Lemon Sauce, Endive with 141
Lemon-Basil Dressing 72
Lemon-Butter Crust 108
Lentil Soup 54
Les Halles Onion Soup 50
Lettuce:
    Bibb Lettuce 20
    Boston Lettuce 20
    Bunching Lettuce 20
    Buttercrunch Lettuce 20
    Butterhead Lettuce 20
    Cos Lettuce 20
    Crisphead Lettuce 20
    Iceberg Lettuce 20
    Loose-leaf Lettuce 20
    Romaine lettuce 20
Lima Beans 10
Lima Beans & Sausages, Oven-Baked 123
Limas & Onions in
    Sour Cream 144, 148-149
Lime Dressing, Oil & 71
Linguine with Vegetables &
    Provolone 124-125
Loose-leaf lettuce 20

M
Main Dishes 112-131
Marinated Four-Bean Salad 81
Marmalade-Glazed Parsnips 139

Marnier, Carrots Grand 147
Marrow Squash, Italian 28
Mayonnaise:
    Greek Garlic Mayonnaise 166
    Mustard Mayonnaise 162
    Pistachio Mayonnaise 162
    Provençal Mayonnaise 35
Meat Sauce 113
Meat Sauce, Spaghetti Squash
    with Greek 128-129
Meatballs, Florentine 41
Mexican Corn & Squash 148-150
Mexican Corn Bread 178
Mexican Dressing 76
Mexican Jícama & Orange Salad 76
Mexican Salsa 169, 171
Mexicana, Chayote 152
Microwave Cooking 8
Milanese Torta Rustica 100-101
Milanese, Asparagus & Eggs 88
Minestrone 53
Monterey, Gazpacho 45
Moo Shu Pork 117
Moussaka, Mushroom 113
Muffins, Super Healthy Carrot-Bran 180
Multi-Layered Gazpacho Salad 64, 74-75
Mushroom:
    Abalone Mushrooms 21
    Champignon de Paris Mushrooms 21
    Dutch Babie with Mushroom Center 87
    Enoki Mushrooms 21
    Fresh Mushroom Soufflé 83
    Green Bean & Mushroom Salad 67, 90
    Grilled Shiitake Mushrooms with
        Cheese 41
    Hot Mushroom & Sausage Triangles 42
    Italian Sausage & Mushroom Pizza 98
    Mushroom 21
    Mushroom & Almond Pâté 34
    Mushroom-Filled Soufflé Roll 88
    Mushroom Filling 88
    Mushroom-Gruyère-Salad 68, 74-75
    Mushroom Moussaka 113
    Mushroom Puff Pastry 110
    Mushroom Risotto 163
    Sherried Mushroom Soup 53
    Shiitake Mushrooms 21
    Stuffed Mushrooms 43
    Tiny Mushroom Pastries 42
    Tree Oyster Mushrooms 21
    Wild Rice & Mushroom Soup 49
Mustard Greens 18-19, 22
Mustard Mayonnaise 162
Mustard Vinaigrette Dressing, Shallot- 77
Mustard-Tarragon Dressing 71

N
Napa Cabbage 12-13
Nasturtium Blossoms, Garden Greens
    with 71
New Potatoes with Caviar 138
Nicoise, Salade 65
Nordic-Style, Asparagus & Shrimp 120
Nutrition 6

O
Oil & Lime Dressing 71
Oil & Vinegar Dressing 77
Okra:
    Okra 22
    Okra & Corn Stew, Southern 154
    Okra & Tomato Medley 144

Index

Omelet, Swiss Potato 89
Onion:
    Bavarian Onion & Bacon Pie 99
    Golden Puree with Caramelized
      Onions 143
    Green-Onion & Parmesan
      Loaf 148-149, 174
    Green Onions 22-23
    Les Halles Onion Soup 50
    Limas & Onions in Sour
      Cream 144, 148-149
    Onion & Bacon Filling 99
    Onions 22-23
    Sausage-Stuffed Onions 143
Orange Carrots, Brandied 147, 148-149
Orange Salad, Mexican Jícama & 76
Orange-Carrot Cookies 180
Orange-Glazed Beets 147-149
Orange-Glazed Yams 138
Oven-Baked Lima Beans & Sausages 123
Oyster-Stuffed Tomatoes 38-39

P
Paella with Seafood 119
Pancakes, Sour-Cream Vegetable 104-105
Parboiling 7
Parmesan Loaf, Green-
    Onion & 148-149, 174
Parmesan-Coated Zucchini 151
Parsley 23
Parsley, Fried 172
Parsley-Vinaigrette Dressing 65
Parsnips 23, 26
Parsnips, Marmalade-Glazed 139
Pasta Bolognese 99
Pasta Salad Provençal 72
Pasta with Fresh Tomato & Basil 101
Pasta with Pesto Primavera 109
Pastries & Pasta 94-111
    Hot Mushroom & Sausage Triangles 42
    Tiny Mushroom Pastries 42
    Cream-Cheese Pastry 42
    Sweet Butter Pastry 183
Pâté, Mushroom & Almond 34
Pattypan Squash 28
Pattypan with Cheese & Chilies 152
Pea Pods:
    Chinese Pea Pods 11, 24
    Chive-Stuffed Pea Pods 38-39
    Edible Pea Pods 11, 24
    Pea Pods & Cucumbers, Stir-Fried 133
    Pea Pods & Shrimp, Chinese 121
Peas:
    Curried Pea Vichyssoise 56
    Peas 24
    Peas with Prosciutto 142
    Saffron Rice with Peas 142
    Snap Peas 11, 24
    Snow Peas 11, 24
    Sugar Peas 11, 24
    Sugar Snap Peas 11, 24
    Yellow Split-Pea Soup 54
Pecan-Coated Sweet-Potato Casserole 139
Peperonata 157
Peppers:
    Bell Peppers 24
    Green Peppers 24
    Hot Peppers 24
    Peperonata 157
    Red Peppers 24
Persian Vegetable Pie 91

Pesto Primavera, Pasta with 109
Pesto Sauce 168
Pesto Sauce, Quick 151
Pesto Sauce, Zucchini with Quick 151
Pickled Beets 78
Pickles, Zucchini Bread & Butter 169-170
Picnic Cake, Carrot 181
Pie, Persian Vegetable 91
Pie, Praline-Topped Squash 182-183
Pie, Taco Pizza 96-97
Pilgrim Stew in Butternut Shells 130
Pissaladière Pastry 111
Pistachio Mayonnaise 162
Pistou Soup 59
Pizza:
    Basic Pizza Crust 98
    Cornmeal Crust 96-97
    Italian-Sausage & Mushroom Pizza 98
    Taco Pizza Pie 96-97
    Tortilla Flats 100
    Vegetable-Toppped Whole-Wheat
      Pizza 95
    Whole-Wheat Pizza Crust 95
Platter Salad, Vegetable 69, 74-75
Platter, Summer Vegetable 156
Pocket Sandwiches, Vegetable-Stuffed 98
Pods, Chinese Pea 11, 24
Pods, Edible Pea 11, 24
Pork, Moo Shu 117
Pot-au-Feu 58
Potatoes:
    Bacon & Potato Squares 86
    Baked Potatoes with Toppings 136
    Chocolate-Potato Cake 186
    Creamy Scalloped Potatoes 138
    Danish Hash 117
    French-Fried Potato Skins 43
    French Potato Salad 71
    Garlic-Buttered Potato Dollars 135
    Garlic-Potato Bread 176
    New Potatoes with Caviar 138
    Orange-Glazed Yams 138
    Pecan-Coated Sweet-Potato
      Casserole 139
    Potatoes Anna 135
    Ranch-House Stuffed Potatoes 136
    Spuds & Sausages Bandit-Style 118
    Swedish Whipped Rutabagas &
      Potatoes 135
    Sweet Potatoes 25, 29
    Swiss Potato Cake 137
    Swiss Potato Omelet 89
    White Potatoes 25
Praline-Topped Squash Pie 182-183
Preparation, Vegetable 6-7
Preserves, Gingered Cherry 168-169
Pressure Cooking 8
Prosciutto Timbales, Zucchini- 93
Prosciutto, Peas with 142
Provençal Mayonnaise 35
Provençal, Pasta Salad 72
Provence, Herbs of 111
Provolone, Linguine with
    Vegetables & 124-125
Pudding, Carrot 185
Pudding, Southern Corn 92
Puff Pastry, Mushroom 110
Pumpkin:
    Cheese Soup with Pumpkin 61
    Early California Soup in a Pumpkin
      Tureen 60-61

    Pumpkin 26
Pumpkin-Eggnog Bombe 184-185
Pumpkin-Walnut Bread 175
Squash Flambé 179
Squash Soufflé Custard 178

Q
Quiche:
    Leek & Italian Sausage Quiche 103
    Spinach & Chèvre Quiche 102
    Zucchini & Walnut Quiche 103
Quick Pesto Sauce 151
Quick Pesto Sauce, Zucchini with 151

R
Radishes:
    Herb-Coated Radishes 146
    Radishes 26
    Shredded Egg & Radish Salad 80
Ranch-House Stuffed Potatoes 136
Ratatouille 158
Red Cabbage 12-13
Red Cabbage & Apples 144
Red Peppers 24
Red-Tomato Relish 172
Red-Wine Vinaigrette Dressing 81
Refresh 8
Relish, Green-Tomato 167
Relish, Red-Tomato 172
Rice:
    Green Rice 163
    Mushroom Risotto 163
    Saffron Rice with Peas 142
    Wild Rice & Mushroom Soup 49
Risotto, Mushroom 163
Roll, Ham-Filled Spinach Soufflé 90-91
Roll, Mushroom-Filled Soufflé 88
Rolls, Sausage-Stuffed Cabbage 124
Romaine 20
Root, Celery 14
Rutabaga:
    Rutabaga 26-27
    Golden Puree with Caramelized
      Onions 143
    Swedish Whipped Rutabagas &
      Potatoes 135
Rye Wafers, Hot Artichoke Dip & 34

S
Saffron Rice with Peas 142
Salads 63-81
Salsa Verde 170
Salsa, Mexican 169, 171
Salsify 27
Sandwiches, Vegetable-Stuffed Pocket 98
Sarasin, Galettes 106
Sauces & Relishes 164-172
    Bechamel Sauce 127
    Brandied Hard Sauce 185
    Custard Sauce 113
    Endive with Lemon Sauce 141
    Hot Garlic & Anchovy Sauce 32
    Meat Sauce 113
    Pasta Bolognese 99
    Sesame Sauce 115
    Spaghetti Squash with Greek Meat
      Sauce 128-129
    Spaghetti Squash with Tomato
      Sauce 129
    Spinach Soufflé with Chive Sauce 84
    Steamed Artichokes with Dipping
      Sauces 162

Wine Sauce 43
Zucchini with Quick Pesto Sauce 151
Sauerkraut & Sausage 131
Sausage:
Artichoke & Sausage Frittata 89
Escarole & Sausage Bistro Salad 81
Hot Mushroom & Sausage Triangles 42
Italian-Sausage & Mushroom Pizza 98
Leek & Italian Sausage Quiche 103
Oven-Baked Lima Beans & Sausages 123
Sauerkraut & Sausage 131
Sausage-Stuffed Cabbage Rolls 124
Sausage-Stuffed Onions 143
Spuds & Sausages Bandit-Style 118
Sautéing & Stir-Frying 8
Savoy Cabbage 12-13
Scalloped Potatoes, Creamy 138
Scalloped Squash 28
Scandinavian Vegetable & Cheese Salad 77
Seafood:
Asparagus & Shrimp Nordic-Style 120
Baked Fish & Vegetables Piraeus 120
Chinese Pea Pods & Shrimp 121
Jerusalem Artichoke & Seafood Salad 77
Oyster-Stuffed Tomatoes 38-39
Paella with Seafood 119
Spinach & Clams Hiely 119
Sesame Sauce 115
Sesame Spread, Garbanzo- 33
Sesame-Soy Dressing 73
Shabu Shabu 114-115
Shallots:
Shallot Dressing 79
Shallot-Mustard Vinaigrette Dressing 77
Shallot Salad 79
Shallots 23, 27
Sherried Mushroom Soup 53
Shiitake Mushrooms with Cheese,
Grilled 41
Shiitake Mushrooms 21
Shredded Egg & Radish Salad 80
Shredded Vegetable Trio 158
Shrimp Nordic-Style, Asparagus & 120
Shrimp, Chinese Pea Pods & 121
Shrimp, Endive with Curried 38-39
Side Dishes 132-163
Skewered Vegetables, Turkish 160-161
Skins, French-Fried Potato 43
Slaw, Sweet & Sour Hot 73
Snaps Voilà, Sugar 142, 148-149
Snow Peas 11, 24
Sorrel 19, 27
Soufflés & Egg Dishes 82-93
Squash Soufflé Custard 178
Soups 44-62
Sour Cream & Chives, Kohlrabi with 139
Sour Cream, Limas &
Onions in 144, 148-149
Sour Hot Slaw, Sweet & 73
Sour-Cream Pastry 101
Sour-Cream Vegetable Pancakes 104-105
Southern Corn Pudding 92
Southern Okra & Corn Stew 154
Soy Dressing, Gingered 68
Soy Dressing, Sesame- 73
Spaghetti Squash:
Spaghetti Squash 29
Spaghetti Squash with Greek Meat
Sauce 128-129
Spaghetti Squash with
Tomato Sauce 129

Spanakopita 104
Speckled Chocolate-Carrot Cake 181
Spicy Dressing 80
Spinach:
Florentine Meatballs 41
Galettes Sarasin 106
Green Rice 163
Ham-Filled Spinach Soufflé Roll 90-91
Hot Spinach & Bacon Salad Flambé 70
Persian Vegetable Pie 91
Spinach 28
Spinach & Chèvre Quiche 102
Spinach & Clams Hiely 119
Spinach & Sunflower Squares 86
Spinach Gnocchi Balls 131
Spinach Soufflé with Chive Sauce 84
Spinach-Turkey Stir-Fry 116
Spanakopita 104
Sprouted Spinach Salad 70
Split-Pea Soup, Yellow 54
Spread, Garbanzo-Sesame 33
Sprouts, Bean:
Bean Sprouts 11
Sprouted Spinach Salad 70
Sprouted Zucchini Brownies 179
Sprout, Brussels 12
Sprouts Véronique, Brussels 155
Spuds & Sausages Bandit-Style 118
Squash:
Acorn Squash 29
Banana Squash 29
Buttercup Squash 29
Butternut Squash 29
Chayote 15, 28
Chayote Mexicana 152
Cocozelle Squash 28
Crookneck Squash
Mediterranean-Style 150
Hubbard Squash 29
Italian Marrow Squash 28
Mexican Corn & Squash 148-150
Parmesan-Coated Zucchini 151
Pattypan Squash 28
Pattypan with Cheese & Chilies 152
Pilgrim Stew in Butternut Shells 130
Praline-Topped Squash Pie 182-183
Pumpkin-Eggnog Bombe 185
Pumpkin-Walnut Bread 175
Scalloped Squash 28
Spaghetti Squash 29
Spaghetti Squash with Greek Meat
Sauce 128-129
Spaghetti Squash with
Tomato Sauce 129
Sprouted Zucchini Brownies 179
Squash Flambè 179
Squash Soufflé Custard 178
Summer Squash 28
Table Queen Squash 29
Winter Squash 29
Yellow Crookneck Squash 28
Yellow Straightneck Squash 28
Zucchini 28
Zucchini & Walnut Quiche 103
Zucchini Bread & Butter Pickles 169-170
Zucchini-Prosciutto Timbales 93
Zucchini Squares 85
Zucchini Tea Loaf 175
Zucchini with Quick Pesto Sauce 151
Steamed Artichokes with
Dipping Sauces 162

Steaming 8
Stew:
Cassoulet 123
Pot-au-Feu 58
Ratatouille 158
Pilgrim Stew in Butternut Shells 130
Southern Okra & Corn Stew 154
Vegetable Garden Stew 159
Stewing & Braising 8
Stir-Fry:
Chinese Cabbage & Tofu Stir-Fry 134
Spinach-Turkey Stir-Fry 116
Stir-Fried Chinese Vegetables 133
Stir-Fried Pea Pods & Cucumbers 133
Stir-Frying & Sautéing 8
Tofu & Vegetable Stir-Fry 116
Storing Vegetables 6
Straightneck Squash, Yellow 28
Stuffed Artichokes, Ham & Cheese 127
Stuffed Cabbage Rolls, Sausage- 124
Stuffed Eggplant Boats 130
Stuffed Eggplant, Yaya's 153
Stuffed Grape Leaves (Dolmas) 36
Stuffed Mushrooms 43
Stuffed Onions, Sausage- 143
Stuffed Pea Pods, Chive- 38-39
Stuffed Pocket Sandwiches, Vegetable- 98
Stuffed Potatoes, Ranch-House 136
Stuffed Tomatoes Avgolemono 126
Stuffed Tomatoes, Oyster- 38-39
Stuffed-Vegetable Platter 38-39
Stuffing, Chestnut & Vegetable 107
Stuffing, Italian Swiss-Chard 110
Sugar Peas 11, 24
Sugar Snaps Voilà 142, 148-149
Summer Squash 28
Summer Vegetable Platter 156
Sunchoke:
Sunchoke 9, 26
Jerusalem Artichoke & Leek Bisque 52
Jerusalem Artichoke & Seafood Salad 77
Jerusalem Artichokes & Celery
au Gratin 152
Sunflower Squares, Spinach & 86
Super Healthy Carrot-Bran Muffins 180
Swedish Whipped Rutabagas &
Potatoes 135
Swedish-Style Cucumbers in Dill 78
Sweet & Sour Hot Slaw 73
Sweet Bell Peppers 24
Sweet Butter Pastry 183
Sweet Corn 16, 29
Sweet Corn with Garlic Butter,
Grilled 160-161
Sweet Potatoes 25, 29
Sweet-Potato Casserole, Pecan-Coated 139
Swiss Buttered Herb Sauce 165
Swiss Chard 14-15, 30
Swiss Potato Cake 137
Swiss Potato Omelet 89
Swiss-Chard Stuffing, Italian 110

T
Tabbouleh 80
Table Queen Squash 29
Taco Pizza Pie 96-97
Tarragon Dressing, Mustard- 71
Tarragon-Vinaigrette Dressing 66
Tart, Decorative Caviar 108
Tea Loaf, Zucchini 175
Techniques, Cooking 7-8

Index

Tempura 37
Tempura Batter 37
The Farmer's Soup 59
Timbales, Carrot 93
Timbales, Zucchini-Prosciutto 93
Tiny Mushroom Pastries 42
Tips for Buying Vegetables 6
Tips for Storing Vegetables 6
Tofu & Vegetable Stir-Fry 116
Tofu Stir-Fry, Chinese Cabbage & 134
Tomatoes:
  Chili Sauce 172
  Cooked Tomato Sauce 168
  Gingered Cherry Preserves 168-169
  Green-Tomato Relish 167
  Mexican Salsa 169, 171
  Okra & Tomato Medley 144
  Oyster-Stuffed Tomatoes 38-39
  Pasta with Fresh Tomato & Basil 101
  Red-Tomato Relish 172
  Spaghetti Squash with
    Tomato Sauce 129
  Stuffed Tomatoes Avgolemono 126
  Tomato Fantasy Soup 46-47
  Tomato Soup Under a Pastry Cap 55
  Tomatoes 30
Toppings, Baked Potatoes with 136
Tortilla Flats 100
Tree Oyster Mushrooms 21
Trio, Shredded Vegetable Trio 158
Turkey Stir-Fry, Spinach- 116
Turkish Skewered Vegetables 160-161
Turnip Greens 18-19, 30
Turnips 26, 30

V
Vegetable & Cheese Salad,
  Scandinavian 77
Vegetable Garden Stew 159

Vegetable Index 9-30
Vegetable Pancakes, Sour-Cream 104-105
Vegetable Pie, Persian 91
Vegetable Platter Salad 69, 74-75
Vegetable Platter, Stuffed- 38-39
Vegetable Platter, Summer 156
Vegetable Preparation 6-7
Vegetable Sauce, California 171
Vegetable Soup, French 50
Vegetable Soup, Fruited 62
Vegetable Stir-Fry, Tofu & 116
Vegetable Stuffing, Chestnut & 107
Vegetable Trio, Shredded 158
Vegetable, Cooking Techniques 7-8
Vegetable, Nutrition 6
Vegetable-Stuffed Pocket Sandwiches 98
Vegetable-Topped Whole-Wheat Pizza 95
Vegetables & Provolone,
  Linguine with 124-125
Vegetables Piraeus, Baked Fish & 120
Vegetables à la Grecque 157
Vegetables, Butter-Glazed 156
Vegetables, Buying 6
Vegetables, Cashew Chicken & 122
Vegetables, Stir-Fried Chinese 133
Vegetables, Storing 6
Vegetables, Turkish Skewered 160-161
Verde, Salsa 170
Véronique, Brussels Sprouts 155
Vichyssoise 45
Vichyssoise, Curried Pea 56
Vinaigrette:
  Basil Vinaigrette 67
  Herb Vinaigrette 67
  Parsley Vinaigrette Dressing 65
  Red-Wine Vinaigrette Dressing 81
  Shallot-Mustard Vinaigrette Dressing 77
  Tarragon-Vinaigrette Dressing 66

Vinegar Dressing, Oil & 77
Vintners' Herb Braided Bread 176-177

W
Wafers, Hot Artichoke Dip & Rye 34
Walnut Bread, Pumpkin- 175
Walnut Quiche, Zucchini & 103
Washington Square Deli Salad 67
Watercress 30
Watercress & Endive Salad 66
Wax Beans 10
Western Cobb Salad 65
White Potatoes 25
Whole-Wheat Pizza Crust 95
Whole-Wheat Pizza, Vegetable-Topped 95
Wild Rice & Mushroom Soup 49
Wine Dressing, Garlic- 64
Wine Sauce 43
Winter Squash 29
Witloof Chicory 17, 20

Y
Yams 25, 29
Yams, Orange-Glazed 138
Yaya's Stuffed Eggplant 153
Yellow Crookneck Squash 28
Yellow Split-Pea Soup 54
Yellow Straightneck Squash 28

Z
Zucchini:
  Parmesan-Coated Zucchini 151
  Sprouted Zucchini Brownies 179
  Zucchini 28
  Zucchini & Walnut Quiche 103
  Zucchini Bread & Butter Pickles 169-170
  Zucchini-Prosciutto Timbales 93
  Zucchini Squares 85
  Zucchini Tea Loaf 175
  Zucchini with Quick Pesto Sauce 151

8.249211656